"Our organizations are at a watershed moment. Their participation in the growing social and environmental problems we face—and their crucial role in finding solutions—can no longer be denied. Activist stakeholders are speaking up and demanding action. *Higher Ground* is the go-to book for those wishing to navigate this tumultuous territory, and Alison Taylor's expertise in this area is second to none."

—**MEGAN REITZ**, Professor of Leadership and Dialogue, Hult International Business School; coauthor, *Speak Up*

"Business ethics books tend to be either unrealistically idealist, unconstructively critical, impractically theoretical, or naively simplistic. Alison Taylor has found the sweet spot with *Higher Ground*. With an impartial, critical eye, she offers valuable practical tools and options for practitioners. A must-read for any business leader."

—**MARTIN REEVES**, Chairman, BCG Henderson Institute

"Corporate ethics is generally thought of as a boring, dry topic. *Higher Ground* un-dries it, makes it lively, and explains how to use it to navigate today's—and tomorrow's—stormy economic waters."

—**BRUNO GIUSSANI**, Global Curator, TED

"In today's volatile, complex, emotional, uncertain, and politicized business world, Alison Taylor provides a set of thoughtful, nuanced, and realistic approaches that recognize the very real challenges facing business leaders. *Higher Ground* is a refreshing antidote to the many superficial approaches that can drive businesses to 'tick the box and miss the point.'"

—**JOE ZAMMIT-LUCIA**, business leadership adviser; author, *The New Political Capitalism*

"In the acrimonious debate about how corporations should govern themselves in a society where freedom of belief is a core value, important common ground can be forgotten. Most Americans believe that businesses should treat their workers, their customers, their communities, and the environment with respect. Alison Taylor charts a sensible path for businesses that want to deliver profits for their stockholders while respecting those whose lives their conduct affects. Her practical recommendations to do the right thing build on common ground, transcending partisan labels at a time when restoring the ties that bind us is an urgent priority."

—**LEO E. STRINE JR.**, former Chancellor and Chief Justice, Delaware; Michael L. Wachter Distinguished Fellow in Law and Public Policy, University of Pennsylvania Carey Law School

"This is a very timely, welcome, and well-written book. Arguments about what companies should and shouldn't do have reached a fever pitch. Extremes on both sides are spouting ideology rather than thoughtful commentary, which is exactly what this book provides. Taylor has very pragmatic views about companies. She recognizes the many conflicts they are facing—some of their own creation—and has some hard-headed, clear-eyed advice about what they should do."

—**ROBERT ECCLES**, Visiting Professor of Management Practice, Saïd Business School, Oxford University; founding Chairman, Sustainability Accounting Standards Board (SASB)

"Engaging, practical, and insightful. Taylor's *Higher Ground* challenges conventional wisdom in the world of business ethics and brings fresh ideas by embracing the complexities of the real world and offering practical guidance. With compelling narratives drawn from experience, ideas, and research, Taylor takes her audience to higher ground with a clear compass and a steady steering wheel."

—**HUI CHEN**, Senior Adviser, R&G Insights Lab; former Compliance Counsel Expert, US Department of Justice

"Authentic, incisive, and practical, whether you're a student who wants to understand how significant ESG and ethical issues are handled by the pros or an experienced executive who believes we never stop learning."

—**SILVIA M. GARRIGO**, former Senior Vice President and Chief ESG Officer, Royal Caribbean Group; professor, University of Miami Herbert Business School

"Standing on higher ground, you see further, and you have a different perspective. Reading *Higher Ground* provides a real step up, a complete tool kit any business leader should have."

"The transition from businesses focusing only on shareholders to a broader focus on stakeholders is not an easy move. Read Alison Taylor's book and use her experience, research, insights, and accessible style to be guided and inspired to become a truly responsible business."

"In a world filled with hypocritical rhetoric and genuine human suffering, spin and legalistic compliance can't pass for corporate ethics. In this groundbreaking book, Alison Taylor shows a way to higher ground, guided by valuing humans."

"The words 'corporate ethics manual' and 'gripping page-turner' do not naturally spring to mind in the same breath, but Alison Taylor makes the pages fly, reminding us, one fascinating, horrifying tale after another, that public norms can seemingly move at the speed of light."

"This book is must-read. Alison Taylor offers a hugely insightful and timely guide for anyone in the private sector committed to moving beyond compliance to integrity and to building an authentic integrity culture throughout all the functions in the company."

"Alison Taylor is a rarity: an experienced, articulate truth teller. Her book is a timely and vital guide to help leaders navigate the polarized and shifting landscape and get far beyond the supposed shelter of banal purpose statements."

HIGHER

GROUND

HARVARD BUSINESS REVIEW PRESS
BOSTON, MASSACHUSETTS

HIGHER GROUND

HOW BUSINESS CAN DO THE RIGHT THING IN A TURBULENT WORLD

ALISON TAYLOR

The web addresses referenced in this book were live and correct at the time of the book's publication but may be subject to change.

Library of Congress Cataloging-in-Publication Data

Names: Taylor, Alison, author.
Title: Higher ground : how business can do the right thing in a turbulent
    world / Alison Taylor.
Description: Boston, Massachusetts : Harvard Business Review Press, [2024] |
    Includes index.
Identifiers: LCCN 2023033107 (print) | LCCN 2023033108 (ebook) |
    ISBN 9781647823436 (hardcover) | ISBN 9781647823443 (epub)
Subjects: LCSH: Business ethics. | Industrial management. |
    Industries—Social aspects—History—21st century. | Social responsibility of
    business—History—21st century.
Classification: LCC HF5387 .T395 2024 (print) | LCC HF5387 (ebook) |
    DDC 174/.4–dc23/eng/20230925
LC record available at https://lccn.loc.gov/2023033107
LC ebook record available at https://lccn.loc.gov/2023033108

ISBN: 978-1-64782-343-6
eISBN: 978-1-64782-344-3

The paper used in this publication meets the requirements of the American National Standard for Permanence of Paper for Publications and Documents in Libraries and Archives Z39.48-1992.

This book is dedicated to Peter Christian Hall, who guided and supported me through a challenging process. For over a decade, he provided inspiration and ideas, edited my drafts, helped spruce up my writing, and sense checked my arguments. I do not know a better editor or writer. I'm so grateful for his help.

CONTENTS

Does it seem to you that something fundamental changed in the business world in the late 2010s? Does it seem as though every day you're walking through a political minefield, everyone is mad about something, everything is moving faster, and generally, it's all just very strange?

You're not imagining it. Since 2015 I have been studying the ways that the internet, social media, and the arrival of the smartphone have shaken up social relationships, the generation of knowledge, the mental health of Gen Z (those born after 1995), and the stability of liberal democracies. Something really big *is* happening. We have just left the Gutenberg era, which began with the invention of printing in the fifteenth century and reached its zenith in the age of mass media in the late twentieth century. In the Gutenberg era, ideas were committed to paper; humanity developed ways of debating, evaluating, and vetting those ideas (always imperfectly); and shared norms could and did spread through a society, community, or industry via communication channels that could reach most people.

That era is over. The arrival of the internet in the 1990s, followed by the paired technologies of smartphones and social media, plunged us into a new era in the early 2010s. We are now in the painful early days of the transition to a world of ever-shifting, lightning-quick networks in place of more stable, more humane communities. The move to a mostly digital existence, accelerated by the Covid-19 lockdowns, promises to bring enormous gains in productivity and wealth, but we have little understanding of what it is doing to our brains, our children, and our institutions—including corporations. Hence, we're confused, apprehensive, and often anxious.

If you need help navigating this very strange and very new world, you have come to the right place. Alison Taylor is the perfect guide. She is my colleague at New York University's Stern School of Business, where we both teach MBA courses on professional responsibility and business ethics. But unlike me, Alison worked for twenty-five years as a consultant to multinational companies, helping them to improve their operations and reduce risk in everything from sustainability and human rights to corruption and compliance. She is no ivory-tower egghead; she knows how messy, confusing, and seemingly impossible it often seems on the ground, even when a company is trying to do the right thing. You'll get no airy lectures on ethics in this book. You'll get sympathy, great stories about real successes and failures, and deep insights into how to navigate these challenges today, when everything is so much harder than it was just ten years ago.

Alison has also been my partner since 2019 as the director of Ethical Systems, a nonprofit that I founded in 2014 to build a bridge between the academic and business communities. Academics do research and are rewarded for their journal publications, not for helping real companies. Business leaders, on the other hand, have long read popular books written by academics on leadership and decision-making, but not on ethics, values, and ethical culture. Alison's charge at Ethical Systems was to make the best research on ethical culture widely available and easily accessible to the business world. She managed our collaboration among twenty-five of the top researchers, led a team that sought out research that we thought would be of use to business leaders, and has given hundreds of interviews and written dozens of essays in places such as the *Wall Street Journal* and *Harvard Business Review* laying out those connections. You'll get no long, dull recounting of experiments in this book; you'll get insights into the dynamics of stakeholder conflicts and everyday interactions that are informed by the latest research, complete with hundreds of footnotes.

One of the most important features of *Higher Ground*, I believe, is that Alison offers substantive guidance on how to figure out the right thing to do for your company. She explains why the answer offered by the political right is unworkable and unwise today. (Just return to Milton Friedman and maximize shareholder value!) She explains why the answer offered by the political left is unworkable and unwise. (Use your company's resources to solve a long list of social ills, while also finding win-win solutions for all of your stakeholders!) She invites you to go back to the first principles about your company and about the social license to operate that societies grant to corporations. Her answer is both simple and inspiring: make your core product well, clean up your messes, do no harm, and treat human beings with dignity and respect.

As for how you actually apply those principles in the maelstrom of modern business life, well, that's what *Higher Ground* will show you.

—Jonathan Haidt

Rethinking Ethical Business (Just Don't Say "Ethics")

I n spring 2023, Laxman Narasimhan held his first earnings call with investors as the new CEO at Starbucks. He spoke of "a crisis of disconnection, where loneliness, division, and polarization have become far too common," and said that "the everyday ritual of coffee is a powerful way to make connection happen with others and with yourself."[1] Emphasizing the strengths of the culture at Starbucks, where employees are called "partners," he cited "a strong partner-first mentality that is both top-down and bottom-up."

While there are reasons to imagine that a global chain of coffee shops could play a positive and profitable role in countering an epidemic of social isolation, Narasimhan had weightier considerations in mind that afternoon.

His inspiring words contrasted with sharp criticism of Starbucks's response to unionization drives at hundreds of its nine thousand company-operated US stores.[2] Two months earlier, even some white-collar employees and managers at headquarters in Seattle had taken the risky step of backing baristas in an open letter to leadership protesting both the company's return-to-office mandate and its contentious resistance to unionization. "We believe in Starbucks, we believe in its core values, and we call for a return to those values," said their letter.[3] On the very day it was publicly posted, a labor law judge ruled that Starbucks was engaging in "egregious and widespread misconduct" in repeatedly violating federal labor law in Buffalo, New York.[4]

Far from backing leadership in its efforts against unionization, investors soon voted at the company's annual meeting for an independent review of its commitment to freedom of association and collective bargaining.[5] Outgoing CEO Howard Schultz had to testify in a Senate hearing on Starbucks's labor practices.[6] Two days later, a barista who had fought to unionize lost her job.[7] Then, after Starbucks shut down all three off-campus outlets whose staff had voted to unionize, students pressed Cornell University to find a "new, ethical" campus coffee vendor. (Cornell later chose not to renew its contract.)[8]

As Narasimhan was taking the reins, Starbucks had just facilitated an extraordinary level of connection and unity among key stakeholder groups: workers, managers, customers, and investors. It just wasn't the kind of "stakeholder capitalism" the company's leadership had in mind.

Starbucks had long and effectively taken pains to establish itself as an enlightened, even progressive force in US retail. By most measures, the world's third-largest restaurant chain is a *leader* in inclusion, equity, and employee rights. It maintains 100 percent pay equity for workers, discloses wages and diversity efforts, conducts human rights audits, and offers relatively good benefits and work-life balance. Even its dogged resistance to unionization is normal in corporate America.[9] JUST Capital, which rates companies' environmental, social, and governance (ESG) efforts, rates Starbucks the second-best employer in its sector.[10] The company has won extensive praise from credible organizations for its commitments on climate change and environmental responsibility.

So had Starbucks blown it on the values front? Was it still the "good," ethical, responsible enterprise it touts to customers and investors? Did its dogged opposition to unionization negate efforts in other realms?

"You now have the expectation of employees that they want consistency—not only formal consistency of rules but also consistency with general ethical principles," Philippe Montigny, who has long helped European companies build ethics programs, tells me. "This is not just about anti-bribery or compliance issues but including harassment, including relationships to the environment. For me, this is the main revolution."[11]

The idea that corporations might step up and do the right thing sounds so appealing. Corporations are powerful actors in society, and their decisions matter profoundly to everyone. In the classroom, I hear every day from students who want to work for and buy from companies whose values align with theirs.

But responding to these calls brings unwelcome scrutiny and unexpected turns. So how is any leader to proceed? There's no capsule answer, no magic pill to help you understand what it now takes to establish and maintain a good, trusted business. In writing this book, I intend to explore and map the warrens and dead ends that can confound the best-intentioned executives, and then outline ways for you to guide your organization to higher ground.

You will come to regard "purpose" in a fresh light. Purpose can prove useful in a practical sense, but only if it goes beyond common win-win framing. It can—and must be—deployed as much more than a marketing gimmick. You will learn to weigh your company's potential impacts on human beings before and after you make significant moves. You will discover that comprehending the myriad ways in which your company affects the world can bring your business a far more solid foundation than basing decisions on risk and reputation.

Eventually—once we've trekked through challenging terrain to reach a nice overview—I'll share my thoughts on what and how Starbucks might do better. For now, let's ponder why it has become so difficult to grasp what being a good, trusted business takes today.

To start with, the scope and range of issues that a business leader must track and respond to has expanded dramatically. For example, in 2014, a teenager named Michael Brown was fatally wounded by a police officer and left on the street for hours in Ferguson, Missouri. While this sparked some of the earliest #BlackLivesMatter protests, corporate leaders at the time saw no reason to speak up on a divisive and distressing issue that bore little direct connection to running a business. On social and political controversies, the default position was to stay neutral and avoid taking a stand. As Michael Jordan had quipped in the 1990s: "Republicans buy sneakers, too."[12]

That neutral middle ground crumbled in just seven years. During the early months of the Covid-19 pandemic, George Floyd was publicly murdered by officer Derek Chauvin in Minneapolis, and corporate America abruptly faced a broad reckoning over its commitment to social justice and the amelioration of systemic racism. Leaders of companies including Reddit and CrossFit resigned to make room for more diverse leaders, and the CEOs of many of the largest businesses in the United States signaled commitments to diversity, equity, and inclusion by issuing impassioned personal statements on injustice.[13]

That was an astonishing departure. During the late twentieth century, we had settled for several decades on a clear vision of the scope and limits of the corporation's responsibilities: focus on shareholder value and don't break the law. In 1970, Milton Friedman crafted a compelling case for how and why the logic of business is simply to maximize profit.[14] Morality is the domain of humans, he argued, not corporations. Business leaders are the agents of shareholders and should not misuse investor capital to pursue social priorities or political agendas. A proper leader should maximize a corporation's self-interest while working within the rules of the game, which are set by governments. When corporations pursue economic gain, they help spread individual choice, freedom, and prosperity. That's the best they can do for everyone.

In line with this vision, "business ethics" was implicitly equated with legal compliance and treated as the responsibility of lawyers, auditors, and human resource teams. These functions were charged with protecting corporate value from legal incursions, reputational scandals, and fines.

I spent more than a decade helping to build and secure these defenses. I conducted due diligence, investigated fraud and corruption, and designed and implemented compliance programs. This sounds dry and technical, but the reality was messy, often surreal. I've been pressured by bankers to rewrite due diligence reports so they could greenlight lucrative deals with controversial oligarchs. I've watched senior leadership teams mull which prospective scapegoat might best take the hit for their knowing involvement in fraud. I've stepped away from a Christmas dinner in London to attend to frightened anti-corruption investigators stranded in a remote stretch of northern Mexico after their armed driver absconded with the car. I've advised companies on coping with human rights abuses committed by their private security forces, revelations of child labor surfacing in their supply chains, and surveillance by hostile host governments. Again and again, I saw that legal compliance is not always a good proxy for business ethics. Culture and leadership matter.

In search of greater insights on how companies might wield a more positive impact in society, I then made my way into the emerging field of "corporate sustainability." Like Alice in *Alice Through the Looking Glass*, I encountered an unfamiliar realm festooned with impenetrable buzzwords. I learned how to advocate for social impact, regeneration, value chains, sustainable development goals, net zero, the triple bottom line, inclusive economies, resource stewardship, community engagement, and climate justice. Again, I found that inspiring terms are no match for the disorder of real life. I have made the business case for sustainability to powerful executives all over the world—as their eyes glazed over. I've watched companies lose sight of core principles in their zeal to capitalize on the financial upsides of ESG. I've heard sustainability leaders exaggerate their public commitments while privately dismissing their effectiveness. I've seen committed CEOs exit and their promising sustainability programs collapse. I've helped companies respond to shareholder resolutions inspired by community protests as far afield as Pakistan and as close as Pennsylvania. I've advised them on cleaning up the damage after employees leaked sensitive internal information on social media.

I've never come across a company that gets everything right, and I cannot name good or bad businesses—only better and worse ones.[15] In real life, organizations evolve constantly. Even more important, they tend to build expertise by responding to friction. Activists target the best performers as well as the worst, and an absence of criticism isn't necessarily a reassuring sign. Anyone who has spent time working on responsible, ethical business knows the neat win-win arguments we're expected to push; these often stymie open discussion of strategies and approaches that are actually effective. In fact, I've found that some of the best ideas are generated in controversial sectors, by companies facing existential challenges as they strive to recover from serious mistakes.

It made sense for a long time to treat branding, culture, sustainability, risk, and ethics as separate disciplines that required distinct approaches. But internal teams can't afford to pursue misaligned agendas for long in a digitally paced world.[16] Any company lacking rigorous internal coordination will soon look disjointed and hypocritical.

Even then, it's no small task to implement a globally consistent approach to doing the right thing, and it's getting harder by the year. Our personal values reflect culture, upbringing, religion, politics—even our genes. Contemporary society is so fragmented (both within and among countries and cultures) that the very concepts of capitalism and democracy are being contested. Nonetheless, calls for businesses to intervene in high-stakes questions of worldwide import keep getting louder. Such crises as climate change, Covid-19, and geopolitical turmoil continually spotlight a glaring lack of consensus on *how far* companies should pursue efforts to address systemic societal and environmental challenges. It's easy to say companies should register a positive impact and help society flourish, or listen to stakeholders and balance their interests. The devil lurks in *how*.

Even with the best will in the world, it's challenging for any business leader to judge when to directly address a stakeholder concern, when the government might be better placed to step in, and when a business can—and should—compensate for governmental weakness or failure. These questions are not addressed by the standard corporate frameworks of compliance, ESG, or sustainability. And because academic approaches to business ethics are grounded in moral philosophy, they can seem impractical, even contradictory. I have yet to attend a meeting where executives debate whether it's better to apply a utilitarian or a deontological framework to a decision.

Amid so much confusion and risk, corporations find themselves in a tense, ambiguous position. They bear much responsibility—both direct and indirect—for our complex array of tax cuts, deregulation, and influence peddling. At the same time, they have global reach and are more trusted and responsive to public pressure than many nation states. Survey after survey shows that the public prefers business to take the lead on social change rather than await government initiatives.[17]

Business faces such pressure because of its scale—and society's dire needs. For example, a 2022 article in the *MIT Sloan Management Review* argued: "As social justice issues move to center stage in the political sphere, the stakeholder rubber has hit the strategy road."[18] But saying that business must intervene simply because we're desperate offers no coherent argument for how business should try to solve societal problems, or how far it should go.

CEOs struggle to respond to such inchoate demands, for good reason. It's impossible to be all things to all people for long, and people change their minds. Understandably, companies default to bland statements that are hard to tell apart. Research at MIT found that most companies cite from three to seven values, with two-thirds of them avowing a commitment to "integrity."[19] A previous study found that corporate values statements converge around integrity, teamwork, and innovation.[20]

Since pledging integrity won't get you very far in this mistrustful era, how is your company to navigate the swamps of our contradictory expectations? Where's a solid path to higher ground? A well-marked one leads back to Milton Friedman's shareholder value, but how would today's consumers greet a company's declaration that making a profit is its sole mission?

Instead, companies are expected to balance conflicting stakeholder interests and demands; to follow clear global principles while adapting to local conditions and cultures; to solve societal problems while maintaining shareholder value; and to be transparent and authentic, with no empty talk or inconsistencies. Whether or not you personally believe in the emerging story of stakeholder capitalism, you and your team face these pressures. Any failure to at least assess them can carry swift and devastating consequences.

In rethinking ethical business, then, let's start by acknowledging that no business is a black box or a singular, self-interested personality that can be protected from political, social, and environmental pressures by a nexus of contracts. Once-reliable demarcations between internal and external issues have blurred. In our daily, lived experience, any company is an open social system that sits within—and relies on—economic, political, social, and environmental networks to survive and thrive.

The uncomfortable truth is that the accepted terms "corporate responsibility" and "sustainability" often describe corporate efforts to offset prior damage wrought by core business models by offering sunny, distracting narratives. Indeed, amorphous, confusing jargon is not a bug, but rather a persistent feature of the business ethics landscape. In these unruly, transparent times, corporations must cater to a powerful appetite for accountability. This means, first, that corporations must be more candid and realistic about problems they suggest they can take on. Second, business must acknowledge that legal, political, and regulatory institutions should not be manipulated or undermined to serve corporate interests. These institutions exist to level the playing field for everyone, not least companies. Both goals could be achieved if leaders were to spend less time claiming to make the world better—and more time making their businesses better.

This book's journey toward higher ground will feature both big-picture vistas and detailed practical tools. You need both for a good climb. In part 1, "A Turbulent, Transparent World," chapter 1 will recount how we arrived at today's stressful status quo. In chapter 2, I'll review the tools currently at hand to help us traverse the thickets we face—and explain why we need fresh thinking and new equipment. Doing the right thing in this heated era is particularly challenging because values, impact, and culture cannot be considered in isolation; they interact incessantly to create positive or negative feedback loops.

In part 2, "Business Doing the Right Thing," we'll look from the inside out at a company's effects on the world, starting with a discussion of the frameworks aimed at helping businesses manage and respond to stakeholder perceptions. In chapters 3 and 4, we will examine how companies can cogently consider common advice to balance stakeholder interests and set effective environmental and social priorities. For enterprises of any size, it's hard for leaders to delegate these imperatives, and conflicting advice abounds. I will discuss how to reliably determine your priorities and find direction amid the noise.

Calls to balance stakeholder interests and consider external impacts do not intersect neatly with traditional legal compliance efforts. So, in chapter 5, I'll discuss what the evolution of anti-corruption strategies teaches us about the benefits—and limits—of compliance. If regulation can no longer serve as a North Star, where else can you find guidance? In chapter 6, I will describe why a company can more readily and reliably decide where and how to act in response to an enormous range of pressures if it bases its ethical commitments on its *impact on human beings*. Whatever our politics, religion, or values, everyone wants agency, bodily autonomy, dignity, and respect.

Indeed, a corporation's impacts on human beings constitute the very roots of its legal, operational, and reputational risks—even if *how* those risks might manifest is unpredictable. Those who wish business to pursue an ambitious societal agenda should agree that it's unwise to try to address everything at once. Those who wish to address the climate crisis should agree that technical, scientific messaging has had limited success, and that efforts anchored in human impact and behavior offer a more promising route to higher ground. I will establish that making your best effort to do no harm ought to take priority over involving your company in tangential popular causes.

This raises questions about how to manage impacts and risks that are partly or fully out of your direct control. In chapter 7, I will explore how to engage more effectively with the political process. As business has become more overtly political, it has fallen prey to undemocratic, partisan agendas, internal conflict, and unrealistic expectations. Any credible approach to responsible business must grapple with them. In chapter 8, I'll turn to the promise and peril of transparency, reflecting on how demands for constant communication and disclosure can easily trap corporations in a reactive, paranoid mode.

In "Leading and Shaping the Future," the third and final part, we'll turn our gaze inside the organization to examine how societal shifts affect culture, leadership, oversight, and voice. In chapters 9 and 10, I will look at how novel pressures on business are transforming culture and leadership. In chapter 11, I'll discuss what this means for compliance, rules, and oversight. In chapter 12, I will review how speaking up by both employees and corporations has expanded and transformed—and what to do about it. In the conclusion, I'll explore what it really takes to implement corporate purpose and find a view from higher ground.

This book reflects my personal perspective and career experiences, but I haven't rested on them. From June 2021 through August 2023, I interviewed two hundred experts, practitioners, activists, executives, and academics around the world. Some of their candid views are quoted; many were shared with me off the record because the challenges we discussed are difficult to acknowledge, even taboo. And while the book addresses leaders and readers everywhere, such issues as the availability of reproductive choice, corporate political funding, and the acceptability of ESG ratings are particularly volatile in the United States.[21] Given the global reach and impacts of US-based businesses and American culture, I will address certain of these matters in detail.

While researching this book, I was fascinated by how many experts told me they try to avoid using the word "ethics" at all because it sounds judgmental, punitive, and old-fashioned. While this is understandable, the further insistence of many commentators that ESG has nothing to do with being an ethical business also causes considerable confusion. So, when I use the word "ethics" in this book, I'll rely on a definition from the Ethics Centre in Sydney, Australia, which views ethics as a process of collective exploration: "the process of questioning, discovering and defending our values, principles and purpose."[22]

Ascending tough terrain always requires focus, courage, and stamina. A company can neither separate from society nor solve every societal challenge it encounters. Shaping a better business will require that you exercise practical curiosity over your impacts on the world, muster your energy, respect your inherent limitations, and then help the vital systems you rely on to function better. Let's get started!

PART I

A TURBULENT, TRANSPARENT WORLD

1

Why Running a Business Got So Complicated

Today's corporations are bigger and more powerful than ever, yet they remain so vulnerable that colossal, time-honored brands can vanish in a blink. Even corporate value has become less material. It once rested in such physical assets as plants, machinery, buildings, and cash. But by 2020, the *Economist* was reporting that "61% of the market value of the S&P 500 sits in intangibles such as research and development, customers linked by network effects, brands and data. The link between the CEO authorizing investment and getting results is unpredictable and opaque."[1] This, in turn, has put a soaring premium on trust and relationships inside companies and between companies and their stakeholders. That reliance on human capital and brand reputation—and the prospect that technological change might upend it all—renders some of our mightiest business empires *intangible*.

At the same time, the power of government to address societal problems has faltered. Tobacco, opioids, and sugary snacks have caused expensive public health crises, and state capacity to address them is limited, partly a result of corporate efforts to evade accountability. The prevailing business models for oil, car, clothing, and food companies are environmentally unsustainable. Downward pressure on wages has heightened inequalities among and within nations. And now investors, consumers, employees, and voters want corporations—*your company*, in fact—to help solve big challenges, even as they differ ferociously on how to define them.

Relying on even the most seasoned corporate affairs team to craft a narrative about your corporate responsibility efforts can no longer suffice in this fast-moving, interconnected, image-dominated era. Managing reputational risk cannot ensure your trustworthiness—it is more a funhouse mirror than a balanced accountability mechanism. Activism among employees, customers, and investors is surging in a social media environment rife with a "gotcha" mindset, polarization, and fake news. In May 2022, Ron Williams, a former CEO and chairman of insurer Aetna, told the *Wall Street Journal* that in the face of social and political turmoil, "running the business turns out to be table stakes."[2] (In business, "table stakes" is the bare minimum you must offer to be considered a viable entrant before any consideration of competitive advantage.)

Globalization once offered companies enormous growth opportunities while reducing oversight from national legal and political institutions. Now it exposes them to a fragmented, at times chaotic, map of social and political risk. Since 2008, popular discontent has accelerated in frequency and scale.[3] While each upheaval is unique, dissent is rising under authoritarian and democratic regimes and in developed and developing countries. Headlines cite unrest over fuel prices, fare hikes, ethnic division, corruption, immigration, homelessness, and headscarves, but the protests are fired by a potent cocktail: economic pressure, plus rage over common transnational themes of elite greed and corruption, environmental and social injustice, and individual rights and empowerment.

Meanwhile, a revolution in how information is accessed and then regenerated by the public has rendered corporate impacts on society—both positive and negative—far more visible and contentious, forcing companies to engage much more actively with stakeholders. Missteps are common and costly.

Before we begin delving into what companies can do about this, let's pause to ask how on earth we got here.

How Business Became Political

Companies everywhere now find themselves caught between the Scylla of political risk and the Charybdis of social license to operate.[4] Western enterprises encountered unprecedented pressure to close their operations in Russia when it invaded Ukraine in March 2022. As prominent Yale professor Jeffrey Sonnenfeld was fashioning a spreadsheet to help the media track which companies were in and which were out, CEOs with operations there had to decide almost instantly whether to keep paying employees, evacuate Russian nationals, sell the assets, or try to stay put.[5] (Western companies perceived to have handled the issue well soon found themselves facing questions about their operations in such authoritarian countries with poor human rights records as China and Saudi Arabia.[6])

Far from Moscow, HSBC struggled to balance support for racial justice in the United States with its tacit acceptance of crackdowns in Hong Kong.[7] Telecommunications company Telenor sold its Myanmar operations to a Lebanese investment firm after the 2021 coup made it impossible to meet human rights commitments, only to be criticized afresh over the manner of its withdrawal.[8] Multinational brands face demands from Western consumers to address poverty, pollution, and human rights abuses in their supply chains. Those consumers still want the stuff they ordered, right now.

In a sharply polarized US environment, corporations encounter loaded dilemmas at every turn. A 2022 decision by the US Supreme Court terminating any national claim to abortion rights left companies wrangling with distressed staff, state-level medical restrictions, and threats of political retaliation should they take steps to help employees obtain certain procedures.[9] (While assisting access to abortion might strike overseas observers as a limited business priority, most US companies provide core health-care benefits to employees, and their specific offerings are important to employees and potential hires.) Similarly, it was left to many businesses during the Covid-19 pandemic peaks to decide whether to enforce requirements for masks and vaccines. And disparate gun regulations in many US states force companies to choose whether to allow firearms in their offices or stores.

These are certainly matters of geopolitical risk in a multipolar world, but this lens is too narrow. As University of Chicago professor Luigi Zingales pithily put it, "We now have the politicization of the corporate world because we have corporatization of the political world."[10] Globally, the public sees business as more responsive to its dictates than nation states and expects it to play a more active role in a world reeling from political and regulatory failures. Some companies wind up implicated in these problems by virtue of previous lobbying, tax avoidance, and corruption. Others are simply caught in the tailwinds of shifting expectations. Anxious customers, shareholders, and employees have embraced activism. Corporations are their target.

I first experienced this transformation in my own work when communities situated around mining and infrastructure projects began reframing long-standing complaints about water pollution and relocation as human rights violations, and then connecting them to a wider struggle against corporate irresponsibility. Soon I was being cornered at parties in New York by people eager to discuss how offshore finance and money laundering were pushing up property prices.

What made ordinary people so angry? To start with, the 2008 financial crisis was ameliorated by the injection of vast public subsidies into private companies, swiftly followed by severe and continued austerity in public spending. The disruption's aftermath undermined the sense that bankers and policy makers could be trusted to act like the adults in the room. No meaningful retribution met those perceived to have caused the crash, and scant reform was applied to the financial system.

In 2011, Occupy Wall Street, the Indignados of Spain, and the Arab Spring flourished as early examples of intersecting sociopolitical frustration.[11] In 2014, protesters in Hong Kong and the United States commonly used the same hands-up gesture to signify opposition to repressive police tactics.[12] In 2019, as Catalan militants in Barcelona were waving the flag of Hong Kong, and Lebanese protesters were hoisting anti-Brexit placards, Chile's government released a statement blaming protests on international influences and media—including Korean pop music.[13]

Protests abated during Covid-19 lockdowns, but frustration kept mounting. Rapid urbanization in many developing countries badly strained government services, even as it begat communities of underemployed youths with little to do but organize around grievances. Environmental and climate stresses became key stimulants for protest in many nations, with schoolchildren at the forefront. At the same time, demonstrations erupted over governmental environmental initiatives that threaten to raise fuel costs and reduce jobs in mining and fossil fuels.

Evidence suggests that only a minority of the world's population trusts governments, many of which tend to respond to crises by vacillating or indulging authoritarian impulses.[14]

When critical stakeholders push companies to take on more overt social and political roles, it's tempting to meet this emerging demand. Many CEOs now pitch *themselves* as activists and their organizations as agents of social change. A 2021 global survey by GlobeScan and Oxford University found that 75 percent of companies now have "some appetite" or a "strong appetite" for corporate activism.[15]

CEO activism emerged decisively in the United States during the early stages of Donald Trump's presidency and, by 2018, was being described as the "new normal" by the *New York Times*.[16] The proximate cause was the Trump administration's zest for drawing business leaders into chaotic policy conflicts that might inflame the domestic culture wars. But Trump's divisive leadership was merely a catalyst—the most visible sign that old assumptions are no longer reliable or even relevant.

Big business had carefully avoided polarized messaging for decades. The status quo was to avoid controversy and maintain alliances across the political spectrum. As that neutral middle ground shrank, CEOs and their teams discovered that well-timed ideological appeals could galvanize customers and workers. When the Trump administration withdrew from the Paris Agreement on climate change, scores of businesses responded: "We Are Still In."[17] Nike's sponsorship of quarterback Colin Kaepernick and his football protests drove its stock price to an all-time high, while Chick-fil-A profitably doubled down on its conservative agenda.[18] When Kenneth Frazier of Merck became the first CEO to resign from Trump's manufacturing council after violent right-wing protests in Charlottesville, Virginia, he was widely applauded.[19] My students no longer regard political neutrality as a realistic option for companies; many are surprised to hear it was once customary.

Those ideological appeals had unfortunate second-order consequences for both internal culture and societal divisions. CEOs at Coinbase and Basecamp moved to ban internal debate over politics in order to return to their companies' core missions; their employees quit in droves amid a wave of critical press reports.[20] Then came more organized backlash. In the United States, Republican politicians denounced "woke" branding efforts by which corporations sought to appeal to younger workers and consumers. Meanwhile, Democrats continued urging companies to speak up on controversial questions, and investors to divest from oil and gas.[21] When Disney's CEO infuriated both employees and politicians by vacillating about LGBTQ rights in Florida, corporate leaders started to worry about getting "Disneyed." He was soon replaced, though the controversy was just getting started.[22]

Old assumptions and accepted wisdom no longer offer reliable solutions. Indeed, the corporate tendency to favor siloed, piecemeal responses frequently worsens matters. Are climate change and racial justice political issues? Or are they deeply personal? That depends on whom you ask.

It's very hard to draw back from taking stands once you're begun. Proclamations that core values are as important and fundamental as profit shifted the Overton window (the range of ideas and policies the public will accept at a given moment) and opened the corporate arena to negotiation, debate, and pressures from all quarters. Taking a stand on any issue now invites suspicion of hypocrisy and scrutiny as to whether your company's actions—and political spending—match your rhetoric.[23] Doing the right thing is far more demanding than it looks.

So now that everyone is yelling at you, how do you decide whom to listen to?

How Transparency Became a Weapon

Back in 2009, I began to see a tectonic shift in the weaponization of information. I had spent much of 2007 working for an insurance client that wanted to know who was responsible for dumping five hundred tons of toxic chemicals in Côte d'Ivoire, burning lungs and flesh and triggering vomiting and severe headaches in at least thirty thousand people. The foul-smelling waste had reached Abidjan in 2006 on a ship named *Probo Koala*, registered in Panama and chartered by a Singaporean commodities trading company known as Trafigura.[24] The noxious material had then been spread across big, public areas by a newly incorporated local enterprise called Tommy.

At the time, few West Africans had internet access, there was no free media, and the documents we gathered from the dusty files of Ivorian government departments were laughably unreliable. We built a vast, circumstantial case and our client seemed grateful, but we couldn't conclusively prove intent. Trafigura's time-honored playbook was to agree to settlements without admitting liability—all the while moving aggressively to forestall critical media coverage. Its model would have worked perfectly had an Australian programmer named Julian Assange not founded WikiLeaks. In 2009, the nonprofit group published parts of Trafigura's own internal investigation and email discussions, sparking one of Twitter's early social media storms and enabling an informal consortium of major newspapers across Europe to evade Trafigura's libel injunctions.[25] It seemed to me that a thrilling new means of holding companies accountable was at hand. If corporations could no longer function dependably as black boxes, everything would surely change.[26]

A year later, WikiLeaks released a fascinating trove of data: a set of classified diplomatic cables that invited unprecedented insight into the US government's overseas machinations. The files, which became known as Cablegate, included detailed descriptions of the assets and lifestyle of Tunisia's longtime ruler. They were framed by a blunt, undiplomatic assessment: "Corruption in the inner circle is growing." In despair over police demands for bribes, a local fruit seller set himself ablaze on camera, and Tunisia erupted in protest and ousted its president.

This was the first in a wave of Arab Spring uprisings in countries across the region, coordinated on social media and fueled by fresh awareness of how corruption blunts individual opportunity. In 2013, WikiLeaks shared Edward Snowden's riveting revelations about the technological reach of US intelligence agencies. In 2016, persistent allegations of corruption dogged both US presidential candidates, and Hillary Clinton's leaked emails fueled grievances on both sides. Confidentiality provisions were not yet dead, but in just ten years they had become utterly unreliable.

In 2009, only 1 billion of the world's people had internet access. By early 2020, almost four times as many were using social media, and adoption has continued to surge in the Global South. This revolution has transformed every aspect of our lives, including how we do business. Indeed, the most valuable companies in the world used to be in natural resources. Today's titans are in technology.

If you manage a business, one of the most profound consequences of mass internet access is that you can no longer control your narrative.

Simply put, anyone with a smartphone can instantly give fellow citizens intense, detailed glimpses into environmental disasters, labor rights violations, and grassroots protest movements. Or shabby customer service: in 2017, we watched security staff drag a doctor from an overbooked United Airlines flight, giving him a concussion and a broken nose and the airline a slipping share price and huge litigation expenses.[27] Viewing a stranger's live footage offers visceral impact that after-the-fact reporting and spin can't match.

Back in the twentieth century, public relations was simply about effective communication, not underlying culture, values, or behavior. Mainstream media was concentrated—and reluctant to trigger libel actions or risk losing ad revenue—so companies could largely direct messaging through friendly, predictable channels.[28] Today, the public crowdsources opinions on where to work and what to buy, and then skeptically compares them to the corporate narrative in question.

In his 2014 book *Revolt of the Public*, Martin Gurri pointed out that elites have lost their monopoly on information. If your business can't shield itself from the gaze of the outside world, your risks multiply exponentially. You cannot suppress critiques or keep secrets, and you can be thrown dramatically off course by misunderstandings and misinformation. No one can rely on the old-fashioned reputation management playbook: public relations, advertising, and employee-confidentiality provisions.

Today's activists start with hashtags and online petitions because social media is the tail that wags the dog of mainstream coverage—and even shareholder resolutions. Cozy relationships among big nongovernmental organizations (NGOs) and corporations have turned less dependable. Reputation management now involves playing whack-a-mole with faceless activist groups on the internet, whose viral successes seem to spring from nowhere. Consider the wildly successful #BoycottNRA hashtag that followed the Parkland, Florida, school shooting in 2018. Why this particular mass murder out of thousands in the United States? The answer lies in the agency and passion of some teen survivors and their parents. After Parkland, Walmart ceased to sell guns; Citibank, Bank of America, and JPMorgan Chase stopped serving the firearms industry; and companies including Delta Airlines and MetLife ended partnerships with the

National Rifle Association.[29] (A Republican backlash later brought retaliation in certain states.[30])

Social media can enable localized problems, conflicts, and concerns to gain global reach as never before. What's hardest is figuring out which issues might catch fire, which of your mistakes might come back to bite you as reputational risk. There's no predictable formula.

In 2016, investors were utterly unprepared when grassroots protests to block ongoing construction of the Dakota Access Pipeline (DAPL) blew up into a powerful metaphor for attacks on human rights in the United States. Compared with the risks of operating in failed petrostates like Equatorial Guinea or Venezuela, bankers had regarded domestic pipelines as a no-brainer investment. Loans to DAPL's owner, Energy Transfer Partners, had sailed through due diligence checks, and respected banks had provided financing.

But the pipeline was designed to cross sacred Native American lands, threatening leaks and spills that could taint water supplies. The Standing Rock Reservation's objections during the permitting process were largely ignored. When construction began, youthful protesters organized an activist group called ReZpect Our Water, put up a social media hashtag (#NoDAPL), and launched a cross-country run to raise awareness.[31] Protest camps at Standing Rock quickly drew thousands of supporters, with millions of Facebook check-ins. In September 2016, Americans watched YouTube footage of attack dogs being used against protesters.[32] Security forces in riot gear then used water cannons on them in freezing weather. A young woman nearly lost an arm in an unexplained explosion.[33]

Almost overnight, DAPL became a viral illustration of investors' complicity in human rights abuses. Shareholders launched proxy resolutions against the seventeen banks that had provided US$2.5 billion to fund construction. Protesters turned up at bank headquarters and branches to urge customer boycotts. CEOs were bombarded with emails and phone calls. A group of socially responsible investors with US$653 billion in assets under management signed a letter in support of rerouting the pipeline.[34] Shareholder resolutions aimed at specific banks amassed record-breaking vote totals. The strength, speed, and effectiveness of the DAPL protests shredded the banks' standard risk calculations and due diligence checklists and mired everyone involved in litigation and controversy.[35]

Participating banks sold off shares in the parent companies and dumped loans they held.[36] I spent most of 2017 helping a prominent US bank comprehensively revise its environmental and social risk policies and procedures, in direct response to a shareholder resolution over DAPL. As I write this, the pipeline is operational, pending a new environmental impact assessment, and US pipelines have become a riskier, heavily scrutinized investment.[37]

This fraught, new landscape for external risk isn't even the biggest challenge. Corporate affairs teams, exhausted from countering unwelcome images and complaints from the public, face more daunting threats from within. What began as CEO activism quickly morphed into a far more powerful, bottom-up phenomenon.[38] Unfiltered employee views now slip regularly from the corporate grasp and onto social media. We are constantly given opportunities to peer into the chasm between images a company takes care to project and what it's actually like to work there.

The weaponization of embarrassing internal information first flourished in the rarefied atmosphere of Silicon Valley, where open debate was long an article of faith. Staff at Google raised ethical concerns about projects for China's government and the US Department of Defense. Then twenty thousand Google employees took part in a walkout over millions of dollars in exit packages given to executives who'd been accused of sexual harassment.[39] At Facebook, gig workers violated their contracts to speak to the media about the trauma entailed in their work as content moderators.[40] In early 2022, a former government affairs executive at Uber gave the media 125,000 damning internal documents, including a message in which an executive said the company was "just f---ing illegal."[41] By the end of that year, Twitter employees were offering blow-by-blow accounts of the chaos following Elon Musk's acquisition.[42]

Employee activism quickly spread to other sectors. Workers at Wayfair challenged senior leadership about the company's contracts with US Immigration and Customs Enforcement; when they didn't get a satisfactory response, they organized a walkout via a new Twitter handle that garnered seventy thousand followers in twenty-four hours.[43] Employees protested work by Whole Foods and Ogilvy for government immigration agencies, and Harvard students took issue with working at law firms that serve oil and gas clients.[44] Employees at all the major accounting firms in Hong Kong issued an anonymous advertisement supporting protests there.[45] A senior account manager at public relations giant Edelman became a prominent climate whistleblower after unearthing huge contracts to provide PR to ExxonMobil.[46] A day after KPMG's UK chairman dismissed unconscious-bias training as "complete crap" in an internal meeting, his comments appeared all over the news, and he was out of a job.[47] Reduced to admitting that the firm is a "leaky sieve," KPMG took to imploring employees to use its internal hotline, not the media.[48]

These incidents are the visible tip of a fundamental reckoning over the balance of power between workers and leaders. A 2019 global survey by Herbert Smith Freehills found that 80 percent of C-suite respondents foresaw growing worker activism in the coming decade, with 95 percent expecting more employees to take up sharing their views on social media.[49] Even MBA students have been avowing greater skepticism about capitalism.[50] Beyond perception surveys, control of damaging information is slipping away from corporate control. In February 2022, as an increasingly global, viral movement embodied in the #MeToo hashtag continued to build against sexual harassment and abuse, President Joe Biden signed into law a bill ending forced arbitration in sexual assault cases. Draconian nondisclosure agreements came under sustained pressure, too.[51]

Before the mass adoption of digital discourse, the messy innards of corporate life were revealed only in the wake of scandalous revelations. Now anyone with an interest can dissect clumsy emails, assess tense town hall meetings, chortle over toxic gossip posted on Slack, and roll their eyes at accounts of drunken groping at charity fundraisers. In response, companies have deployed abundant new tools to track and monitor workers, suppliers, and customers.[52]

It won't suffice. Wise executives now assume that anything they say or do may become public knowledge.

How the Professional Became Personal

When I was recruited for my first proper consulting job at age twenty-six, I knew that my priority would be to project a professional identity and adapt to my employer's norms—not the other way around. I bought business-casual outfits at Banana Republic and prepared to suffer long hours and tedium until I could amass enough seniority to tell other people what to do. I would not have known how to respond to the current notion that I should be able to "bring my whole self to work."

How anachronistic those views are now. My students at NYU Stern do not aspire to find careers that align with their values and enable them to have a positive impact. They expect it.[53] As Doug Pinkham, CEO of the Public Affairs Council, tells me: "Employees want to work for a company with purpose—that has values and sticks to them and isn't hypocritical about it. They want to know: Are you doing something good for the world? Am I part of something positive, as opposed to just a money machine? Some companies were never able to answer that before. Now they can say, 'Well, you know what? We actually step up and do what's right.' So the pressures to get involved in social issues are enormous."

We can already see the impact on organizational culture in sectors dominated by the young and educated: technology, consulting, the media, nonprofits, and social enterprises.[54]

But while young people are often characterized as monolithically progressive and woke, the reality is far more complex.[55] In the United States, a high proportion of Generation Z and millennials feel alienated from political parties as they fret about the future of democracy.[56] There is strong bipartisan alignment among them around environmental sustainability and diversity and inclusion, as well as support for more governmental intervention in the economy. They serve company leaders who are still overwhelmingly middle-aged and male. You might call the pace of change "glacial"—back when glaciers still melted by the inch.

Hierarchical, intergenerational tensions are hardly novel. Their latest iteration might have played out gradually if the Covid-19 pandemic hadn't abruptly dissolved the boundaries between our personal and professional lives. Longer working hours, incessant communication, intensified employee surveillance, burnout, and mental health challenges were already on the rise. Rumblings over gender and racial inequalities were growing louder, too. They've become another new front as conflicts over power, control, opportunity, and inclusion play out in organizations.

Well before the pandemic, companies eager to collect ever-greater insights into workers were assuming control over anything that might have a tangential impact on employee motivation and productivity. New tools are presented as objective, data-driven methods to drive efficiency and reduce fraud, and they lure managers into monitoring everything from employees' sleep to the wording of their emails.[57] Managers and compliance teams find it difficult to resist tools that might reduce rule-breaking, but these can be invasive and threaten to undermine employee trust and motivation.

Just as corporate power has advanced in tandem with avowals of higher corporate purpose, all-consuming, unrealistic notions of the spiritual, ideological, intellectual, and emotional satisfaction our careers should provide have surged alongside those calls to bring your whole self to work.

Are these shifts here to stay? Exhibit A is the heightened concern over psychological welfare among our youngest workers, who are still powerfully motivated by dreams of personal fulfillment and financial security.[58] Numerous studies show that even before the pandemic exacerbated mental health issues, rates of anxiety, depression, and suicide in Gen Z were rising fast, particularly among women.[59] Graduating students are used to accommodation in academia to help them cope with anxiety or ADHD, and they expect comparable treatment in the workplace. Young employees seek flexibility and freedom, but they also want socialization and mentorship. In 2019, Starbucks was one of a growing roster of companies offering workers twenty annual mental health sessions.[60]

The idea that you should be able to bring your whole self to work is a tenet of the diversity and inclusion movement.[61] Having to hide such core aspects of your identity as your beliefs or sexuality might limit your ability to speak freely or share ideas, so this is well grounded and well intentioned. Still, it leaves us with yet another paradox: organizations must now set and establish clear values and cultural norms while responding to expectations that they will adapt to individual needs and demands, not the other way around. Even with the best intentions, that's far from straightforward.

As open social systems, companies cannot shield themselves from societal turmoil over equity, inequality, and inclusion. Pressed to diversify their ranks and make newcomers feel welcome and included at all levels, managers struggle to drive an overnight transformation of recruitment pipelines, promotion and retention, speaking up, and representation. It's natural to grope for turnkey solutions that don't exist, whether it's buying unconscious-bias training packages or expecting flagship hires to single-handedly achieve cultural transformation. But there's little evidence that any of this effectively increases belonging or inclusion.[62]

Here, too, young employees are weaponizing internal information to push leaders further and faster. Black staff members at Nike, Glossier, Adidas, and Everlane created Instagram accounts to share their experiences at work. Walmart sent an internal survey to gather perspective on the company's culture from senior Black employees, and its unflattering conclusions swiftly leaked to Bloomberg News.[63] Shareholder resolutions on diversity are multiplying.[64] For all the rhetoric about inclusion, companies face mounting litigation risks and criticism from all sides.

The culture wars will rage on and multiply. Employee activists are targeting historic discrimination that was long de-emphasized in favor of a narrative that played up meritocracy and colorblindness. It's important to note that today's focus on generational, gender, and racial categories comes as a backlash to chronic failure. Even good-faith efforts cannot change the entrenched power structures atop our organizations fast enough to satisfy these expectations.

Many corporations are used to operating on the assumption that leadership is simply a matter of setting direction and incentivizing underlings to perform. But younger employees no longer see experience and power as synonymous with authority. They want more democratic input on decisions. This raises difficult questions about how you can listen to and benefit from employee voice without slowing the pace of work and generating perpetual conflict. Managers are struggling with the perceived need to be as nurturing and supportive as a cherished teacher or cool parent while trying to fulfill financial goals and drive employee performance.[65]

Navigating this rugged and tumultuous world would be tricky in the best of times. But as the earth shifts underneath, we're using leaky boots and worn-out tools to keep from being dragged into the muck. Since we cannot reliably shield ourselves from turmoil, we should pause to review some of the shaky precepts that got us here. The path to higher ground calls for better footing and firmer foundations.

How "Responsible Business" Became a Tangle of Traps

I n responsible business, the perfect is truly the enemy of the good. Consider Yvon Chouinard's announcement in September 2022 that he would transfer the ownership of Patagonia Inc., which he'd founded in 1973, to a nonprofit trust.[1] The media responded with initial enthusiasm to the eighty-three-year-old eco-entrepreneur's declaration that "Earth is our only shareholder. Instead of 'going public,' you could say we are 'going purpose.'" But within days, commentators were noting that the underlying business model would still rely on plastic, the deal's structure would facilitate tax avoidance, and Patagonia's employees would get no stake.[2]

Even turning your profoundly successful company into a charity won't suspend society's "gotcha" mindset for long. In a feverish atmosphere where polarization and misinformation flourish, there is no reliable way to avoid criticism, please all stakeholders, and manage reputational risk. When the ground is shifting, neither higher walls nor a faster pace will help. It's time to seek firmer footing.

We all humanize companies. We give them personalities and discuss what they fear, decide, and intend. Long before the onset of consumer spectator sports like Coke versus Pepsi and Microsoft versus Apple, the urge to anthropomorphize the great forces in our lives came naturally to human beings. People readily project personhood onto nations, storms, ships, teams, flags.[3] Even professional journalists report vividly on what the businesses they cover think and dream.

But the idea of the corporate person isn't just an appealing metaphor. It is fundamental to business law. From the Babylonian Code of Law through regulations in ancient India, imperial Rome, medieval guilds, Renaissance banking, the British Empire's joint stock companies, and various innovations in the United States, private enterprise has evolved to attain what we call corporate personhood.[4] What we know as the corporate "principal" has a singular identity and set of interests. Everyone in an enterprise must answer to it. Contrary to what you may have heard, not even shareholders own or control it. They merely partake in its profits.

But in our daily lives, a corporation does not present itself as a singular, self-interested citizen. It's not a person with a character we can root for or against. A company doesn't have a brain; it decides nothing. It's an open system in constant motion, comprising real human beings who form groups and negotiate over power, resources, strategy, and direction. The group dynamics just happen to play out behind a complex curtain of corporate lore and received wisdom.

This has always been true. But as corporate value becomes less tangible and corporate culture more vulnerable, thinking of corporations as good or bad becomes less and less useful. For companies to do better, we'll need new metaphors and fresh ways of seeing their role in the world.

I invite you to join me now in critically examining the common clichés, myths, and misunderstandings about responsible business that confuse and paralyze us. They carry unintended, troubling, even dangerous consequences. By making some simple adjustments, you can avoid the booby traps.

Companies Can Balance the Interests of Their Stakeholders

In 2019, the Business Roundtable redefined the purpose of the corporation with a message that quickly sprouted into a mantra: corporations should not focus exclusively on shareholder value, but ought to balance the interests of all their stakeholders: customers, employees, suppliers, communities, and (finally) investors.

This is hard to argue with, but that's because it's banal. For one thing, "stakeholder" is an elusive buzzword. A stakeholder can be defined as someone who has an interest in your business today—or might tomorrow. By this definition, all companies "engage" their stakeholders. Critics quickly pointed out that although the Business Roundtable had framed its assertion as a fundamental shift in corporate governance, few of the CEOs involved consulted their boards on the matter.[5] They may have signed on because the statement seemed to reflect business as usual.

Moreover, the call to balance stakeholder interests is vague and falsely suggests that win-win solutions are always available. If you're a leader trying to execute this in a practical fashion, you will quickly be overwhelmed. Should you pay attention to employees who contend that your enterprise ought to stop doing business with oil companies? Or to union leaders pressing you to hike wages above market levels? Should you respond to politicians who oppose "woke capitalism," or to staffers who expect you to serve as the last bastion of support for their reproductive rights? What will you tell activists who want you to focus on tackling inequality? Or those who see animal rights—or plastic waste—as your biggest priority?

This is less about finding balance than exercising practical curiosity to identify blind spots and alternative angles—and then mustering the courage to make tough trade-offs. While there's risk in having key interest groups say you're ignoring them, it's riskier to anchor your decisions in the shifting sands of opinion. That would never please everyone and might well leave you looking skittish and indecisive.

An even bigger problem is that while the idea of balancing stakeholder interests *sounds* new, it still assumes that stakeholders constitute threats to the precious corporate principal. Take this statement from prominent Columbia University law professor John Coffee Jr.: "[Do] boards owe a fiduciary duty to stakeholders? This is a legal contradiction in terms; by definition, a fiduciary owes a duty of undivided loyalty to his beneficiaries, and one cannot owe such a duty to natural adversaries."[6]

Here, Coffee acknowledges that from a traditional corporate governance perspective, stakeholders—the customers, suppliers, employees, and communities that any business *relies on to survive*—are to be treated as *natural adversaries.*

This is no mere legal mindset. Charles Fombrun shaped the notion of reputational risk in the 1990s when he contended: "A company's reputational capital is the value of the company that is 'at risk' in everyday interaction with stakeholders."[7] There it is again: stakeholders are seen as *threats*. This shows us how the hard work of building a social license to operate can easily become downgraded into the instrumental goal of accumulating reputational capital.

If your primary goal is to protect the corporate principal from dangerous incursions, no wonder it's such a struggle to implement stakeholder capitalism! Our old metaphors blind us to the potential of collaborating for mutual value. Worse, they limit envisaged solutions to those a company can achieve on its own.

You will never please all the people all of the time, and opinions shift with the breeze. In chapter 3, I will explore why comprehending your impact on stakeholders is so much more useful and grounded than trying to deflect reputational risk. Starting with impact gives you the chance to build truly resilient relationships that can guide you through turbulent times.

Environmental and Social Responsibility Is Always Good for the Bottom Line

It's been hard to miss the exponential growth in investors' enthusiasm for integrating environmental, social, and governance (ESG) factors into their decisions. In January 2018, Larry Fink, CEO and chairman of BlackRock—and by many measures the world's most powerful shareholder—set forth his thesis that "every company must not only deliver financial performance, but also show how it makes a positive contribution to society."[8] Advocates for ESG investing (whose title is often conflated with sustainability, and which is morphing as political struggles over the underlying issues mount) argue that good ESG performance will invariably lead to stronger financial performance over the long term, so long as you survey the range of issues and identify those relevant for either risk reduction or value creation. Historically, investing for social impact had been a niche activity that meant accepting lower returns. Then Fink and other mainstream financiers began to argue that any perceived tension between morals and money reflects a false dichotomy.

Fink had been circulating annual missives to CEOs since 2012, but this one hit a nerve. Within days, it seemed as if every executive in America wanted to discuss the "Larry Fink letter" with me. With influential people wanting to hear more about the business case for ESG, I was suddenly being asked to provide evidence that doing the right thing would help their companies make more money. Exhilarated by so much fresh momentum, I sought to oblige. Soon I realized that we'd maneuvered ourselves into a circular argument that shareholder returns are the best way to evaluate an approach originally conceived as a counterweight to the overwhelming obsession with . . . shareholder returns.[9]

Fink's position largely drew on an influential article by Michael Porter and Mark Kramer, who contended in 2006 that businesses needed to identify and prioritize initiatives that would create shared value by benefiting society and generating profit at the same time.[10] This thinking also manifests in the notion of the "triple bottom line" whereby you measure your efforts according to "people, planet, profit," and you "do well by doing good."[11]

Why are these memes so appealing? They tell us something we want to hear: what's good for stakeholders will be good for shareholders—and vice versa. But these broad, long-standing arguments provide little guidance on what to do about the numerous issues for which doing the right thing costs your company more and takes more time, and where the rewards are longer term, uncertain, and out of your control.[12]

Sustainable finance advocates love to insist that their efforts are just smart capitalism—not designed to help companies do the right thing so much as to manage external risk. For example, Hortense Bioy, head of sustainability research at Morningstar, said, "There are still people who inappropriately conflate sustainability and ethics."[13] Her view is understandable, given the aggressive effort by a subset of political actors to falsely frame ESG as an ideological, "socialist" movement.[14] Nonetheless, suggesting that sustainability and ethics are entirely unrelated is a conceptual booby trap.

Big environmental and social missteps can certainly wreak enormous damage on your reputation, leading to financial underperformance. But these missteps result from disregarding your negative impacts on human beings. ESG issues present today's corporations with a spread of profound intertemporal and cross-functional challenges. It is impossible to navigate among them or set priorities unless your organization can clearly differentiate between a material risk and an opportunity to create value. Further, you will need to set priorities among impacts that may not *yet* present a material risk or opportunity but might do so in the future.

An overwhelming number of examples demonstrate that if you wait until reputational risk manifests, you've waited too long. It was only after George Floyd's murder in 2020 that lagging on diversity, equity, and inclusion presented companies with significant reputational risk. Despite its government's track record of unprovoked aggression and corruption, it was only when Russia invaded Ukraine that operating there brought significant reputational risk. And for all the evidence that plastic waste was harming the environment, it took a David Attenborough documentary about companies' packaging practices for reputational risk to manifest. The root cause of reputational risk is always negative impacts.

Questions of morality and money now converge with blinding speed. Every company must judge how and when a negative impact might become a risk, though this can be fiendishly hard. For every shared value example of an energy-saving initiative that reduces operational costs, or a social investment that enhances customer loyalty, we can find a less comfortable result. It can cost a business money to ensure better labor standards in its supply chain, or to reduce pollution when it's not legally required—and the long-term financial benefits can't be predicted with certainty. But an individual corporation can easily make a business case for investing in favorable regulatory treatment and tax avoidance. Public rage over inadequate social services, human rights violations, or corruption will not affect all businesses equally or at once. These things can't always be quantified, and they don't fit neatly into a spreadsheet of costs and returns.

This makes fixating on achieving better ESG ratings as an end in itself a singularly ineffective way to lead and manage a company today—and not just because the ratings are so inconsistent. If you understand ESG only as a scoring system to help attract investors and generate higher returns, you can certainly tick that box. But you'll be missing the point.

You should never try to convince anyone that you can meaningfully prioritize dozens of complex ESG issues. That's impression management.

In chapter 4, I will discuss why a better approach is to identify a tiny number of issues—one is ideal—that are strategically significant because they present existential threats *and* potential financial opportunities. Then you focus on truly addressing these issues and integrating the effort into your business. A one-size-fits-all approach won't work. Success demands that you incentivize innovation while penalizing irresponsibility and ethical violations. This can't be done unless we're clear on which is which.

Business Ethics Is a Simple Matter: Just Don't Break the Law

If expecting so much from companies is unrealistic, and balancing stakeholder expectations impossible, was Milton Friedman right after all? Are we overcomplicating this? I might seem to be making a case to just go back to basics and stick to not breaking the law. However, legal compliance has never been a simple, binary matter, and it's growing ever more complicated. Hong Kong–based financial services firms need to honor contradictory Chinese and US regulations, while asset managers in the United States face conflicting strictures on ESG from state governments.

I worked on anti-corruption efforts for twelve years. I watched the field ramp up, and I tracked the transformation in corporate compliance that resulted. My experience confirms that regulatory attention can dramatically nudge corporate norms and behavior in a positive direction. It also illustrates the limitations of legal compliance frameworks when it comes to influencing corporate conduct.

An obviously negative manifestation of corruption is when government officials seek bribes from companies in return for access to services, contract awards, information, or favors. But paying bribes was long deemed unavoidable; companies reasoned that it's "just the way they do business over there."

After that attitude brought US Senate hearings and reform legislation in the 1970s, the heat temporarily subsided. But as globalization advanced following the end of the Cold War, institutions like the World Bank and IMF began focusing on how government corruption undermines development, wastes natural resources, and distorts competition.[15] Then the 9/11 attacks triggered greater focus on preventing money laundering and terrorist financing. The anti-corruption enforcement boom took off first in the United States, then globally. In mere decades, a remarkable international consensus emerged.

The zeal for enforcement continues and comes with copious advice from regulators on how to design a good anti-corruption program.[16] A decent one can even serve as both operational and legal defense in the event a bad-apple employee is caught paying a bribe. Your company almost certainly has a zero-tolerance anti-corruption policy. It's likely that your international business partners are familiar with the US Foreign Corrupt Practices Act and similar internationally binding laws, and know they must sign agreements promising not to pay bribes if they wish to secure your business.

Corporate anti-corruption programs have thus reached the kind of advanced state that climate change activists dream of. Yet corporate bribery scandals continue, and corruption as a societal challenge remains unresolved.

In chapter 5, I will show that while compliance efforts against bribery are essential, they are insufficient to tackle the wider challenges of corruption. First, you need to consider whether your company's goals and targets incentivize employees to operate unethically. Are internal reward systems addressed in your compliance framework? As for bribery, zero tolerance won't help much in countries where corruption is so endemic that your staff cannot function without facing extortion or physical threats.

Ruling out payments and favors won't reliably address nepotism, regulatory capture, and rising pressure over lobbying and campaign finance. Moreover, doing business in a kleptocracy doesn't necessarily mean bribing the power brokers who control lucrative relationships; working with them is a condition of entering the market. In such a market, winning a contract guarantees nothing: shifting political winds can topple kleptocrats and lead to retaliation, even expropriation. So if you ban bribes but don't consider wider questions of power and political risk, it can all end very badly.

Tackling corruption risk effectively in a given country requires more than legal controls. It starts with gaining a practical understanding of how corruption affects your sector. Then you must build business and political relationships to make your company resilient in the face of ever-unpredictable shifts. You'll need to build an organizational culture whose incentives and rules do not conflict, and your employees must be empowered to raise questions and use their judgment.

Business Ethics Is an Oxymoron

Viewing business ethics as an approach to deflect regulatory risk served companies well enough for a long time. But society has grown too transparent, too angry, too unpredictable to let legal risk continue serving as some sort of anchor to guide corporate decision-making. If you view your efforts in terms of defending the corporate black box from scrutiny and the law, you'll be confined to a reactive mode.

Recognition of this is a primary driver of the renaissance in talk of corporate values, with "purpose" a favorite. But even with the best intentions, focusing on values puts companies in a bind that carries . . . risks. Values are contentious, political, and ideological. Taking a strong stance will inevitably alienate some stakeholders. Potentially, you will create a subset of resentful employees and encourage internal conflict over what your priorities should be and when to take a stand.

Where does this leave business ethics?

As I discussed in the introduction, many experts shun the term on the ground that "people expect you to start singing hymns." Even executives who love to rhapsodize about ethics in speeches confine their formal, written commitments to terse, forgettable pledges to "lead with integrity." Their vagueness reflects warnings from legal professionals that issuing more ambitious, concrete commitments could expose their enterprises to litigation. (Corporate lawyers can cite cases.)[17] What results is a corporate penchant for unmemorable statements that don't convince anyone.

Is there a worthy alternative?

Yes, though it requires work and fresh thinking. Being an ethical business is about undertaking a process of discovery about your *real-world impact* and then basing your values and supporting principles on what you find. What has your company been doing that generates negative and positive impacts? (Economists call them "externalities.") How do you affect the external environment? How does it impact you? How might you alter these results?

Companies have historically struggled to manage notions of impact because it's simpler and more direct to assess risks and returns. That's too bad, because rising concern over the negative impacts of powerful corporations is what's actually driving this messy paradigm shift. In the 2020s, impact is the most promising anchor for any notion of what it means to be an ethical business.[18]

Considering corporate impact is not as exotic or esoteric as it might sound. Every business aims to provide a service, meet a need, or solve a problem. It seeks to generate profit by delivering a positive impact, perhaps many. The darker side—treating negative impacts as irrelevant externalities, the way industrial wastewater used to be shed in public channels—is no longer a smart or defensible practice. Seeking to do no harm and manage your own impacts is a far better-grounded approach than seeking to impose values on people who may not share them. It is pluralistic and respectful of individual rights and freedom. It can help build your social license to operate while averting ideological distraction.

As I will describe in chapter 6, a final advantage in treating values as a question of impact is that there's plenty of thoughtful guidance on how to consider impact. It is fresh, too—codified as recently as 2011—and it comes from the field of business and human rights.[19]

Making a commitment to human rights, dignity, and inclusion shows that you know these issues aren't optional social priorities or means to an end. They're critical matters for every company that employs human beings. They are internal and external, personal and political, universally applicable—yet culturally determined. They encompass environmental, social and governance challenges, but unlike the instrumentalism of ESG, they rest on a coherent body of international law that at least considers the ethical obligations of business and how they relate to the ethical obligations of government.

Responsible Business Isn't about Politics

This notion is popular among both opponents and proponents of responsible business. It's appealing to frame one's own goals as obvious and rational while only the other side has a political agenda.

To steer clear of politics was a long-accepted dictum for big business everywhere: Who wants to alienate potential customers with divisive public positions? But the bright line demarcating business and politics has never been more than a convenient story. Pursuing the singular goal of making as much money for shareholders as possible has made it de rigueur to deploy lobbyists with vast budgets to secure favorable regulations and lower tax rates. As Raghuram Rajan, a former governor of the Reserve Bank of India, astutely commented, "shareholder value maximization . . . completely turns a tin ear to politics."[20]

The tin ear exists by design. Businesses do not wish to draw attention to the shadowy work of their government relations teams. Even as pressures to address corporate externalities have risen, we prefer to frame environmental and social responsibility as a set of objective performance metrics. Facing backlash from Republican politicians over ESG, Larry Fink wrote in 2022: "Stakeholder capitalism is not about politics. It is not a social or ideological agenda. It is not 'woke.' *It is capitalism.*"[21] (A year later, he declared he would no longer employ the term ESG and said he was ashamed at how it had been politicized.)

But as we saw in chapter 1, stakeholder capitalism arose partly from political failure. With activists and employees so focused on hypocrisy in the C-suite, it has grown harder to divorce a company's ESG priorities from policy questions. If you've committed to the Paris Agreement, it is hard to justify your business's lobbying against climate legislation. If you have made noise about empowering women, it's a stretch to support candidates who favor undermining reproductive rights. However awkwardly, companies cling like limpets to this split-screen approach.

It is simply disingenuous to treat corporate responsibility and political influence as unrelated topics, not least because every company confronts environmental and social dilemmas it cannot solve alone. Any attempt to define social or environmental responsibility must implicitly take a position on the appropriate role of corporate voluntary action versus government oversight. While maintaining knee-jerk opposition to regulation and tax increases might seem in a corporation's self-interest, this stance has dumped a lot of painful public policy problems on companies' laps. If there isn't an agreed carbon price, it's up to you to figure out the costs and benefits of adapting to climate change across a range of unpredictable scenarios. If wildfires are raging, it's up to you to figure out what to do about corporate travel, office air quality, and employee health conditions.[22]

Corporate political responsibility is a hot topic, and I will explore emerging pressures and responses in chapter 7. Trade association memberships, lobbying, tax avoidance, and government subsidies are undergoing sustained scrutiny. A useful response will require much deliberation. You will need to limit outreach and to ensure that your efforts to achieve political influence don't conflict with your public statements. This is further reason why pursuing sharply focused environmental and social priorities is a far better strategy than ticking the ESG box or seeking brand advantage from empty words in reaction to public events and furors.

Transparency Drives Accountability

If any single idea unites today's businesses, regulators, investors, and NGO activists, it's the power of transparency to drive accountability.[23] There's plenty of evidence that transparency *is* powerful and is transforming the operating context. For example, opaque corporate ownership and contract award processes decidedly increase corruption risk, and nondisclosure agreements have long shielded perpetrators of harassment. As we've seen, corporations can no longer dependably control their reputations or rely on confidentiality provisions. This is at once a cause and consequence of heightened transparency.

Corporate transparency is seen as both a means and an end. The term has become a common shorthand for all sorts of information disclosure. But our devotion to transparency as a solution has taken on a quasi-religious quality. If you admit to reservations about transparency, you must have something horrible to hide.

When we ask tough questions, complications soon emerge. Transparency is said to promote trust in business because consumers and investors can use corporate disclosures to "vote" by withdrawing funding, business, and social approval from bad actors. In other words, if we mandate disclosure, "good" companies have nothing to fear: transparency guarantees a reputation-enhancing win-win.

None of these arguments pays much attention to the *receiver* of information. For transparency to lead reliably to accountability, we must agree on what good performance looks like. We must first be able to access the necessary information. Then we need the expertise and capacity to interpret it, and the power to force a response.

These conditions are lacking in the real world. Even when humans receive the simplest information, we respond according to our existing biases and beliefs. Business disclosure is never simple, even when a company is not trying to obfuscate. While this is true of financial information, it is exponentially more so when it comes to disclosing environmental and social performance. "Consider the amount of water it takes to produce a one-liter bottle of Coke: The Coca-Cola Company's own estimates have varied from less than two liters of water to 70 liters, depending on the methodology used," Ken Pucker, former COO of Timberland, observed in 2021.[24]

Because there is no objective measure of what "good" looks like, and no agreement on the ultimate goal of the push for transparency, companies have little incentive to spill their guts onto the operating table and trust they'll benefit from the procedure. Indeed, academic research on activism suggests that *both* leaders and laggards are targeted: the more transparent and responsible you claim to be, the more criticism and scrutiny your company will generate.[25] Keep your head down and stay in the middle of the pack, and it's likely that you will avoid being targeted.

So corporate leaders are wary of transparency, though they can't admit it. The consequences abound in carefully curated disclosures that frame corporate actions in the best light possible. These are often viewed with suspicion as "greenwashing," "purpose washing," and "woke washing." The result? We spend far more effort and energy playing endless games of cat and mouse than changing anything.

It is when companies have nothing left to lose that they stop trying to tell their stories and we see truly promising transparency efforts. Such candid disclosures show the true potential of corporate responsibility as a messy, dynamic, and useful process of improvement. In a general atmosphere of exasperation over unconvincing corporate spin, putting forth an authentic account of your efforts and their limits can prove much smarter and less risky than you've been told. In chapter 8, I will argue that admitting to imperfection can be a powerful way to build trust. It can even generate competitive advantage.

Becoming an Ethical Company Is Just a Case of Removing the Bad Apples

An alternative set of clichés about good and bad companies begins with a classic. What if being a good company is simply a matter of finding and removing the bad *people*? Specifically, compliance programs aim to prevent employees from stealing, cheating, or bribing. In this way, they protect the corporate principal from the selfish actions of its human employees, or agents. (This is known as the principal-agent problem.[26])

When ethics scandals hit the headlines, it's common for the unfortunate executive at the microphone to assure us that the problem is merely a few bad apples. This claim conveniently absolves leaders of personal responsibility while implying that ethical oversight is a simple matter CEOs can delegate while they focus on more important things.

If building an ethical business is simply a matter of removing rogue employees, all that companies need to do is impose clear policies and rules, mandate training to enforce them, provide a whistleblowing mechanism to enable employees to speak up, and investigate and fire wrongdoers.

Unfortunately, it's not so simple. Human personality does matter—some. But we're far more influenced by our social environment than we like to admit, even to ourselves. Dividing people into good and bad isn't much more useful than dividing companies into good and bad.

Nor will compliance procedures necessarily address situations in which employees are incentivized to behave unethically *for the benefit of the company and its leaders*. Compliance teams can, and often do, become captives of the systems they oversee. Problems in the run-up to Credit Suisse's collapse included a US$5.5 billion trading loss from the collapse of Archegos Capital, the launch of employee surveillance, and breaches of Covid-19 restrictions by the board chair. These were not so much compliance failures as leadership failures that reflected poorly on the compliance department's mission and authority. Compliance at Facebook had no legal alternative but to hand over private messages to authorities in Nebraska who intended to pursue a mother and daughter for seeking an abortion; Facebook had the data because its business model broadly rests on capturing and monetizing sensitive personal information.[27] In other words, if how the company makes money is the issue, there's a clear limit to what compliance can achieve.

In practice, companies harbor ethical problems because of a flawed tone at the top that's underpinned by widespread willful blindness, toxic incentives, and mechanisms that deflect scrutiny. These conditions existed at Wells Fargo, VW, and Boeing, to cite a few examples. Such conditions seem to persist and metastasize. If we really want organizations to be ethical, we need to focus on designing cultures that make being ethical as easy as possible. In chapter 9, I will explore how to build resilient, ethical organizational cultures in our transparent, angry era.

It's All about Tone at the Top; Ethical Leaders Ensure an Ethical Business

If bad apples serve as a convenient explanation (if not a very useful one), what about another perennial cliché, "tone at the top"? This notion is more compelling because leaders are responsible for socializing employees into an organization. While we all sign a code of conduct when we join a company, it is watching what leaders prioritize—and whom they reward and punish—that tells us what behavior might help us succeed. Leaders therefore need not be personally involved in wrongdoing to bear some responsibility for it.

Still, tone at the top suggests we need only find and select good leaders and our problems will be resolved. Organizational realities are far more complex, and it's never enough for a leader to simply be a good person. Ethical leaders take oversight seriously, broaden capacity for moral decision-making, and focus on instilling trust and psychological safety throughout the organization. Otherwise, tone at the top inevitably gives way to tone in the middle, where inconsistency is a huge problem. In the classroom, for example, I hear every day from middle managers who are told to prioritize *both* high performance and individual well-being.

Becoming a leader creates a power distance that blunts sensitivity and judgment. Some 91 percent of leaders surveyed by Deloitte in 2022 believed that employees felt leaders cared about them; only 56 percent of the surveyed employees agreed.[28] As we will discuss, leading companies have come to view employee voice as an asset and consciously build checks and balances to compensate for the inevitable blind spots at the top. In chapter 10, I'll explore how to design organizations with these realities in mind.

We Should Have Zero Tolerance for Unethical Behavior

Proclaiming zero tolerance is how you signal a robust commitment to removing those pesky bad apples. It's a boilerplate statement for good reason: publicly admitting you allow some unethical behavior is about as unthinkable as querying the benefits of transparency. But as professor and business ethics consultant Bettina Palazzo tells me: "It sounds very brave, but it's a sign of helplessness. Somebody started this stupid phrase, and everybody just copied it—like very often in business ethics."

Signaling a robust approach to wrongdoing is unquestionably important. But too often, zero tolerance results in strictures that force employees to learn irrelevant rules and procedures that undermine the individual judgment and voice you actually need them to develop.[29] Worse, many companies combine rhetoric about zero tolerance with lax enforcement, especially at senior levels. Scandals such as the 1MBD fraud at Goldman Sachs and others at large corporations, including GSK and Wells Fargo, show how common it is to award impunity to high performers while not looking closely at what it took for them to achieve so much.

Under pressure to signal firm intent to regulators, many compliance teams generate pointless rules and processes.[30] Generic online training and overly bureaucratic approvals are plainly alienating. Compliance teams that hound staff in lower ranks often lack the authority to impose these processes on senior leaders. This helps explain why the compliance industry, notwithstanding its exponential growth, has failed to curb ethical scandals.

The most important priorities for any compliance program are to encourage good behavior and ensure that punishment for bad behavior is credible, fair, and proportionate. But while some challenges come with stark outlines, many more are shrouded in shades of gray.

In chapter 11, I will explore why it's best for compliance efforts to contain zero tolerance to a limited number of critically relevant rules, conduct investigations without fear or favor, and give compliance teams the formal charge to hold senior leaders accountable. On a broader scale, it's best to help employees develop judgment and critical faculties so they learn to navigate fraught questions and to raise and discuss concerns when they feel uncertain. That's a more reliable way to resolve problems before they become scandals.

Employees Should Have the Courage to Speak Up about What's Right

Today's corporations spend a lot of time entreating employees to speak up without exploring why it requires so much courage in the first place. The realities of hierarchy almost always make whistleblowing a career-limiting move. Regulatory obligations require anonymous speak-up lines, but even when employees know they exist and how to use them (far from certain), the procedure is commonly mistrusted.

A bigger problem is that speaking up has become a far broader, more dynamic process. Weaponizing information is today's preferred whistleblowing mode. Speak-up lines were built for a quieter era, whereas whistleblowing is now about coordinating employee protests, or collectively leaking your organization's secrets onto social media.

The legacy speak-up framework was designed *solely* to identify any regulatory risks from fraud, corruption, discrimination, and harassment. While contemporary employees may agonize over fraud, they are just as likely to be upset about inaction on climate change. Since no one is going to call the whistleblowing line to complain that their boss is valuing profits over purpose, such frustrations wind up being expressed on social media. This can wreak enormous damage.

In chapter 12, I will argue that a resilient business won't try to ban all expressions of discontent. It will benefit from realizing that an expression of employee discontent effectively invites leadership to anticipate and head off what might otherwise become a public relations crisis. Leaders need to find balance between ensuring that critical employee voices will be heard and seeming to suggest that every corporate decision can be interminably debated or opened to a democratic vote. If you listen carefully and explain your decisions well, employees will be able to decide whether your company is a good fit for their values and ambitions.

Employees Should Bring Their Whole Selves to Work; Jobs Should Align with Personal Values

The belief that work should align with personal values has grown popular, along with the idea that we should bring our whole selves to work. These aspirations have found an outlet in the corporate "purpose" movement, which aims to leverage employee passion for meaning at work. Paul Polman, the former CEO of Unilever, has maintained: "You cannot be a purpose-driven company if you're not purposeful yourself, finding your purpose, fighting for things you believe in. . . . So live what you preach."[31]

Purpose statements abound. Some are forgettable and inoffensive; others sound like grandiose, manipulative bullshit. (When using this word, I will follow Harry Frankfurt's definition of bullshit not as a lie but rather as a "statement made without regard to the truth."[32]) There's a toxic, self-serving underside to the notion that a workplace might be like family, or that being a billing coordinator or plant supervisor will provide spiritual fulfillment. The approach creates more problems than it solves: some companies that unwittingly fostered conflict over contentious values issues are now pressed to speak up on every controversy that surfaces in the ranks.

In this book's conclusion, I will explore how to make purpose more than a marketing gimmick. Taking concrete steps to value and listen to your employees—and to provide rewards they care about—will prove far more effective than an aspirational rebrand. If staff do not feel valued during the workday, any organizational commitment to a higher purpose will rest on quicksand.

I do not maintain that tackling these myths will be easy. Each is deeply embedded in established approaches to corporate ethics and responsibility. As with most clichés, all contain kernels of truth—and long tails of misunderstanding, wasted effort, and vested interests. With so much in flux, these tools and ideas are no longer fit for the tasks at hand.

There's a fresher, firmer way to navigate tangled, thorny underbrush and make our way to the clearer views and brighter skies of higher ground. Let's start by discussing what it means to get serious about stakeholder trust.

PART II

BUSINESS DOING THE RIGHT THING

3

Building Stakeholder Trust

I n 2022, Coca-Cola stumbled into a maelstrom of criticism after signing an agreement with Egypt's government to sponsor the COP27 climate talks in Sharm el Sheikh.[1] The company had earlier disclosed that it annually produced 3 billion tons of plastic packaging and had pledged to recycle a bottle for each one sold by 2030.[2] A commitment made back in 1990 to recycle 25 percent of its bottles by 2015 had flopped spectacularly, but the beverage giant's long-running partnerships with some big environmental NGOs, including the Ellen MacArthur Foundation and the World Wildlife Fund, had always constituted an effective reputation management playbook.[3] Indeed, this blend of disclosures, pledges, partnerships, and sponsorships is the legacy corporate approach to stakeholder engagement.

But when a tiny activist organization launched a petition against Coca-Cola's COP27 sponsorship, the grassroots campaign took off.[4] Coca-Cola's COP27 sponsorship was suddenly portrayed as the latest turn in a bad-faith, manipulative relationship with the public. A spate of reports contrasted decades of the company's avowed targets and commitments with its lobbying strategies and found scant evidence of a meaningful commitment to change.[5]

Managing reputational risk is a contained activity. It treats corporate messaging as an end in itself that's divorced from questions of a company's underlying conduct. A domain of PR focuses on "reputation laundering."[6] By contrast, any effort to generate trust must begin with an appreciation of reciprocity. What it means to trust an organization is hotly debated, partly because trust is so difficult to define. But we might best regard it as mutual confidence that one party will not exploit the other.[7] Trust means anticipating reliability, honesty, fairness, competence, respect, and transparency. This aligns with how most of us believe a business *should* behave.

A company that makes the effort to understand its impacts on stakeholders and aims to build trust (rather than merely enhance its reputation) is likely to prove resilient. A study called "Not All Sparks Light a Fire" examined the background to corporate crises in the mining sector and showed that if you have deep and trusting external relationships, you'll get the benefit of the doubt when a crisis strikes. If you lack such trust, any hole you are in is likely to keep getting deeper.[8]

How, then, can companies go about building reciprocal, resilient relationships? Many corporations and mainstream investors have endorsed an approach called "stakeholder capitalism": companies should engage their stakeholders and balance various interests to secure a broad social license to operate. Recent frameworks, including the EU's Corporate Sustainability Reporting Directive and the UN Guiding Principles on Business and Human Rights, go further.[9] They aim to drive a shift away from exclusive consideration of *risks to* corporations, and toward seeking a deeper understanding of the *impact of* corporations. This change in mindset cannot be accomplished by peering out at the world from inside your headquarters. You'll need to exercise humility and curiosity about your company's impacts, solicit the perspectives of those affected, and then determine how to proceed in accordance with your capabilities and relationships.

There's a dearth of practical guidance on how to achieve this. A lot of confusion stems from a big buzzword: Just what is a *stakeholder*?

R. Edward Freeman, one of the most influential voices in stakeholder capitalism, defines a stakeholder as "any group or individual who can affect or is affected by the achievement of the organization's objectives."[10] This stakeholder landscape includes anyone who has a material interest in your business today, or who might have tomorrow. Primary stakeholders are "customers, employees, suppliers, communities and shareholders."[11] In making practical decisions, companies might also need to consider such secondary stakeholders as regulators, government agencies, industry associations, and NGOs—even the environment itself.

This adds up to a cacophony of voices. As Judy Samuelson of the Aspen Institute has pointed out, "the term [stakeholder] is too generic and the concept is both too facile and hard to grasp as a starting point for real change."[12] And as business ethics scholar Muel Kaptein rightly argues, the stakeholder literature is rarely, if ever, specific about who is *not* a stakeholder. The result, Kaptein wrote, is literature that "suggests that the ethical responsibilities of companies are unlimited and incessant."[13]

Trying to balance stakeholder interests can draw criticism from all sides. It entails deciding whose interests to heed, when to collaborate, and when to compete. That's a far more complicated process than the Business Roundtable makes it sound: "Each of our stakeholders is essential. We commit to deliver value to all of them, for the future success of our companies, our communities and our country."[14] Understandably, many leaders find this language generic and confusing.

Whatever they call their process, CEOs determine whose interests to prioritize in everyday decisions on how to allocate resources and authority, hire and reward people, make social investments, influence the political system, and set values and supporting principles. These judgments can help you build deep, resilient networks or they can leave you vacillating when problems crop up.

Moreover, companies cannot singlehandedly solve many of the environmental and social challenges they face. Whether you're trying to improve supply chain oversight, transform your energy usage profile, or adapt your product line to new demands, collaboration can be as important as competition.[15]

Stakeholder engagement is a mindset as well as a process. When your goal is to manage reputation, you'll perceive stakeholders as threats to corporate value and your task will be one of messaging, deflection, and neutralization. If instead you seek to build trust, you'll focus on developing a practical understanding of your company's impact. You'll need to ensure that your efforts aren't siloed into a single team. You must then proceed carefully and deliberately in any exchange of views. Nancy Mahon, chief sustainability officer of the Estée Lauder Companies, tells me, "Stakeholder analysis is not fixed in time. It really does need to be a dialogue. And the good news is that people don't expect perfect companies, but they do expect transparent companies."

The Messy Realities of Stakeholder Engagement

I've worked on dozens of projects involving stakeholder analysis and engagement. A high proportion amounted to generic virtue signaling with no clear point. That's because the teams I was working with tended to lack strategic influence: conducting a stakeholder interaction for its own sake rarely brings value. If undertaken with commitment, though, stakeholder engagement rewards enterprising companies that consciously acknowledge a need for insight into at least one high-stakes question that demands difficult trade-offs.

Even the largest multinational cannot manage all of its stakeholder interactions with equal intensity. Corporations tend to develop expertise in dealing with the stakeholder groups most important to their business models; that's where they face the most friction and pressure.

If you spend time working in responsible business, you'll find again and again that an absence of controversy never affirms good performance, and a visible effort never inoculates a company from scrutiny. Charlotte Moore is a managing director at Sigwatch, an organization that tracks activism and advocacy efforts targeting corporations. "Activists target the most well-known companies in a particular industry, and singling out a particular company sharpens that criticism. This can certainly be the most notorious, like ExxonMobil. But they also pick out the companies who see themselves as leaders on sustainability and human rights," she tells me. "Activists are looking to drive change, and so targeting companies already making moves in the sustainability space increases the likelihood that some of their demands will be met, thus forcing the less receptive competitors to meet a new industry standard."

Most exposés by media and activists about supply chain challenges target companies in the consumer goods sector. That's for good reason: in addition to questions about their packaging, these organizations face intense scrutiny over the origins and safety of the raw ingredients they use. The most advanced supply chain mapping and engagement work I've done has thus been for companies selling the public physical products:

food, clothes, medicines, smartphones. These organizations need to trace their impacts all the way to workers and source communities, so they find themselves at the forefront of efforts to develop more resilient, trusting relationships with distant farms, factories, and mines.

Each sector has its own profile of stakeholders and hot-button priorities. Procurement practices in the mining sector, for instance, draw far less scrutiny than those in consumer goods, so its companies pay less attention to oversight of their corporate supply chains. What they take very seriously, however, are direct human rights impacts: mineral extraction has huge effects on the quality of life in surrounding communities, and customers and investors are keen to avoid financial and reputational repercussions from any perceived ethical violations. This hardly means that all food and apparel companies perform well on supply chain sustainability, or that mining companies all adhere to best practices in human rights. It simply means we can learn much by looking at the practices of companies at the forefront of intractable sustainability challenges.

In the remainder of this chapter, I'll describe how to build stakeholder trust. Listening to stakeholders is a process that invites companies to learn, address their internal blind spots, and build resilient, reciprocal networks to tackle challenges for which good solutions don't yet exist. It's not about recruiting unpaid external agents to advance your corporate agenda. Although details, context, and stakeholder profiles vary almost infinitely among companies, thinking consistently—with humility—will invite success.

Getting to the Point Faster

The best reason to embark on systematic external engagement is to better comprehend your company's *impact on human individuals and communities*. Gaining this fundamental understanding of impact will enable you to determine environmental and social priorities, shape resilient ethical commitments, manage your externalities, and develop trusting relationships. Understanding your impact is a precondition for any coherent approach to ethical, responsible business. Indeed, as I will argue, your impact now offers the best grounding for your ethical commitments.

This is not an elementary process. Since a company of any size affects thousands, perhaps millions of people, seeking to understand your impact can quickly overwhelm you and your team. In practice, most companies either conduct focused engagements on specific topics or seek to establish an ongoing governance mechanism, which might be a stakeholder advisory board or external committee.

Focused engagements often start with a specific question, concern, or location. One way to make your approach more practical is to focus on stakeholders who are experts on a priority issue or are at the frontline of your impacts, which might include plastic waste, water use, deforestation, animal welfare, and so forth. (We'll explore how to identify your priority issues next, in chapter 4.)

Your need for input on a high-stakes question will prompt you to consider the interests and agendas of various parties broadly and deeply. It will bring to light tensions that might remain obscure in any generic engagement effort. It's important to be straightforward from the start about the problem you wish to address.

A prime challenge in seeking to grasp your company's impact is that the people most affected by your decisions may lack the voice, capacity, or recourse to influence *you*. Advocates for sustainability and human rights tend to recommend engagement with vulnerable groups without fully appreciating the burden it places on those parties. Human rights proponents, for example, say investors should conduct their own human rights due diligence on top of any such work undertaken by a company.[16] To steer clear of exploitation, an alternative is to seek out local civil society and community groups that can represent local perspectives.

Good practice in human rights goes further. It suggests you build stakeholder considerations into formal governance mechanisms. That's the idea, for example, behind seeking "free prior informed consent" from local communities on new projects and investments.[17] Mining company Antofagasta has made local investments on its Somos Choapa project in Chile in conjunction with local municipalities rather than impose its decisions on stakeholders.[18] I'll discuss human rights impacts in greater detail in chapter 6, and internal governance in part 3, "Leading and Shaping the Future."

If you aim to build robust ethical commitments . . .

Since legal obligations are no longer a reliable proxy for ethical ones, you need to reckon where to ground your efforts. By definition, ethical challenges are dynamic and divisive. Leading companies use a consultative process to ensure that their commitments are robust and reflect likely real-world effects.

Maarten Hoekstra, who leads ethics at ABN Amro in the Netherlands, tells me how the bank approaches ethical questions. It starts with the creation of a process to consider and legitimize choices, based on an evaluation of all stakeholders' interests:

> Our purpose is banking for better, for generations to come. And while we are very good at playing with numbers to know what is commercially attractive, and very good at playing with words to know what is legal or not, in the moral domain we found we lacked a grammar to explore what is good. We know that goodness cannot be captured. It's controversial and it's volatile. We explore what is at play—what are the values, what are the interests, what are our options? We help senior management on an ad hoc basis to basically correct the moral code for complex issues that we are facing.

Far to the west, leading technology companies raise similar issues. "The billion-dollar question is: Whose ethics?" says Paula Goldman, chief ethical and humane use officer at Salesforce. Like ABN Amro, Salesforce uses an external multistakeholder process to establish ethics policies—in this case, regarding how customers use its products. "We created an ethical use advisory council that includes, notably, frontline employees, executives from throughout the company, and external tech ethics experts. And so when an issue comes our way, we will debate it from multiple angles," she tells me. "We'll take it through this process, and we'll make a recommendation to leadership on how to deal with a particular issue."

If you aim to manage a crisis . . .

Extreme circumstances can necessitate the forging of deeper relationships. (If a crisis is self-inflicted, the effort might be dismissed as too little, too late.) A paper by Stavros Gadinis and Amelia Miazad noted how companies responded to Covid-19's initial surge in 2020 with deliberate efforts to understand the impact on important stakeholders: "[F]rom a substantive perspective, management recognized that without input from affected parties it would be making decisions in the dark. . . . Stakeholders are firsthand witnesses of corporate activity on the ground. . . . They can also monitor company practices, note strengths and weaknesses, and suggest improvements."[19]

Their paper cites a number of examples of how companies successfully managed difficult trade-offs by consulting affected groups. Clorox swiftly chose to prioritize hospitals over its strategic retail relationships. Airbnb extended its cancellation policy so local communities wouldn't be overwhelmed by stricken tourists. Levi's provided financial support so its long-term suppliers could stay in business as demand collapsed. These companies took pains to swiftly obtain the external perspectives needed to shape vital strategic decisions.

If you aim to anticipate critiques . . .

A very good reason to connect with external groups is to better anticipate and understand emerging concerns. We've seen how major multinationals like Coca-Cola form relationships with prominent NGOs, partly in the expectation that they will be informed in advance of disparaging campaigns or reviews. In the face of unpredictable online campaigns, broader outreach to stakeholders can unearth budding issues before they bite.

With research suggesting that effective activism can transform industry norms, it's worth trying to sort signals from noise.[20] This is tricky. You might grant the loudest, most confrontational faultfinders disproportionate time and attention and still fail to win their support. You might give a minor issue extravagant focus, sparking opportunistic criticism from other groups. In their own campaigning, NGOs often rely on scholars and small specialist groups for original insights. So it's more useful to build relationships with leading academic experts on bioplastics or green chemistry than to rush a response to the latest online petition about plastic straws. If your company is targeted in an ill-informed campaign, you needn't respond; the crowd will probably pivot to a new issue tomorrow. But if an external issue is *both* strategically important to your business and salient to your stakeholders, you'll need all the expertise you can get.

If you aim to innovate . . .

A further reason to connect with external groups is that collaboration can bring strategic insights. The people or organizations in question may well possess perspectives and knowledge that are difficult for you to gain, not least because internal biases and blind spots are inevitable. In Africa, French telecommunications company Orange launched partnerships with NGOs and government institutions to help it develop products and services for local markets. Western Union has worked with experts in education to develop financial offerings for the global education market.[21] External perspectives helped both companies expand in ways that served customers well.

When you are researching a core business opportunity, you should always properly compensate end users participating in facilitated group discussions with your product development teams. Respect the line between collaborative innovation and exploitation.

If you aim to take coordinated action . . .

Sometimes companies work *together* to address intractable challenges. This requires that antitrust concerns be overcome, but it's not impossible. Apparel makers teamed up after the Rana Plaza collapse in Bangladesh to coordinate on safety standards. Companies came together to design an industry code of conduct governing conflict minerals and ethical standards in the electronics supply chain. The Global Network Initiative, founded in 2005 to address emerging human rights and technology concerns, has shaped critical thinking on how companies can balance user privacy and freedom of expression, as well as respond to governments that seek users' data to undermine human rights.[22] The World Economic Forum's First Movers Coalition aims to use the purchasing leverage of more than fifty companies to guarantee a market for some emerging technologies that aren't yet commercially attractive.[23]

While coordination can diminish scrutiny from regulators, that's not the objective here. Suppliers, for instance, can benefit by meeting broad, consistent requirements from customers around worker safety or environmental goals, rather than having to satisfy disparate contractual provisions. Still, big collaborations tax company resources and can become frustrating, even counterproductive, so it's best to be extremely selective. Don't dilute your credibility and attention by joining zombie coalitions. You needn't sign up to every voluntary standard or pledge.

Proceed with Respect

The rhetorical embrace of stakeholder capitalism is not yet reflected in how companies go about making important decisions. For all the corporate statements about how working with "our stakeholders" helps drive value, it's more productive to establish core engagement principles aimed at building trust and making better decisions. Outreach that adheres to clear processes and procedures is far less likely to backfire.

The most important principle is respect. Respect for stakeholders should be the basis of such key public commitments as your code of conduct, supplier agreements, customer acceptance policies, and social investment strategy. This means starting with an appreciation of your own power and influence and how it impacts human beings. It means properly valuing external expertise, too.

I recently worked with qb. consulting on a project in several major US cities for a telecommunications company to define its biggest gaps in servicing and capabilities. The ultimate goal was to better develop new products and services, so the project team was careful to be clear with stakeholders about the company's commercial interest. This meant organizing candid, live discussions with no company employees present. The participants were compensated for their expertise and were able to add it to their CVs and share their experiences with friends, neighbors, and colleagues.

Be clear about the problem you are trying to solve. It's easy to get overwhelmed, and it's impractical to try to communicate with everyone at the same level of intensity. Monitoring and messaging can be important, but this isn't about telling your story to a passive audience. You should always be clear about what you intend to learn or achieve. For example, a press report entitled "Puma opens up supply chain, sustainability effort to Gen

Z scrutiny" described how Puma had hired four influencers to evaluate its efforts.[24] My students weren't impressed. They pointed out that the influencers in question were not members of Gen Z, weren't from nations where Puma manufactured, and lacked the expertise to evaluate supply chain oversight. It's now important to recruit influencers to help appeal to young customers. And it's important to secure external expertise to improve the rigor of your supply chain oversight. Mixing the two missions betrays a lack of clarity.

Ask someone what they think, and you will activate expectations. Many of us have filled out employee pulse surveys soliciting our views on culture and leadership. When our opinions aren't acknowledged and changes aren't made, we shrug it off as a bad-faith exercise. It's no more acceptable for you to work with external stakeholders without intending to listen. If you know there's no possibility that their perspective can alter anything, the exercise will simply stir resentment and cynicism.

The point is to learn. Some groups and individuals are easier to identify and reach than others. Some are more inclined to work with business. You will benefit from consciously seeking alternative perspectives and actively listening, rather than just pursuing your agenda. If you speak only with the biggest, most strategic suppliers in your dominant markets, for example, or with the loudest and best-funded activists, you'll be unlikely to learn anything new.

Explain your decisions to the people you consulted. You should always share summaries, actions, and outcomes with participants—and ideally, with the public. Social media content-moderation decisions, however fraught and contentious, provide an example of leading practice. Stakeholder governance models are emerging fastest in this sector because of its intractable tensions: while most of us are uncomfortable with the notion of private companies controlling online content, government regulation seems equally problematic. For example, Facebook (while far from consistently transparent) hosts community dialogues on content-moderation decisions and makes the minutes publicly available.[25] Similarly, before Elon Musk's acquisition gutted its content-moderation efforts, Twitter consulted more than sixty-five hundred people to develop its policy on synthetic and manipulated media and allowed all users to comment on its initial draft.[26]

Make the Exercise Practical

Stakeholder analysis can be helpful in coping with complex, high-stakes problems. It's how you avoid a one-size-fits-all approach or (worse) reflexive efforts to placate the loudest complainer. Still, mapping and analysis are resource intensive. It's not a simple case of handing a junior team member an Excel spreadsheet and asking them to fill in criteria you've provided. Such spreadsheets wind up somewhere in the cloud, incomplete and outdated.

In seeking a broader perspective, you cannot be too generic and vague, or your exercise will fail. Common criteria to analyze stakeholders include influence, expertise, hostility, vulnerability, and impact. Select criteria that align with your goal.

If you aim to reduce negative externalities or meet a human rights commitment, you must comprehend the vulnerabilities and capacities of each stakeholder. Grasping the potential for collaborative or hostile relationships will help drive how you approach any negotiations.

If you aim to anticipate and reduce risk, you'll need to assess each stakeholder's level of influence over the risk in question, their expertise and overall credibility, and whether they're motivated by a collaborative or combative agenda. This approach will help you understand issues such as whether your relationships heighten your exposure to corruption or extortion, a topic we'll revisit in chapter 5.

If you aim to create value and innovate, it's paramount to gauge a stakeholder's level of insight, expertise, and capability. Your criteria might include the present level of mutual trust and the stakeholder's organizational and technical capacities. These could inform whether you ultimately seek a strategic partnership or merely compensate the stakeholder for insights provided.

In a particularly high-stakes situation, network analysis can help. This entails mapping relationships among groups that have no direct contact with you, and identifying shared connections, ownership networks, political agendas, and so forth (see figure 3-1). Understanding these wider

FIGURE 3-1

Network analysis

In these high-stakes, uncertain situations, it may be more useful to map the key players across the ecosystem and explore their influence on each other. This can help identify stakeholders who may shape the future trajectory of an issue, even if their direct influence on the company is currently low.

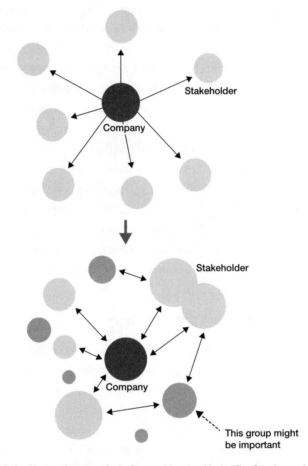

Source: Alison Taylor, Charlotte Bancilhon, Cecile Oger, and Jonathan Morris, "Five-Step Approach to Stakeholder Engagement," BSR.org, 2019, https://www.bsr.org/en/sustainability-insights/download/stakeholder -engagement-five-step-approach-toolkit. Reprinted with permission from BSR.

stakeholder relationships can help you gain clarity and avoid nasty surprises. At first glance, a community group might seem to possess limited leverage and online presence, but you'll need to determine whether it has local politicians on speed dial and might be able to block approvals for licenses you need. I've conducted network analyses that helped companies navigate relationships among competitors and corrupt politicians, thereby averting retaliation and exposure to compromised third parties.

In 2016, I worked with an energy company that was expanding into Myanmar, a high-risk frontier market undergoing dramatic political shifts. The company's identified project area was located far from national and state capitals; there we organized village town halls, meetings, and interviews with community leaders and local NGOs to gain insights we could use in planning community investment and the project's socioeconomic baseline. But we also worked at state, national, and international levels to determine the agendas of international and local NGOs, regulators, politicians, and competitors, along with the activities of rivals awarded nearby exploration permits. We managed to anticipate and reduce the prospect of intercommunity conflict and political retaliation by considering the relationships among stakeholders as well as the relationship and influence each stakeholder group had with our client. These insights helped us develop scenarios that aided the company in preparing for and managing human rights demands from the international community and US government, political and commercial turmoil in Myanmar, and the tensions posed by these contradictory pressures.

Consider Who Does the Work—and Why

A significant omission in much advice about how to engage stakeholders is that it pays little attention to who does the engaging—and on what topics. In the real world, "companies" don't engage "stakeholders." The procurement team interacts with suppliers, the business development team with customers, and so on. People interact with people. Not accounting for this can muddle important questions about who is tasked with representing the company and where their loyalties might lie. Your employees have independent agendas and opinions, and what they do will shape stakeholder perceptions in turn.[27] (For this reason alone, it makes sense to treat employees as your most critical and impactful stakeholder group.)

Think very carefully about who sits at the nexus of corporate and stakeholder interactions. It is common to suggest that stakeholder interactions should be delegated to the sustainability team, as if demonstrating that you are a good corporate citizen is a distinct task from the creation of shareholder value in the core business.[28] At the same time, well-intentioned efforts to win over vocal interest groups will fail if they are mounted as ends in themselves. Now commonly derided as "greenwashing," such moves are likelier to heighten scrutiny than deflect it.

This is why delegating all stakeholder relationships to your sustainability team can backfire. Sustainability employees may feel relatively isolated, powerless, and ambivalent about their work in what is hardly a corporate profit center. Some may perceive themselves as activists on a mission to reshape the company, and this poses risks. A friend who's toiled for decades on sustainability issues tells me: "You need to be careful of your own mental health because you're going to be banging your head against the wall. But without you, they wouldn't be doing anything. You have got to understand it won't all change overnight."

Any organization that truly prizes voice and fortitude seeks out and values such diligent employees. Still, delegating external relationships to them can bring unintended consequences for stakeholder trust. Some teams might grasp at straws to reassure stakeholders by exaggerating the company's commitments. Demoralized colleagues might express frustration to outsiders. Both can potentially fuel critical activism. And if contact teams lack cohesion and internal influence, external stakeholders might get mixed messages from employees in varied contexts and conclude that the company is not acting in good faith.

Everyone, from senior executive to customer service specialist, plays a role in whether your company is perceived to be trustworthy. You cannot expect external messaging to be perfectly consistent unless all communications are rigidly controlled. Since that's a tall order over time, your efforts with stakeholders will flourish best if your organizational culture emphasizes treating them with dignity and respect.

Daniel Korschun, a professor at Drexel University, looks closely at "boundary spanning employees" because how much they identify with—and bear loyalty to—the organization's interests affects their behavior and responses to external interests.[29] Korschun sees particularly devoted employees as likelier to treat external stakeholders as hostile "out groups." He writes that the best way for a company to foster meaningful collaboration is to encourage staff to perceive *relevant* stakeholder interests as vital to the organization's purpose. This involves framing "the mission of the organization in societal terms, highlighting that the organization is not motivated purely by self-interest but is also based on the varied interests of a wider collective that includes key stakeholders."

Building stakeholder trust is no ordinary process. It involves cultivating a fresh mindset across an entire organization. A good starting point is to recognize all challenges and to plan interactions thoughtfully and with humility. It can be very useful to focus on a few strategic priorities, as we will discuss in chapter 4.

Choose the Right Format

If you intend to seek input on a specific issue or to answer a single question, you might organize a group discussion. While one-on-one meetings can provide conceptual and personal depth, they are time consuming. They won't help you build consensus, and they provide little insight into the dynamics and relationships among stakeholders. Live group discussions take up more time, but they facilitate personal trust and intimacy among participants. That's very hard to replicate online or in one-on-one meetings.

Whichever format you elect to pursue, it's critical that all parties be informed, prepared, and genuinely aware of why you seek their input. You should share your expectations clearly and ask participants for theirs. If you invite questions and suggestions in advance, you'll be less likely to encounter confusion or unanticipated conflict.

It's crucial to focus discussion and allow contributions in a variety of formats. Not everyone finds it easy to speak up in a big group, particularly amid significant differences in power. Retaining skilled, external facilitators and inviting participants to contribute anonymously, if they prefer, can help stakeholders appreciate that you know the company is just one actor in a wider system.

Thinking through issues of language, format, accessibility, and expense is important. While providing no compensation is exploitative, paying the stakeholders can suggest you're trying to secure a particular outcome. It should be made plain that any payment is to cover their participation and expertise and entails no expectations. Hiring third-party facilitators and avoiding direct participation by the company can reduce some risk of misapprehension, but it's critical that stakeholders be clear as to your involvement, funding, and agenda.

Share an accurate written summary of what happened with all participants soon after the event takes place. Most important, it should lead to a robust set of actions you can share with everyone involved. This could mean publicly admitting that your efforts were imperfect to begin with—something corporations prefer to avoid. If you are not going to take action, perhaps because the discussion did not help as much as you'd anticipated, you will need to explain this, too.

For all these reasons, stage such conversations only around critical issues that present clear dilemmas and on which you need—and intend to use—external perspectives to help shape strategy. If your goal is really just messaging, communication, or winning the stakeholder over to your position, a live dialogue is the wrong format. It might bring negative, unintended consequences.

Stakeholder Governance: Establishing an Advisory Board

If your company can establish a continuing relationship with a network of critical friends, this will prove more valuable than any internal committee, risk assessment, or social media analysis. The most radical and decisive way to do this is by exploring new corporate forms, such as employee cooperatives.[30] But even if entrenched interests are reluctant to transform corporate governance, there are ways to move beyond answering specific questions by incorporating stakeholder perspectives more meaningfully into your decision-making.

Many companies establish ongoing stakeholder advisory panels that can shape strategic and ethical decisions (or help ensure that your proposals make sense). While involving members of your board of directors will increase a panel's influence, securing active participation by senior executives is more important for translating advice into operational change. Any mandate must be clear. It's wise to expect the panel to do something concrete, not just show up and opine periodically so you can tick an engagement box. For example, Vodafone and Nestlé established panels of experts to help them avoid "greenwashing" allegations.[31]

A stakeholder advisory panel can provide deep technical expertise that would be too costly to maintain on the payroll, as well as a level of independence no employee or director could provide. Because members are not directly involved in, or accountable for, business results, maintaining a panel affords an excellent way to challenge embedded assumptions at the senior level. Term limits will help maintain the panel's independence and enable the company to adapt as new questions emerge.

Members you recruit will need to be sufficiently trusted and credible that you take their opinions seriously; this is why so many companies select people who bring recognized personal stature. Bear in mind, though, that many senior nonprofit leaders, academics, and specialists who are esteemed may lack recent working experience. Any shortage of practical expertise will inevitably undermine a stakeholder advisory panel's credibility in action, however well its lineup might read on your website.

A large stakeholder panel can serve a big, diversified business by enabling the gathering of perspectives from people in varied disciplines. This is probably the best way to identify emerging trends and disruptions while covering a range of bases, but it can grow unwieldy over time. A tighter, more focused group will better enable meaningful teamwork and trust.

Collegiality is important. So are direct and honest critiques. Many boards of directors fail at oversight because consensus and mutuality are valued above genuine debate and accountability. An external panel should be given the brief to challenge and critique groupthink in your organization.

Before I consider which issues to prioritize for stakeholder engagement (and broader corporate strategy), let's summarize our journey so far.

STEPS TO HIGHER GROUND

Your goal should be to build trust and reciprocity with stakeholders. This should be clear from your code of conduct and other written statements of your values and commitments. But you also need to engage in a process that starts with understanding your impact on human beings and results in concrete action to address harm and provide benefits.

The shift to stakeholder capitalism has come with confounding, generic rhetoric about balancing stakeholder interests—and without much practical guidance. Too often, this defaults into more traditional, defensive efforts to manage reputational risk. I've worked on stakeholder engagement projects for teams that either lacked internal influence or had little interest in learning to do anything different. It's no longer a good idea to expend limitless energy seeking to defend corporate value from stakeholder perceptions.

The sheer scale of stakeholder inquiries can overwhelm and prompt you to default to generic communication efforts. Start by focusing and clarifying the problem you're trying to solve, exercise practical curiosity about your impacts, and then ensure that you communicate honestly and transparently about changes you conclude are needed.

It's dangerous to delegate stakeholder interactions to the sustainability team, or to treat this process as a siloed effort divorced from decisions about strategy, values, and capital allocation. To build trust, grant appropriate seniority and influence to the employees you select for stakeholder engagement.

4

Setting Social and Environmental Priorities

I f you want your business to be trusted, you won't get far unless you pay heed to how it impacts human beings. Making a genuine commitment to seek stakeholder perspectives is a crucial step. Understanding your impact on stakeholders is also a critical factor in determining which environmental and social issues you intend to prioritize.

Strategy is the art of choosing what not to do. Let's be clear up front that on environmental and social issues, choosing what *not* to do is difficult. Numerous factors, not least the breadth of stakeholder pressures and demands, weigh against taking a strategic approach. For example, you can make a huge investment in reducing carbon emissions, but it won't protect your company from scrutiny over wages and benefits. This perceived consistency challenge has left sustainability teams tasked with hustling to project neat, credible accounts of achievement instead of focusing on problems their companies could actually address.

Most enterprises are reluctant to place clear limits on the scope of their efforts. For one thing, it would mean publicly acknowledging an unpalatable truth: you cannot act ambitiously on every relevant issue. The pressure to cover all bases is real and reflects genuine societal needs and demands. But it invites problems. One is that you'll never reach the point at which your efforts will be deemed sufficient. Just ask Unilever.

Along with Patagonia, Unilever is a sustainability poster child. In awards, ratings, press coverage, and business school case studies, Unilever is a leader, an acknowledged model for other companies. Paul Polman's decision to stop issuing quarterly reports two days after he became CEO in 2009 is legendary among sustainability practitioners who yearn to encourage longer-term thinking.[1] On assuming leadership of the company in 2019, his successor Alan Jope declared that "brands without a purpose will have no long-term future with Unilever."[2] He also highlighted that the company's twenty-eight "Sustainable Living" brands grew 69 percent faster than the rest of the business while contributing 75 percent of its overall growth.[3]

These achievements hardly immunized Unilever from criticism by investors and investigative journalists, or from lawsuits by activists. As soon as financial results proved less than stellar, the company came under sustained fire from activist shareholders complaining that Unilever's commitment to purpose and sustainability was undermining its performance.[4] A contentious legal battle with its Ben & Jerry's subsidiary over selling ice cream in the Israeli-occupied territories was framed in the press as a reckoning for the notion of corporate "purpose."[5] Meanwhile, the company's perceived failure to fulfill stated commitments to reduce plastic waste in developing countries prompted detailed exposés from Bloomberg and Reuters.[6]

A lot of advice on how to manage environmental and social issues glosses over nuances and tensions to take either a minimalist or maximalist position. Milton Friedman's original argument suggested that companies should altogether ignore environmental and social issues. This still has plenty of advocates, including entrepreneur Vivek Ramaswamy, who established an "anti-ESG" investment vehicle with plenty of powerful backers and ran for the US presidency.[7]

At the other extreme, many advocates for responsible business suggest you transform every aspect of your business model to account for all of your direct or indirect impacts, pursue social justice, and solve societal problems at scale.[8] For example, the authors of a 2022 report from EY called "Enough" wrote: "Sustainability needs to revert to being a noun and not a verb. Sustainability is not an activity, nor is it an industry or a theme—it is a specific point at which economic activity is maintained within sustainable limits. It is that, or it is nothing. . . . And if this means that sustainable corporations shrink to an exclusive group that dare to push the boundaries of the possible then so be it."[9]

Neither position provides robust grounding for a corporate strategy. Ignoring environmental and social pressures is not a realistic option. Nor is tackling them all at the same time, with the same intensity and no clear end goal in mind.

Witold Henisz, a leading academic working on ESG at Wharton who collaborates closely with activist hedge fund Engine No. 1, tells me a strong element of judgment is needed for any robust approach to ESG: "Companies face challenges when they try to understand how to manage an issue like climate change or human rights risk in the supply chain. The issue will affect some revenue or cost structure, but perhaps not for a few years, and the problem will often manifest first in a function that is not responsible for managing the risk."

The leaders I meet genuinely wish to run better, more ethical businesses. They recognize the need for an approach that's less instrumental and better grounded in impact. Figuring out how to get to higher ground is the issue. If they accept that sustainability efforts should never be piecemeal or inconsistent, is their business suddenly supposed to address dozens of societal challenges, regardless of how they affect financial performance—or whether the company even has relevant expertise to contribute? If that's what it will take to become a sustainable company, no business in the world will ever qualify.

If your efforts can never suffice, and you can never satisfy public expectations, how are you to proceed? Where should you focus? And how will you know when and if your actions are adequate? I'm sometimes asked: "Is anything *not* a sustainability issue?"

So how *are* you to set a course through these daunting pressures?

Every company can and should take the time to identify where to focus and how it can contribute. Jim Massey, who became chief sustainability officer at a small biotech company after a long stint at AstraZeneca, tells me: "You need to take the time to identify what is core to the identity and mission of the business, or you will never get internal traction. I've worked in large multinationals and small startups, but the key to success and momentum in any organization is focus. It is dangerous—both for your team and the company—to react to every demand and falsely suggest you can solve intractable problems where you have limited leverage. The organization will lose patience, and you will get nothing done."

A sharp focus will make it easier to cut through noise. This calls for a prioritization process, usually known as a materiality assessment. (Materiality is just another word for relevance.) While people debate what makes an issue relevant, the conditions might include risks (climate change might make it harder to source certain ingredients); opportunities (Could you capture more market share if you prepare for the energy transition better than your rivals or anticipate shifting customer priorities earlier?); and ethical imperatives (Does your business have a long-term future if it depends on fossil fuels or worker exploitation?). Every company faces a mix. A single issue might encompass all three challenges.

Companies have historically been incentivized to view their impacts on society as irrelevant unless the legal system dictates otherwise. Economists treat an impact as an "externality" if "the effect of production or consumption of goods and services imposes costs or benefits on others which are not reflected in the prices charged for the goods and services being provided."[10] Financial accounting has not yet caught up, but it's critical to revisit these assumptions. In an era of intangible value, you can no longer reliably wall yourself off from the consequences of external impacts with legacy approaches.

For honesty and coherence, it's better to identify a small number of existential issues and then tackle them ambitiously. Every company I've ever worked with, no matter its sector, faced at least one such issue. Ambition is not honored with ill-advised commitments to address societal challenges on which you lack expertise. Poorly grounded pledges distract and dilute, frequently doing more harm than good.

Let's look at some common pitfalls.

Obsessing about your ESG score

I've performed materiality assessments in almost every sector. Many were motivated by nascent interest from a board or CEO in getting a better ESG score, a lower cost of capital, and an improved reputation. I've frequently been asked to present the business case for ESG in order to secure the internal budget needed for the initial assessment.[11] But ratings for ESG, whatever it's called, exist so investors can compare companies in order to generate better returns; such ratings necessarily incentivize breadth of disclosure. Seeing the exercise as a way to pump your stock price might get you a bonus, but it won't leave you with much guidance on where the business should actually focus.

ESG frameworks and ratings agencies can certainly help you identify the spectrum of relevant issues. But even the largest, best-staffed multinational will struggle to act on dozens of environmental and social initiatives simultaneously. It's worth noting that the oft-cited cliché "you manage what you measure" was originally a warning against pointless measurement for its own sake.[12] Not everything that can be measured matters, and not everything that matters can be measured.

Managing the message, not the issue

Until recently, the default approach was to aim financial reporting at shareholders and sustainability reporting and disclosures at all other stakeholders, including the public, employees, activists, and NGOs. This didn't reflect cynical intentions so much as a tendency to treat stakeholder perceptions as a messaging challenge, not a strategic one. Even with the best intentions, it's hard to manage a cacophony of critiques. So we get reports laden with impenetrable jargon, euphemisms, and thin, misleading pledges, and illustrated with photos of smiling women in hard hats and happy children in developing countries. I've worked closely with more than a few sustainability teams to identify clear priorities for meaningful change, only for the efforts to be overridden by a perceived need to get behind a popular cause.

If you read a company's sustainability report and then peruse its core risk and financial disclosures, they commonly feel like discussions of two different companies.[13] This split-screen approach is ever less credible.

Herding together for safety

Most big public companies issue sustainability reports, with the foremost realizing they can't tell one story to shareholders and another to everyone else.[14] Still, the need to appeal to multiple audiences results in an exhaustive list of metrics. Sustainability reports and disclosures painfully illustrate the tension between requirements to *disclose data* and align with sectoral norms on a broad range of environmental and social issues and the need to set forth a sharp, strategic focus for concrete action.[15]

A review from Teneo in 2022 of more than two hundred sustainability reports showed significant convergence, with most companies projecting breadth over depth and herding together to avoid being called out.[16] While that's understandable, given the quality of current expression in the field, it does little for your company or the world.

Don't succumb to the most common pitfall—an assessment that ends up sounding as if almost everything is material. Adopting a strategic focus will help you concentrate on a small number of concerns that belong in your core corporate strategy. Your sustainability priorities should then be clear, even to a casual observer.

Ignoring the elephant in the room

Corporate sustainability efforts often seek to distract from the negative externalities companies exploit, and even rely on, to drive profitability. There's a tendency to focus on the important at the expense of the existential. Social media platforms tell us about their renewable energy initiatives but not the impacts of their core product on mental health, democracy, and extremism. Retailers address the environmental requirements they impose on their suppliers, not why they don't pay employees a living wage. Junk-food manufacturers emphasize consumer choice rather than acknowledge that they design products to be addictive.[17] No wonder so many ballyhooed sustainability efforts are written off as corporate responsibility theater.

It's unusual for companies to acknowledge and tackle existential challenges to their business model. Those that do tend to be pitching for survival in a threatened sector. While Philip Morris International remains controversial, it has departed from its sector's preferred storyline by acknowledging the risks presented by tobacco.[18] "ESG disclosure pressures are so comprehensive that a company can choose what story it wants to tell about its risks, opportunities, and impacts," says Jennifer Motles, PMI's chief sustainability officer. She continues:

> That has, historically, allowed companies in the tobacco industry to focus their sustainability-related disclosures on topics like decarbonization and supply chain workers, which are less material. The most material issue for the tobacco industry is the health impacts of the core product; tackling this successfully while transparently reporting progress should be at the core of any tobacco company's sustainability strategy. I'm a human rights lawyer, and I took this role because of the opportunity to transform the business to tackle this existential issue. My work is central to corporate strategy and enables me to influence incentives and capital allocation decisions.

Ørsted, once one of the most coal-dependent companies in Europe's energy sector, really stands out. Having pledged in 2009 to embrace renewable fuels, it now creates and operates wind farms offshore and onshore, as well as solar farms, bioenergy plants, and facilities to store energy.[19]

Some companies in controversial sectors have the most advanced sustainability strategies because they seek to recover from historic mismanagement of their impacts on society. Even if your business faces less controversy, there's much to learn from those that have opted to aggressively refocus.

Misaligned goals and incentives

It's challenging to embed environmental and social priorities into core business decisions. With their emphasis on reputational pressure rather than operational substance, companies tend to place environmental and social challenges, opportunities, and risks into a big bucket of sustainability "stuff."

These efforts will fail unless you know whether tackling the issue in question means you must incentivize innovation (which can be managed using existing business metrics), manage risks (in some cases, this means taking steps to reduce exposure and mitigate consequences, while other risks also provide strategic opportunity), or determine ethical imperatives

TABLE 4-1

Prioritize environmental and social issues with a materiality assessment

Step 1	Identify the full landscape of relevant environmental and social issues.
Step 2	Consult friends, critics, and critical friends, both internally and externally.
Step 3	Prioritize ruthlessly. Identify strategic issues that are important to both internal and external stakeholders.
Step 4	Determine when and how to act. Differentiate between risks, innovation opportunities, and impacts that might become risks if you do not act.
Step 5	Embed priorities into corporate strategy.

(which need policies, prohibitions, and oversight, and are best grounded in your impacts). If you can't distinguish among these imperatives, you'll have no chance of designing coherent goals or incentives.

Conducting a rigorous materiality assessment isn't just about selecting and reporting on everything that might possibly be relevant. Let's look at how to prioritize in a smart and strategic way. (See table 4-1.)

Step One: Identify All Relevant Issues

The first step is to identify *all* of the environmental and social issues that are *directly relevant* to your business operations. These will vary according to your industry, size, and business model. If yours is an oil and gas business, climate change is plainly a material issue. If you manufacture food, how you source ingredients is a material issue; working conditions might have a more immediate and direct effect on your suppliers. Every business will have a range of material environmental and social issues that clearly and directly affect commercial performance and operational risk—the "outside in" impacts and risks.

To identify these issues, many companies start by reviewing sector taxonomies from the Sustainability Accounting Standards Board.[20] These are sectoral assessments of the externalities most likely to have a direct financial impact on a company. In SASB's own words, its frameworks are designed to measure "corporate activities that maintain or enhance the ability of the company to create value over the long term." This detailed work informs the metrics that ESG investors and ratings agencies use. It's a great place to start but might not give you the full picture. It still uses financial performance results as the selection criteria, and it focuses only on core operational considerations—the issues under your direct control.

Next, consider your risk landscape. There's commonly an internal disconnect between risk management and sustainability priorities. As recently as 2017, the World Business Council for Sustainable Development found that only 29 percent of the areas deemed "material" in a company's sustainability report were also disclosed as risks in the company's legal disclosures.[21]

Viewing risk and materiality assessments as entirely distinct exercises is a prime example of problematic legacy thinking. Traditionally, investors require risk disclosures, while voluntary sustainability efforts are implicitly framed as a "nice to have" wherein companies go beyond risk and compliance to be good corporate citizens. This distinction between voluntary and regulated efforts makes less and less sense as the field continues to mature. Human rights due diligence, for instance, has become a regulatory requirement in the EU, though not elsewhere, and climate disclosures are becoming a nexus of regulation and litigation all over the world.

All this means that before you go further, you should review corporate risk assessments that may carry ESG implications. Some risks are purely financial or operational: think of currency fluctuations or tariffs. But your external risks should appear on any list of material issues, and you should at least ensure that risk and materiality assessments use the same terms and concepts.[22] Many companies also maintain lists of emerging risks (those that are not yet strategic priorities but could become so). Include these in your issue landscape.

It's great to encourage deep relationships between risk and sustainability teams; I've seen it enhance the quality of analysis and levels of influence for both.[23] Some of the most successful work I've done has stemmed from long-term scenario planning workshops on material issues with senior executives and their risk, sustainability, and compliance teams. Note that this does *not* mean equating sustainability only with risk reduction; it helps you clarify both risk and opportunity.

Now consider your impacts on the world. When ordinary citizens think about which issues a business should pay attention to, they don't qualify them according to the company's risk profile or financial exposure. They mull impacts: Does your business pollute, defraud customers, cause deforestation, exploit workers, support autocracies, or lobby in ways that seem to undermine popular opinion? If you don't seem to be held accountable for these actions—or may be making *more* money as a result of your negative impacts—the public will become even angrier. So it's important to clearly evaluate your impacts. (This doesn't mean you need to respond apologetically to every ill-informed critique that surfaces.)

Some of your business's impacts in going about its core activities will be obvious (you need to manage waste or employee safety), others less so (How does your procurement strategy affect wages in your supply chain?). The extent and ferocity of criticism in social media are not reliable gauges. It's much wiser to exercise some practical curiosity about how your business impacts stakeholders, as I've already argued. At minimum, you need to look closely at the issues on which activist NGOs, civil society groups, leading academics, and socially responsible investors are focusing in your sector.

Research on how pressure from activists affects company behavior supports Charlotte Moore's contention that it is most effective in raising standards across an industry, specifically by encouraging average corporate performers to anticipate future pressure and enhance their sustainability ambitions.[24] This makes it worth the effort to anticipate how campaigns in your sector might evolve over the coming decade. Some of the toughest decisions you'll face will be about prioritizing impacts that do not present profound risks or opportunities at this time but might pose problems if left unaddressed. (Maybe you aren't getting targeted for your water use yet, but drought is recurring in key locations.)

At the end of this information-gathering phase, you will have compiled a long list of potential environmental and social issues, *all of them relevant.* They will include external risks and compliance requirements (such as product quality and safety, or waste management), as well as opportunities and aspirations (a diverse workforce, perhaps) and industry-specific issues (responsible research and development, clinical trial access, and so forth).

Finalize your issue landscape. You'll now consolidate this list into a clear set of no more than thirty issues. This will encompass the landscape of issues you need to understand, track, and disclose, but it's not yet a guide for where to *act*. You will come to better understand your risks, opportunities, and ethical imperatives by selecting priorities from this issue landscape.

Now combine any similar concepts or ideas, taking care to ensure that none embodies a predetermined agenda. "Sustainable packaging" is a good choice, while "eliminate plastic waste" presupposes a goal. If an issue is mainly about your business growth, with a tenuous link to social or environmental impact, you can drop it. Try to avoid vague terms such as "empowering communities" or "advancing public health." Aim for clear terms and write a brief description of what you mean; if you can't define the issue in a short sentence, it's not robust enough.

You have now developed your assessment framework and can move on to detailed information gathering.

Step Two: Consult Friends, Critics, and Critical Friends

Next, you need to ask a broad range of informed people, both inside and outside the company, which issues they think your company should prioritize from this defined landscape. Even if it's already clear where you need to focus, you'll benefit enormously from these stakeholder perspectives when taking action.

You'll collect the most comprehensive insights if you combine an internal survey with detailed internal and external interviews. Since they provide a wealth of additional strategic insights and can serve as a first step in helping you form longer-term relationships with critical friends you need, interviews can be worth the expense and effort. More limited endeavors rely on social media analysis; they are better than nothing but will probably lack depth.

Interview senior leaders. Inside the company, it's important to talk to leaders in all key functions. However, anticipate that leaders of specific divisions and functions will make selections that reflect their own obsessions and agendas. Defensive politicking is common. Chief compliance officers tend to say that corruption risk is so well managed that it isn't an issue, while procurement leaders highlight the resilience of the company's supply chain. To avert such distortions, it's important to emphasize that this is about the issue's *inherent* importance to the business, not a question of how well it is being addressed.

Begin interviews with a wide-ranging discussion on the future of the business and its strategic priorities—and how much environmental and social concerns affect them. This is a wonderful opportunity to make connections to the wider context. How might hurricanes and wildfires disrupt your operations? How could public concern over human rights affect your work with suppliers in China? After this discussion, ask interviewees to rate the importance of issues on a scale, bearing in mind that numeric rankings are not going to give you the full picture.

Don't ignore other employees. It's smart to broaden your assessment beyond the senior leadership team, so this is the time to gather the views of your other employees. The wider workforce has generally been excluded from materiality assessments, but given the rise of employee interest in sustainability topics, it's wise to involve everyone in considering priorities and trade-offs. While conducting focus groups with staff in a range of regions and functions is ideal, a survey can be a good alternative. Relatively junior employees might focus more on pet concerns but are also likely to care less about status, loyalty, and reputation. In fact, when feedback from the workforce differs significantly from the leadership team's views, you will have unearthed a good indicator of latent frustration or misalignment.

These conversations will teach you much about internal sources of pressure, enthusiasm, pain, and tension. You will better understand what employees expect and value. You may identify people who can lead initiatives and make decisions. In short, you'll be positioned to get something done once the assessment is complete.

Identify and consult external stakeholders. Now you must capture critical commentary from outside the company. This is an even trickier process that requires a representative range of perspectives from customers, suppliers, investors, governments, and communities. If you haven't yet conducted the stakeholder analysis I describe in chapter 3, identifying and building relationships with people that can help inform your priorities is a great way to get started.

You will already know your roster of strategic investors, customers, regulators, and suppliers, and you will wish to speak with as many of them as possible. But don't restrict yourself to contacts that are familiar at headquarters. The usual suspects won't suffice.

Ask important customers about their own priorities and goals; many will already be looking to impose them on your company. Seek perspectives from suppliers in Dhaka, not just Detroit. Probe regulators for insight into how your company compares with peers—and the big emerging trends they foresee. Consult a range of investors for their views, which are likely to be less predictable than you expect.

Finally, you need to consider everyone else: the people and groups your business affects. They may lack formal influence over you—unless your company infuriates them.

A full corporate human rights impact assessment is the best way to understand your real-world stakeholder impacts. Materiality assessments and human rights assessments are usually treated as distinct exercises with different purposes.[25] However, it's a great idea to use a human rights assessment as the basis for the stakeholder axis of your materiality map. (While a human rights impact assessment can help populate your materiality map, it can do much more. We will return to this in chapter 6.) At minimum, you must consciously seek to understand the most hostile perspectives about your business, however unjustified you might deem them.

These conversations can help you form fresh networks and relationships, which you might even want to formalize into an advisory board. They can help you identify common misunderstandings about what your business can and can't directly influence. And they can help you anticipate resistance you might encounter as you proceed.

Step Three: Prioritize Ruthlessly

Once you comprehend the landscape and stakeholder opinions, you must prioritize *ruthlessly*. You will have identified a broad range of relevant issues and may be tempted to think they should get equal priority for balance and consistency. Without clear choices, though, you'll wind up stuck in a swamp of undifferentiated virtue signaling.

Now things will become uncomfortable. The rigorous assessment you've put so much work into can easily be derailed by internal power dynamics. You'll face pressure to escalate some issues and downplay others that might draw negative attention. You can easily wind up trapped between external critiques and internal resistance. That's how a process that starts with materiality ends up as checking a box. An independent voice in the room can help, but only if that voice has internal credibility.

Still, this task is essentially a matter of identifying priorities. A good approach is to create a four-quadrant matrix with external stakeholder priorities along the y axis and internal priorities along the x axis. Now you can visualize which issues emerged as top internal priorities and compare them to the top external priorities. (See figure 4-1.)

Place each of your material issues on the matrix according to how internal and external interviewees prioritized them. Which ones fall where? (With enough data, you can create specific maps for particular stakeholder groups and views from certain regions or divisions.) While many materiality assessments recommend detailed quantitative analysis, this isn't a scientific process. It's impossible to be utterly objective.

FIGURE 4-1

Prioritization matrix

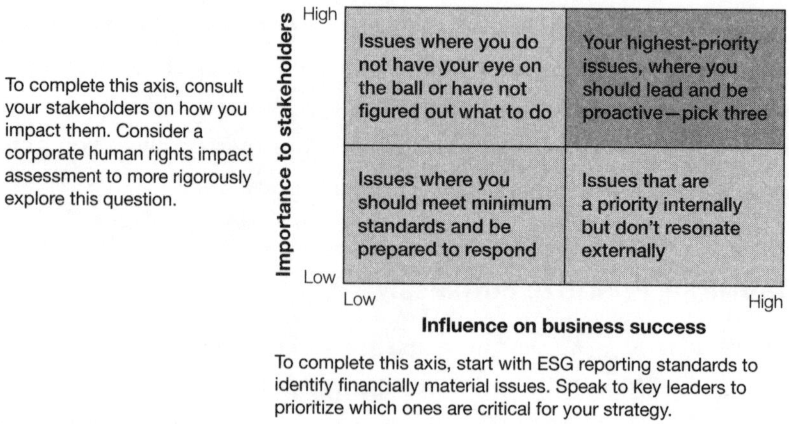

To complete this axis, consult your stakeholders on how you impact them. Consider a corporate human rights impact assessment to more rigorously explore this question.

Importance to stakeholders — High / Low

Issues where you do not have your eye on the ball or have not figured out what to do

Your highest-priority issues, where you should lead and be proactive—pick three

Issues where you should meet minimum standards and be prepared to respond

Issues that are a priority internally but don't resonate externally

Low — Influence on business success — High

To complete this axis, start with ESG reporting standards to identify financially material issues. Speak to key leaders to prioritize which ones are critical for your strategy.

The most important question is which quadrant an issue appears in. Those in the bottom-left quadrant are your lowest priorities. They will need to be monitored, tracked, and assessed, but they won't be active priorities.

Now consider the issues in the bottom-right quadrant. These seemed critical to insiders looking out but less important to external observers. Here, you're likely to see core operational risk priorities and compliance obligations. This quadrant might also include flagship initiatives that don't resonate among external stakeholders. The problem might lie in how the company is communicating or framing them, or they might be issues stakeholders pay little attention to unless things go wrong, like industrial accidents.

Turn to the issues at top left: stakeholder priorities that are not (yet) getting much internal attention. Here, you will tend to find such major societal concerns as public health, climate change, animal rights, and the social impact of technology. Stakeholders may overestimate your degree of influence over the issue, or the extent of your impact. If that's the case, you may ultimately need to hold your nerve against external pressure. That's how you can avoid chewing up valuable bandwidth on marginal concerns—or being pressured into prioritizing climate change when your pharmaceutical company could make a more immediate, positive difference by increasing access to your medicines in developing countries.

Be careful. This quadrant might include issues on which your company has not joined the dots, is not ready to act on decisively, or simply has no interest in being held accountable for. Perceived responsibility for the issue might be fragmented across leaders and departments, meaning that there's no internal clarity on how to manage the issue, despite its importance at the organizational level. Such a matter might contain the seeds of a future ethics crisis and could become the focus of a fiery activist campaign. You may need to manage these issues via your stated values or the requirements in your code of conduct. Think of this quadrant as an early warning system.

Step Four: Determine When and How to Act

Most important is the top-right quadrant. Here, you'll see the environmental and social issues deemed critical by *both* internal and external observers. Each issue in this quadrant is likely to be multidimensional; it presents risks and opportunities and ethical and commercial imperatives.

In this quadrant, you'll find the areas where close, ongoing dialogue with key external experts and other stakeholders will be most valuable. If you look for connections among these issues, you might see that they all relate to the same root cause (such as climate change or worker rights). This is the time to engage in robust debate in order to shape a distinctive position aligning rhetoric and action. It's best if you can confidently select a single area of focus. Choose more than three issues, and you will be biting off more than you can chew.

If you've conducted your analysis rigorously, priority issues will include those that are critical—even existential—for your core business model. If your company manufactures medicines, you'll see product liability and safety. If it makes clothing, there's no avoiding questions of environmental impacts and worker rights in your supply chain. It's common to view these issues solely as risks or problems, but you should be mindful that they may present significant opportunities for innovation and strategic advantage.

Suppose your company makes technology hardware. Your upper-right quadrant might include employee development and engagement, responsible sourcing, and data protection or privacy. The issues in your bottom-right quadrant might be health and safety, operations management, waste, water, and energy use (internal priorities that stakeholders will ignore unless you stumble). In the top-left quadrant, you might see stakeholder concerns over such issues as human rights, product use and integrity, and the social influence of technology. Taken together, this might tell you that workers are your biggest source of opportunity and threat. It's unlikely that this has never occurred to you, but you can now comprehend that you'd benefit from looking just as closely at your supply chain workers as your salaried employees. You might also see that a broad human rights assessment of your core product will be more valuable than a narrow data-protection policy.

Clear prioritization makes developing a strategy less excruciating. You'll be less inclined to put a range of incompatible issues into that bucket of ESG stuff or to concentrate on messaging over substance.

Step Five: Embed Priorities into Strategy

Once you've identified your priorities, you can get down to considering how to incentivize innovation, better manage risk, and/or establish ethical oversight. While you might want to look at what competitors are doing and saying, your objective is differentiation, not mimesis. Sam Hartsock, who runs qb., a sustainability consultancy, tells me: "We explore whether specific issues present operational risks, ethical imperatives, or impact/innovation opportunities. This helped drive deeper reflections, before jumping to solutions."

If your focus is sharply strategic, and you clearly see the challenges and opportunities each issue presents, you'll find it much easier to incentivize the core business to focus on these issues. Even more critical, you'll know what expertise your sustainability team (and board) needs. A failure to focus will mean that instead of recruiting issue experts, your sustainability team's job will default to data gathering, coordination, and impression management. Academic researcher Kim Schumacher has noted a tendency to assign these roles to unqualified employees and said that at the very least, such leaders need to know what they don't know.[26]

General Motors is a good example of a company that adopted a focused strategy on a root-cause issue: climate change. While the slow death of the internal combustion engine posed immense risk, GM saw that choosing how and when to address the risk could be a prime source of strategic advantage. Clearly appreciating that a multidimensional transformation would enable it to manage environmental and social risks while driving value, the company elected to become 100 percent electric by 2035. GM is detailing its investment efforts and working closely with activist hedge fund Engine No. 1 to drive them. It is being transparent about a range of issues, including its need for regulatory support and its anticipation of a rise in emissions in its supply chain over the short term.[27] The business made a meaningful commitment, explained why—and why it's so important—and detailed how it will measure success or failure. GM's only material priorities that do not relate to this core goal are ethical imperatives: diversity and inclusion, safety, and ethical conduct. Contrast GM's active stance with other companies' piecemeal efforts suggesting a broad range of goals and relying on one metric per issue to measure efficacy.

A strategic focus will help you incentivize performance. Trying to cover too many bases can dilute your efforts and undermine their credibility. Take the case of McDonald's. In 2021, the company announced it would tie executive compensation to annual increases in the proportion of women and minorities in senior leadership as part of a raft of new human capital measures.[28] This sounded positive until one considered contemporary media reports about the company's settlement of a lawsuit alleging it had long redlined Black franchisees; McDonald's was accused of pushing them to take on the least favorable locations, requiring unrealistic renovations, and subjecting them to harsher inspections.[29] The company denied any wrongdoing in settling the claims, but the allegations highlight why it's so risky to have too many priorities—and why making a meaningful organizational commitment should not rely on a single metric.

If your materiality process tells you that diversity is essential to meet the expectations of customers, suppliers, and employees over the long term (and therefore, indispensable to the survival of the business), it's important to make it a fundamental strategic goal. What might this look like? Executives could be asked to create plans for how their division or function can address a diversity imperative, then encouraged to compete with each other in testing their innovations. This would stimulate the executives to learn about diversity and ways to advance it.

Nikita Mitchell works on Cisco's Purpose Strategy and Innovation team. "We have twelve Social Justice Actions that are backed by a five-year, $300 million commitment, each of which are deeply embedded across accountable business units and overseen by our board of directors," she tells me. "I'm particularly proud that we publicly share data on our progress for transparency. While we are still on the journey, our commitment is real. More importantly, it's innovative."[30]

A strategic focus helps clarify what behavior you are trying to incentivize. Any credible incentive structure you devise must be clear as to whether the task is to incentivize innovation, reduce risk, or manage negative impacts that are not yet risks but might be in the future. If you don't know which is which, you'll quickly run into trouble. If you're setting a goal to cut carbon emissions, it can help to incentivize executives.[31] But reward schemes need to be balanced with oversight. To take one striking example, executives at Marathon Petroleum got bonuses for reducing carbon emissions in 2018, the same year the company was fined for a major oil spill.[32] Again, holistic consideration of environmental responsibility will be far more convincing to stakeholders and investors than a narrow focus on carbon reduction.

Sharp application and honest assessment will enable you to set the foundation for your company to pursue clear operational priorities, goals, and incentives. Philip Morris International, for instance, has created a set of nineteen ESG key performance indicators that connect the company's core purpose, strategy, financial performance, and environmental and social impacts. These are incorporated into the reckoning of executive compensation to help the company meet its 2025 goal of being a majority smoke-free business.[33]

Thoughtful integration of goals and incentives is still sufficiently unusual to bring you a serious advantage in implementation. Still, you're not quite finished.

A strategic focus will help you identify the problems you can't solve alone. In reviewing and debating your material issues earlier, you will inevitably have identified challenges on which the financial consequences of your impacts are uncertain, and for which even ambitious action might not solve matters. You will have found issues that raise uncomfortable questions. Does your diversity priority suggest that you should set minimum wages above what's legally required? If you've identified a risk of child labor, is it enough to audit your suppliers, or do you need to provide childcare or fund schools? What if this is outside your expertise, or there aren't enough teachers to go around in the country in question? Are your actions likely to have unintended consequences?

A robust materiality process will raise questions about how you respond to efforts by governments and civil society institutions to tackle such corporate externalities as greenhouse gas emissions, deforestation, excessive water use, negative public health impacts, and pollution. They might entail broader policy considerations such as supporting democratic participation or gender equity. You might need to source raw materials from regions with poor human rights records. Here, taking action might appear to pose conflicts between the corporation's short-term financial interests and the public welfare.

This means that if you take doing the right thing seriously, there's no avoiding the legal and policy landscape. We'll turn to the role of the law in chapter 5.

STEPS TO HIGHER GROUND

It's easy to feel trapped between a minimalist and maximalist position on environmental or social issues. But a general shift toward valuing corporate intangibles and a rising awareness of the impact of externalities make it impossible to ignore ESG issues, and unwise to act only after they threaten your bottom line. At the same time, do not obsess over your ESG score, and pause before you attempt to solve problems that lie beyond your control or expertise.

Unless you can focus sharply on a maximum of three critically important issues, you'll have little prospect of accounting for these issues in future business decisions. If an environmental and social issue is truly strategic, you can't manage it via a siloed sustainability effort but must consider it as part of your core corporate strategy.

Conduct an honest, rigorous materiality assessment and identify issues that are critical to *both* the business and its stakeholders. These issues become your strategic focus. Once you've identified core priorities, differentiate among innovation opportunities, operational risks, and ethical imperatives. That will make it easier to design effective incentives. It will also facilitate thinking through and clarifying your values, principles, and oversight structures.

Developing a sharp strategic focus does not let you ignore other issues. At the very least, you'll need to report and disclose information about all the issues on your materiality map. A materiality process helps identify areas where your organization has considerable impact on stakeholders but is unfocused or unprepared to act. It will also help you identify key operational priorities you are simply expected to get right. Being equipped with this nuanced understanding of issues and stakeholder pressures will enable you to proceed confidently.

5

Tackling Corruption
(for Real)

B ack in 2003, I took a job providing corporations with intelligence
to help them manage political and operational risks in the Middle East and Africa. This turned out to be a perfect vantage point
from which to observe how multinationals respond to shifting norms and
laws—in this case, those related to corruption risk.

Most of my clients were large Western multinationals (and their lawyers and bankers) in oil and gas, mining, telecommunications, or infrastructure. For an opportunity to make vast profits, they accepted elevated
risk: foreign investors had to cope with an unpredictable landscape where
success might depend heavily on the whims of government ministers. It
was easy to end up on the wrong side of shifting power dynamics, with
licenses canceled and assets expropriated. My clients wanted help in con-
tending with this—not lectures on ethics. Mention bribery in a business
meeting, and you'd be met with awkward silence.

Gradually, the knotty question of what corporations get up to in those
opaque frontier markets became a pressing concern for corporate lawyers. Around 2005, I started to hear from compliance and know-your-
customer teams that wanted to know more about their clients' bona fides.
Were their sources of wealth legitimate? Was a company secretly owned
by a politician, or perhaps by a friend or relative of one? Did it have a

genuine track record, or was it a vehicle for paying bribes or siphoning off state revenue?

When Siemens came under investigation in 2006 for a sweeping global bribery operation, it was clear that we'd reached a tipping point regarding anti-corruption enforcement.[1] Risks and penalties were increasing, and it was no longer merely an option to have an anti-corruption program. My team was deluged by clients asking us to identify the hidden shareholders of their Nigerian business partner, assess whether their Emirati distributor was laundering Iranian money, or look into whether a competitor had bribed a Congolese minister to cancel a mining license.

I thought this was great news. Not only was my business booming, but I relished the opportunity to pivot from sleazy corporate spy to anti-corruption crusader. I had become convinced that accountability over how Western companies operated in the Global South was long overdue, and I wanted to be part of the solution. But my new remit turned out to present a fresh array of challenges.

One immediate problem we faced was that compliance teams were asking questions that were somewhere between difficult and impossible to answer. When we retrieved corporate filings, we'd find that the names of company owners and directors were fake or listed as trusts in the Cayman Islands. The media were tightly controlled in many Middle Eastern and African countries, which meant local journalists could give me jaw-dropping gossip but had no venues in which to air it; publishing these stories would, in any event, have put their lives at risk. There were simply no neat paper trails. The long nights I spent in hotel bars with well-connected sources usually raised more questions than they answered.

Because hard evidence was so elusive, clients interpreted our findings in accordance with their risk appetite and culture. Some leaders were genuinely concerned to understand how a particular business relationship might affect their reputation, integrity, and competitive position, and we were able to give them useful guidance. Others just wanted to tick the due diligence box and close the deal. I grew accustomed to conference calls in which investment bankers would pick holes in the information we'd painstakingly gathered, order us not to put damning quotes in writing, and dismiss the timid objections of their compliance colleagues. Again and again, I witnessed the relentless pressure placed on oversight functions to bow to the raw power and status of a sales team hunting a bonus. I started to ask tougher questions about what my work was for, and I found few clear answers.

In chapters 3 and 4, I focused on how companies can cope with rising pressure over their environmental and social impacts from employees, investors, customers, and the public. Changing expectations and demands have made it much riskier to focus on simply not breaking the law. Indeed, these issues have gained so much traction precisely *because* a narrow focus on legal risk is grossly inadequate when it comes to running an ethical business.

Reflecting these novel societal pressures and expectations, the vast majority of public companies (and many private ones) make sustainability disclosures. These often reflect a legacy approach that treats sustainability as a "nice to have" signal to stakeholders that your company is a good corporate citizen. Meanwhile, a separate—and usually, more powerful—team called "ethics and compliance" works to meet regulatory requirements and ensure that the enterprise and its employees do not break the law.

The knee-jerk notion that regulatory risk should exist in a separate domain from sustainability accounts for why these internal functions have so little to do with each other—and why their agendas may conflict. This legacy structure *might* make sense if there were a clear, practical distinction between legal requirements and sustainability issues.

There isn't. Legal compliance has *never* been a simple matter divorced from wider questions about the role of business in society. And numerous developments have rendered the status quo unworkable. On big questions such as free speech, climate change, and human rights, national regulations have diverged markedly. Political agendas have polarized within and among nations. Approaches to privacy and free speech, for instance, differ dramatically in the United States and Europe: privacy protections are considerably sharper and broader in Europe, while a constitutional right prizing free speech takes priority in the United States.

A broad advance in environmental and social regulation is underway, too, notwithstanding international inconsistencies. With sustainability disclosures starting to become legally required, the legacy view of sustainability as going beyond compliance no longer makes sense. The EU, the Corporate Sustainability Reporting Directive, and the Corporate

Sustainability Due Diligence Directive will demand far more oversight of environmental and human rights impacts. A host of incipient EU laws imposes requirements on technology companies. Meanwhile, the Securities and Exchange Commission looks to mandate corporate climate disclosures, notwithstanding extreme polarization in the United States.[2]

Even when laws are clear and consistent, ensuring that your employees won't break them grows ever more complicated. Here, too, it's vital to think strategically: efforts to shield the corporation from liability will prove inadequate unless you also learn to think more systematically about your impacts, your relationships, and the scope of your responsibilities. In this chapter, I'll begin to discuss the ways companies manage the regulatory environment—and how and why this is evolving. I will go on to explore questions of internal governance in part 3, "Leading and Shaping the Future."

Social Impact, Political Risk, and the Rise of Anti-Corruption

In my twelve years as a corporate intelligence specialist, I watched the world grow angrier and more transparent, and regulators grow more ambitious and sophisticated. In 2009, a law firm hired my team on behalf of Cobalt International Energy, a Goldman Sachs–backed company keen to invest in oil exploration off the coast of Angola.[3] The Angolan government required Cobalt to have a local partner, and we were called in to do due diligence on the suggested outfit, a newly formed venture called Nazaki Oil and Gaz. It would be difficult to come up with credible information because Angola is a particularly opaque country. Even before we began retrieving documents and asking questions, it was obvious that Nazaki's local backers must be well connected. The sole question for me was which local oligarch stood to benefit from the deal.

For several months, we tried to explain the nature of these corruption risks to our client. We described how Angola's oil industry interacted with its political system and outlined who our sources had told us was backing Nazaki, only to be met with stony silence and direction to stick to "just the facts." Our final report blandly summarized the documents we had retrieved and acknowledged that we could not conclusively prove anything about the ownership of Nazaki. Cobalt went ahead with the deal in 2010.[4]

Although free speech had long been suppressed in Angola, here, too, internet discourse was starting to undermine controlled messaging from the mainstream media. In 2011, an activist named Rafael Marques de Morais alleged online that Nazaki was controlled by three of the country's most powerful men, and the following year he launched a formal complaint to the attorney general.[5] One of those he accused was Manuel Vicente, who had been in charge of the state-owned oil company, Sonangol, at the time Cobalt and Nazaki were granted the licenses. The other two were prominent former generals: Manuel Helder Vieira Dias Jr. (usually called Kopelipa), and Leopoldino Fragoso do Nascimento (commonly known as General Dino). We had identified both as likely owners in our due diligence efforts, but we had no proof. Now both men acknowledged their stakes to the *Financial Times,* and I wound up as a witness in a US government anti-corruption investigation.[6]

After years of legal wrangling, the Department of Justice dropped the case. By then the reputational damage was done: Cobalt had dropped the project, taken a huge hit to its stock price, and sold its stake to Sonangol, the state-owned oil company controlled by Isabel dos Santos, the president's daughter.[7] In the face of persistent allegations about her sources of wealth, she had amassed a huge network of international business interests and was invariably listed among Africa's richest, most influential figures.[8]

In 2017, her father, José Eduardo dos Santos, stepped down after thirty-eight years as president. A successor from the same party, João Lourenço, was elected.[9] To the surprise of the dos Santos family, Angola's new government launched a major anti-corruption campaign and began investigating powerful figures, including Isabel dos Santos and the owners of Nazaki. In 2019, the government seized her local assets, bank accounts, and businesses, and international banks started seeking distance amid a deluge of media attention.[10] A year later, a program called *O Banquete* (*The Feast*) debuted on Angolan public TV, describing how a few powerful figures, including Manuel Vicente and Isabel dos Santos, "enriched themselves by embezzling public money."[11] (Critics charged that President Lourenço's anti-corruption campaign was mainly intended to target enemies, not to institute reform.[12])

This anti-corruption campaign received a major boost internationally in early 2020 with the release of the so-called Luanda Leaks by the

International Consortium of Investigative Journalists. This mass leak of off-shore filings showed that Isabel dos Santos and her husband held an empire of four hundred companies in forty-one countries, at least ninety-four of them registered offshore, and had hired Boston Consulting Group, PwC, KPMG, and other credible firms to help her manage them.[13] This embarrassed the firms, which had continued to work with the former president's daughter even as she became a pariah in the global banking system.[14] As I write, dos Santos faces serious legal jeopardy and has been banned from entering the United States.

What does all this mean in general? If we wish to understand what corporations can, should, and will do in the face of regulatory imperatives, assessing the progress and limitations of anti-corruption efforts over the past twenty years provides an unusually revealing case study.

What is corruption? It is defined broadly by Transparency International, a leading NGO, as "the abuse of entrusted power for private gain." Our everyday use of the term is even broader. It's common to discuss how organizations and people become "corrupted." But when we talk specifically about corporate anti-corruption efforts, we are usually discussing a specific type of corruption: bribery is a quid pro quo exchange to gain unfair advantage, most often (though not exclusively) via a government official who wields power over contract awards, information, or approvals.

Bribery is a big problem for companies. It distorts fair competition as deals go to whomever pays for favors, not to the most qualified contender or the one offering the best value. It's also a problem for governments, because officials who seek bribes are using their decision-making power for personal benefit. In both cases, bribery is most often framed as a principal-agent problem: an unethical employee gains financially at their employer's expense.

Corruption is a big problem for society, too. It directly wastes government resources and diminishes the quality of services and infrastructure. High levels of corruption correlate with low growth and investment, high inflation, currency depreciation, disproportionate military spending, poor health care and education, bad environmental policy, terrorist financing, and conflict.[15] Corruption is increasingly recognized as a root cause of human rights abuses, poverty, and underdevelopment.

Corruption has been thorny throughout history. Conflicts of interest, venality, abuse of office, and crooked procurement crop up in ancient and medieval literature. All major religions view corruption as immoral. The record of corporate anti-corruption efforts, however, is startlingly brief. As recently as the 1960s, academics accepted bribery as necessary for overcoming bureaucratic obstacles in developing countries.[16] In the wake of the 1970s Watergate scandal, government investigations into corporate political contributions uncovered huge slush funds for bribes at some of the biggest US companies.[17] In response, the Foreign Corrupt Practices Act, which bans bribery of foreign politicians, became law in Washington. US businesses lobbied strenuously against the FCPA on the ground that it would undermine their ability to compete with rivals from other nations. Although it remained on the books, enforcement of FCPA did not become a practical concern for decades.[18]

Academic interest in how corruption can distort markets and institutions surged shortly after the Cold War ended. Transparency International was founded in Berlin in 1993, a time when corporate bribes were still tax deductible in Germany. The World Bank, which had regarded corruption as "too political" an issue, changed course in 1996 when its president, James Wolfensohn, denounced "the cancer of corruption."[19] International treaties from the UN and OECD followed.

Then came the 9/11 attacks on the World Trade Center in New York, which prompted the US government to zero in on transnational bribery, money laundering, and terrorist financing.[20] As regulators ramped up scrutiny and investigations, I witnessed the evolution of corporate compliance efforts in real time. The 2008 global financial crisis triggered further efforts to increase oversight and risk management. An aggressive approach to these issues in the United States catalyzed the criminalization of domestic and international bribery in such varied nations as the UK, Canada, Norway, China, and Brazil.

Today, international anti-bribery efforts constitute a notable bright spot in white-collar crime enforcement. International cooperation on investigations and litigation has flourished, helping regulators build cases against powerful multinationals.[21] Although mining giant Glencore did this as recently as 2015, you'd be foolhardy today to think that flying bags of cash across Africa in private jets is a risk worth taking.[22] Penalties include multimillion-dollar fines, requirements to pay back ("disgorge") profits obtained by bribery, jail time for senior executives, and debarment from obtaining government contracts. Legal fees and negative media notice carry enormous costs, too.[23]

All this enforcement has brought copious advice from regulators on how to design an anti-corruption program.[24] Consensus holds that a good one includes commitment from senior management (often known as "tone at the top"); a clear code of conduct; risk assessment; due diligence on agents, distributors, and other third parties; training; reporting; and investigation.

Programs against corruption have thus reached the kind of advanced state that an environmental or human rights campaigner dreams about. Zero tolerance for corruption is bound to be avowed in any corporate code of conduct. Prospective business partners anywhere in the world should understand by now that if they want to do business with you, they must sign assurances that they won't pay bribes. This marks an astonishing shift in processes and norms in less than two decades. Meanwhile, the corporate investigations industry has mushroomed into a multibillion-dollar business of auditors, lawyers, forensic specialists, and consultants that the *Economist* called "FCPA Inc."[25]

What impact have all these regulatory advances had? It's hard to say. Concern over corruption has not diminished in either developed or developing countries.[26] In fact, public rage over it spurs ever wider popular protests.[27] Freedom House has found that transparency and accountability in government are diminishing, not increasing.[28]

Over the same period, it's become uncomfortably clear that corruption is not only a problem that happens in the Global South. It is a process broadly and deeply facilitated by Western financial institutions and their agents. Huge data leaks demonstrate that both kleptocrats and respectable multinationals use offshore accounts and trusts—even sharing prestigious lawyers and accountants—to protect their wealth from scrutiny.

Our progress on bribery is worth celebrating, but corruption is alive and well around the world. A rethink is well underway. Robert Barrington, a professor of anti-corruption practice at the University of Sussex and former head of Transparency International UK, tells me: "A focus on victims and harm is increasingly at the center of anti-corruption efforts."

Operating Ethically in a Corrupt Environment

Companies often grudgingly spend money on compliance, as a sort of insurance purchase in case things go wrong. This dismissive mindset does nothing to help them tackle the political and strategic risks posed by corruption. Again, corruption is not merely a legal or ethical risk. It is inherently *political*: as we've seen in Angola, new political leaders often launch anti-corruption campaigns against real or perceived adversaries. This can be devastatingly effective—and popular.

To thwart actual corruption, then, you need a more systemic, considered perspective. A focus on internal processes and contractual guarantees should not come at the expense of efforts to contemplate and assess your operating context.

Let's take a look at what this means in practice.

In markets where corruption is endemic, banning bribes will only get you so far. You won't need to pay them to kleptocrats to secure advantage; any transaction with a foreign company will be gamed to benefit them personally. This usually takes the form of control over natural resources like oil, minerals, timber, land, or cocoa.[29] A corrupt state is one in which ruling networks (whose members may or may not hold formal political positions) use their power to capture and control government revenue streams.[30] This isn't a system with a corruption problem. Corruption *is* the system.

In such places, petty and grand corruption coexist because kleptocratic networks tend to be vertically integrated. What I mean by this is that superiors will demand a cut of each bribe secured by junior officials. All this, along with problems caused by underfunded, ineffective government bodies, feeds the sense of grievance and injustice among the general population. Citizens may be extorted to pay bribes just to get electricity connected, cross police checkpoints, or get goods released from import stations. If your company is big and powerful enough, you might be able to pressure the government to alleviate some problems you face without having to bribe anyone, but you can't rely solely on your internal prevention program.

Soji Apampa is probably Nigeria's best known anti-corruption campaigner, and he offers useful guidance for how to operate in environments with endemic corruption. In the early 2000s, he was hired to build up the public-sector business for SAP in Nigeria, where he had to hone strong diplomatic skills without exposing himself to bribery requests. He tells me:

> The first thing I said was that I have to be high profile so I can establish myself. I got a house two doors down from the American ambassador, and I started throwing a lot of cocktail parties. At the end of the day, I'm a salesman, and people buy from people they know and trust. So I have to play golf with key officials and establish myself, but also wear my anti-corruption credentials on my sleeve. That has to be there from the beginning, but I have to be as warm as possible—the "go to" person.
>
> After a while, I would try to bid for a piece of work, and I'd get a phone call: "Don't bother, it's not for you." And then I would just pipe down. And sometimes I would get a tip-off, and someone would ask if I'd seen the tender and suggest I bid. "You never know what God can do; you might want to give it a try." And then I would know that this contract wasn't already owned by someone—and I could bid. Finally, a huge opportunity arose with a major Nigerian government department. I partnered with one of the big four consulting firms because I knew they couldn't play dirty. And all along I kept saying, "Don't take everything from us, take the best of breed." That helped us not to become the target of every other company trying to pull us down. If it is one player and there are corrupt people needing a payoff, no matter what, they will come to me. But if we are ten in the game, and they already know I don't pay, they are going to go for the other guy.
>
> Most people believe that in a corrupt environment everybody is corrupt, but that's not true. If people arrive with these lies already in their heads, they are willing to compromise because they think there is no other option. But you can actually be selective and find a few companies doing the right thing who can grow with you.

Apampa's experience in Nigeria begins to illuminate what it really takes to operate successfully in a corrupt environment. Internal bribery prohibitions and control processes are necessary but insufficient. What more does it take to resist corruption?

Emphasize quality to beat corrupt competitors. A high-quality product and competitive pricing will help. While that's true in any market economy, in a corrupt environment it's even more important to demonstrate that you have cutting-edge products with customer benefits. While some tenders will be affected by corruption, quality may take precedence if a project is sufficiently complex and of high priority.

Analyze who has power and influence, both formally and informally. You need prime local intelligence and stakeholder relationships. The circles of power are often small. This makes it easy to step on someone's toes. It also means that understanding the agendas and relationships of your clients, partners, and competitors need not be an overwhelming task. Entering a risky market is the perfect moment to conduct the stakeholder analysis and interviews I described in chapter 3.

Power and influence are key criteria to look at here. They place a particular lens on the gap between formal and informal power. It will be important to understand wider networks: if your key competitor is close to the deputy minister who controls the tenders, this may not be an opportunity for you. Note that comprehending the prevailing influence networks is useful for more than anti-corruption efforts; it's critical for building a successful human rights strategy, as we'll discuss in chapter 6.

Constantly communicate your values. Intelligence runs both ways. In addition to maintaining high internal standards, you need to consistently signal to the market that you will not pay. While this starts with policies and prohibitions, companies also need to communicate it constantly, so officials and business partners know who they are dealing with—and what to expect. Once officials know that a certain company is an absolute nonpayer, the incentive to create artificial administrative obstacles will shrink. Nothing can be gained by delaying papers or misclassifying your goods.

By contrast, companies that are known to pay bribes, however reluctantly, are more likely to encounter predatory behavior from officials and politicians. If you ever pay—just once—you'll invite bureaucrats to entertain delays and make administrative errors so your company can pay to "solve" them.

Do not rely on a single broker or partner; build broad local alliances. You need to devote detailed attention to whom you partner with (this might protect you or make you more vulnerable) and whom you compete with (retaliation is common). Some researchers have suggested that you identify which stakeholders are more or less ethical so you can build supportive relationships.[31] It's hazardous to rely on a single local partner to help build your relationships, especially if you are unfamiliar with the environment and will depend on what they tell you. Even if your presence in the country is limited, you need to build broad relationships and networks with civil society, trade associations, the diplomatic sphere, and business groups.

Be realistic about how long things take. You must be realistic about time and deadlines. A perception that you're in a hurry will forfeit any advantage you might have in negotiations. Proper project planning and practical thinking about sales incentives and targets will let you and the world know you needn't cut corners.

Measure the costs. Because the cost of bribes does not appear in company accounts, its financial implications are often invisible to the companies paying them. Awareness of the true cost of corruption should boost internal appetite to tackle the problem. The highly successful Maritime Anti-Corruption Network (to which I will return shortly) was formed partly because shipping companies were tracking the costs of delays from extortion by customs officials. In many companies, such costs go unnoticed.

In a former role leading compliance at AB InBev, Matt Galvin focused on helping his colleagues understand the commercial implications of corruption so they'd understand and support his efforts. Galvin tells me: "I see fighting corruption as so core to wider environmental and social aspirations because it is such an attractor and such an inhibitor. It's rarely the case that you have a rogue employee and a rogue government agent meeting in a back room, and they are just two bad people. The problem usually has more to do with market incentives and how they weigh on both parties. Corruption is both highly contagious and highly inflationary. There tends to be a whole ecosystem of everyone grabbing, and more and more people want in."[32]

Galvin analyzed AB InBev's controls and discounting systems to tackle some of these risks in India, even though colleagues feared he would put sales at risk. Sales dipped and then quickly returned to previous levels.

Ask employees for insight and give them (real) support. Dealing with corruption risk is likeliest to place extreme stress on staff far from headquarters, in sales or business development roles. The wrong way to manage these pressures is to require them to sign documents committing not to pay bribes, even as you pay little attention to how you incentivize or communicate with them. The combination of a high-risk environment, isolation, and pressure to meet sales targets makes a toxic cocktail. Frontline employees can be a powerful source of understanding and insight. You need to do all you can to train them to contend with on-the-ground pressure.

Consider collective action to tackle market challenges. Finally, you might look closely at opportunities for collective action. Although cooperative effort remains nascent, it's critical to forging an advanced anti-corruption approach. Let's discuss this in greater detail.

Rethinking Collective Action

We've discussed how corruption, like most challenges in business ethics, is widely understood as a principal-agent problem. In both business and government, proposed solutions focus on reducing monopoly and discretion while increasing accountability.[33] For solutions, corporations concentrate on legal penalties, diligence, and transparency; governments set up watchdogs and anti-corruption commissions, monitoring mechanisms, and sanctions. When corruption is the norm, however, these tools are very likely to become co-opted and politicized. Corruption becomes a systemic problem that can be effectively tackled only if companies work together.

Smaller companies in particular can benefit from joining with larger players to set standards. "I know a few businesses that do their best to operate ethically in highly corrupt places, and they are very communicative and transparent about the challenges," corruption expert Jane Seabrook Ellis tells me. "But to be honest, the companies that do that are the very big companies, who would really hurt the country economically if they left. Once you start thinking about smaller companies, it is a lot more difficult. You would need smaller companies to form a strong network."

Collective action can therefore be a promising and powerful tool for businesses that are struggling with entrenched corruption. John Morrell, at the Center for International Private Enterprise, oversees a collective action coalition against corruption in Thailand. At first, CIPE homed in on local perceptions by asking a thousand companies operating in Thailand whether corruption was a common and pervasive problem. This made sense: social psychology shows that if we view bad behavior as unavoidable, we're far likelier to engage in it. CIPE found that 99 percent said corruption was bad and getting worse; only 3 percent said it was possible to tackle it.

By the time I spoke with Morrell, though, the situation had transformed. CIPE counts eleven hundred companies in its coalition—60 percent Thai-headquartered and 40 percent international. Almost two-thirds of them had come to agree that it's possible to make progress against corruption.

How did CIPE do this?

"There are teeth behind the program," Morrell says. "In order to be part of the coalition, companies must meet very specific, actionable, and verifiable commitments on internal anti-bribery controls. We don't just take their word for it. Fifty percent fail our assessment the first time, and 80 percent of those come back and try a second time. We have a process where we help them comply, and some have even started rolling the program out to their own suppliers. We have seen hundreds of big Thai businesses change their operations in a way that has had an impact on the wider operating environment."

Apampa, too, focuses on collective action in Nigeria. He considers it the most effective approach in countries with weak governance because, he says, self-regulation and internal controls by a business won't suffice when it is constantly approached and extorted for facilitation payments. And it's naive to expect much from government crackdowns: "You can't expect the people who benefit from the system to regulate the system to their own disadvantage."

Apampa has developed several external accountability mechanisms, including the global Maritime Anti-Corruption Network (MACN) mentioned earlier.[34] Such networks send powerful signals to corrupt actors and the wider market: look elsewhere. "There, it's on your sleeve, it lets people know not to come to you. They know even if they rattle your cage, they're not going to get anything out of you. So they'd rather go down the road to the next person." He says, "It is insurance for you, to get involved in collective action."

Cecilia Müller Torbrand, MACN's CEO, explains that progress can follow when a group of companies (either in the same industry or exposed to the same practices) builds an appetite for joining forces against corruption after clearly identifying common problems and costs plaguing them. This can assist internal compliance, she tells me. "The big advantage of collective action is that it reduces finger-pointing. As an internal compliance officer, it is easy to blame your problems on government officials seeking bribes and view yourself as vulnerable. Get in a room with those government officials and they will say, 'Your staff are going around bribing us.' Only when everyone is sitting around the table will the finger-pointing stop, and you can come up with specific, constructive solutions."

Gonzalo Guzman has spent much of his career trying to tackle corporate corruption challenges, first at GSK and now at Unilever. Unilever is relatively unusual in taking a systemic approach to business integrity that reaches far beyond compliance programs. "We have an external advocacy strategy around key topics," he tells me. "One is beneficial ownership, so we advocate for changing rules on disclosure of company ownership to make it easier to identify third-party risks. A second one relates to ease of doing business more generally, so we advocate for 'e-government' and other efforts to reduce red tape. We are also working closely with the human rights team on risk assessment and support for individuals who defend human rights in the local environment."

Guzman says his work has taught him that sustainability and governance challenges intersect and intertwine in the real, messy world, and that internal prevention is no substitute for meaningful engagement on systemic risk.

Beyond Compliance

In 1970, Milton Friedman didn't merely advise companies not to break the law. He suggested that business and politics operate in sharply distinct realms. If these sharp distinctions don't really exist, and the rules of the game are up for grabs, where does this leave us?

Guido Palazzo, a professor of business ethics at the University of Lausanne, has pondered corporate impact and responsibility for decades. During the 1990s, prominent companies started to be attacked for not taking care of workers in their supply chains, or for causing deforestation. In both cases, the proximate cause was efforts by multinational companies to evade local regulations by moving into countries with governments unable or unwilling to enforce the rule of law. Early corporate responsibility efforts pressed corporations to voluntarily fill these gaps in governance.

"This work was in opposition to Milton Friedman's thesis," Palazzo tells me. "But what I always found fascinating was that when Friedman wrote these things, capitalism was Europe, America, Japan. So when he says, well, governments take care of these things—of course they did, more or less, in these contexts. But after the fall of the [Berlin] Wall, companies started operating in China, Russia, Iran, the Congo. This division of labor didn't work anymore."

· · ·

In this chapter, we've started to explore why legal compliance is far from a binary, black-and-white matter. We've seen that legal frameworks are critical in adapting to shifting norms and practices, but following the letter of the law fails to address all governance challenges. Understanding stakeholder agendas and using your own leverage is a core element of building greater resilience against corruption.

There's enormous value in comprehending and navigating political dynamics. Our collective action examples suggest that businesses can, should, and do play a role in creating an ethical and consistent operating environment.

But how, when, and why must they do this? Are there any limits? And what about the risks of straying into political territory? In chapter 6, let's look at this in detail.

STEPS TO HIGHER GROUND

Ensuring that your company and its employees do not break the law is still a basic operating requirement and remains a considerable practical challenge. But it's become an unreliable anchor if you wish to be considered an ethical business. That broadly explains the expansion of sustainability and stakeholder capitalism—and why companies tend to default to separate teams covering "ethics and compliance" on one hand and "sustainability" on the other.

The history of anti-corruption compliance shows that companies respond decisively to legal imperatives, and this can transform societal norms and expectations. The internal processes that seek to protect the corporation from liability have certainly become necessary, but they do not suffice. The focus of corruption research and campaigns is now shifting to its impact on human society. To address this, or any complex societal challenge, you'll need to better comprehend how your actions impact the operating environment and build sturdier relationships.

Operating ethically in a corrupt environment requires clear standards, good products, strong stakeholder relationships, and consistent communication. You'll need to anticipate deadline pressures so they can't be used against you. And you must design your commercial goals accordingly. Collaborating with other companies, even rivals, can help you address systemic pressures and build strength in numbers.

Adopting a successful anti-corruption approach in difficult environments must begin with exercising genuine, practical curiosity about "the way they do things around here." You must also account for an environment as it really is, not as you'd prefer it to be. This may, in turn, constrain your available choices and options. It is likely to raise questions about where you should seek to use leverage to influence the rules of the game.

Grounding Your Values in How You Impact Human Beings

We've arrived at the crux of the dilemma confronting leaders who would like to know what being a good business means today. Corporate values aren't optional, and they're more controversial and contested than ever. Legal compliance no longer offers a solid foundation for efforts to run an ethical business. On the other hand, aiming to base your values and commitments on the full range of stakeholder pressures and demands is a recipe for incoherence and fragmentation.

No matter how energetically you try to shield corporate values from scrutiny and societal turbulence, you are relying on organizational defenses that have turned porous and fragile. Seeking to shore them up and double down is a logical, predictable response, but it won't work because the original premises are obsolete. Notwithstanding numerous ideological and partisan divisions over the role that business should play in society, most people agree that a corporation should strive to clean up any messes it makes and to treat those it affects with respect.

In the introduction, I argued that a company can most readily and reliably decide where and how to act in responding to an enormous range of pressures if it bases its ethical commitments on its *impact on human beings*.

Putting human rights at the center of your values efforts is helpful because they focus on individual agency, bodily autonomy, and dignity—as opposed to imposing values on people who may not share them. Your corporation's impact on human beings is at the very root of your legal, operational, and reputational risks—even if *how* those risks might manifest is unpredictable. The good news is that by exploring your company's real and potential impacts with an open mind and a systemic approach, you can make your ethical commitments more coherent.

While far from straightforward—and frequently controversial—the best guidance to help companies understand and manage their impacts on the world was created in 2011 and comes from the burgeoning field of business and human rights. Because this is relatively new terrain, many corporate efforts are embryonic. But human rights frameworks offer significant advantages over ESG or compliance, which I'll explain in this chapter. As Paloma Muñoz Quick, an associate director of human rights at Business for Social Responsibility (BSR), a sustainable business network and consultancy, told a newspaper, "ESG is still considered a 'nice to have,' and human rights is not—and should not be—in that category."[1]

A Quick Primer on Business and Human Rights

Immediately following World War II, the neophyte UN General Assembly drafted the Universal Declaration of Human Rights, and every member government committed to it. This historic agreement, an aspirational code of conduct for humankind, focused on protecting human beings from the incursions of the state, not business. In 1966, the UN General Assembly adopted two additional treaties: the International Covenant on Economic, Social and Cultural Rights and the International Covenant on Civil and Political Rights. The three treaties are known as the International Bill of Rights.[2] Numerous subsequent covenants include the International Labour Organization's (ILO) core conventions.[3] A robust body of international law and a set of civil society organizations have sprung up to protect and defend human rights all over the world.

Human rights were initially regarded as duties of government. But as corporations expanded into new markets in the 1980s and '90s, it became clear that they were not only seeking to access the raw materials and cheaper workers available in the Global South but to sidestep stricter regulations in their home countries, too. Over time, the public grew alarmed about business links to human rights abuses and environmental degradation. A chemical leak by US-based Union Carbide in Bhopal, India, in 1984 killed thousands and sickened more than a half-million people. In 1986 came the USSR's Chernobyl nuclear disaster in Ukraine, and then in 1989 the *Exxon Valdez* oil spill fouled Alaskan waters.

Beginning in the 1990s, such big brands as Nike, Home Depot, and the Gap encountered sustained pressure from the public and media over deforestation, child labor, and worker exploitation in their supply chains.[4] Consumer companies under fire reluctantly started to impose governance standards on their suppliers. When it became clear that this could not vanquish controversy, some started to go beyond audits and inspections to such systemic interventions as financing schooling for child laborers.

From an ethical perspective, this seemed logical. Companies entering markets with inconsistent or weak governance or social services seemed to face an ethical imperative to fill these gaps. A 2007 paper by Tim Bartley argued: "Most scholars agree that the globalization of supply chains and the lack of existing regulatory capacity at the global level generate demands for new forms of 'global governance.'"[5]

Globalization thus seemed to be inaugurating an era of corporate citizenship—a wider transformation of the role of business in society. Back in 2005, David Vogel published an influential book called *The Market for Virtue*, which argued: "If companies are serious about acting more responsibly, then they need to reexamine their relationship to the government as well as improve their own practices. And those who want corporations to be more virtuous should expect firms to act more responsibly on both dimensions."[6]

Vogel's call for a reexamination of the relationship between business and government was subsequently drowned out by the noisy rise of ESG and the boom in legal compliance, both focused on external threats to corporate value. All along, however, a framework for business and human rights has been taking shape. When it comes to the ethical challenges that models like ESG sidestep, it offers a promising path toward higher ground.

Consideration of human rights joined corruption in the late 1990s as a prime issue demanding greater attention from business. In 2000, then–UN Secretary General Kofi Annan launched the UN Global Compact; its first principle is to respect human rights and commit not to be complicit in human rights abuses. The same year, oil and gas and mining companies established the Voluntary Principles on Security and Human Rights to better manage the risks entailed in working with government security forces, particularly in authoritarian frontier markets. That initiative followed decades of protest by the Ogoni community against Shell's operations in the Niger Delta, which culminated in the 1995 execution of activist Ken Saro-Wiwa and eight others by Nigerian security forces.[7]

Then, as corruption—or at least, corporate bribery of public officials—became more regulated, human rights efforts were gradually relegated to a voluntary, lower-priority effort. Anti-corruption work became the well-funded and well-regulated province of lawyers and compliance teams, as we saw in chapter 5. Corporate efforts on human rights usually came only in response to extreme public pressure following revelations of egregious violations.

In 2005, Annan appointed Harvard professor John Ruggie to consider the respective obligations of government and business on human rights. Ruggie conducted more than fifty consultations with business, government, civil society, and international organizations around the world, achieving global consensus after prior efforts had collapsed.[8]

The result was the UN Guiding Principles on Business and Human Rights (UNGPs), a detailed set of guidelines that clearly lay out what businesses need to do to *avoid, prevent, mitigate,* and *remedy* adverse human rights impacts.[9] Its scope encompasses human rights violations that business *causes,* those to which a business *contributes,* and those *directly linked* to a company's operations, products, or services through its business relationships. In other words, this breakthrough framework unswervingly addresses corporate complicity in human rights abuses committed by governments.[10]

The UNGPs were respectively endorsed by the UN Human Rights Council and by UN member states in 2008 and 2011. While any government has a duty to *protect* human rights, it is a company's responsibility to *respect* human rights. When business-related human rights abuses occur in a country, the state is required to investigate and punish them, and businesses are to cooperate by providing *remedy* to victims.[11]

Creation of the UN Guiding Principles constitutes the sole comprehensive attempt to address the human consequences of transnational business activity. The principles provide the clearest guidance for a business to consider how it interacts with the wider political and social environment and to establish the scope and limits of corporate responsibility. The UN's own credibility problems are well documented, but its human rights frameworks are the most robust, practical guidance we have about the global responsibilities of business to society.[12]

It's critical to note that effective accountability continues to rely on the creation and implementation of national laws. Before 2011, action was rarely taken against companies for human rights violations. Business obligations regarding human rights thereafter embarked on a gradual shift from "soft law" (voluntary standards grounded in international law but not legally binding) toward "hard law." Initial regulatory efforts focused on forced labor, trafficking, and modern slavery. Much as in the early days of anti-corruption efforts, legal efforts have emerged as a patchwork, on a country-by-country basis.

What Are the Advantages of a Human Rights Focus?

Because business efforts regarding human rights are relatively inchoate, companies may find them exotic and esoteric when compared with the familiar turf of risks and returns. It's well worth embracing the discomfort and hard work, though, because human rights frameworks can help you bring conceptual and procedural rigor to your ethical commitments. Here's why.

Human rights are universal. Often derided as Western-centric, human rights are contentious and politicized. But it's indisputable that no one of any ideology or ethnicity welcomes violation of their rights and dignity. A positive business approach to human rights is compatible with an increasingly heterogeneous and pluralistic international environment and with the rising global focus on the rights of individuals.

Human rights are comprehensive. Media coverage of human rights issues is often narrowly focused on forced labor and trafficking. But a key advantage of the human rights platform is that it encompasses the spectrum of economic, civil, political, security, and environmental issues. In 2022, for instance, the UN General Assembly recognized the right to a clean, healthy, and sustainable environment.[13] Placing human rights at the forefront of an environmental responsibility program can thus help companies avoid the common pitfall of treating environmental and social responsibilities as separate issues. Renewable energy project designers, for example, need to consider human rights impacts in shaping realistic, broadly acceptable strategies to reduce emissions.[14]

Human rights are grounded in responsibility to society. However well executed, ESG and sustainability frameworks leave it for individual businesses to decide what to do and when to act. Rather than view ethical obligations solely through the lens of financial advantage, human rights center on a corporation's obligations to general society. It's not that companies can't seek to effect positive changes; it's that such attempts ought not take precedence over the mission to do no harm (or worse, seek to distract us).

Human rights align with other ethical frames. The human rights framework encompasses both the legal rigor of compliance and the external focus of sustainability. Therefore, it can help you chart a coherent, holistic approach to ethical business. It's important to note that human rights include the right to self-determination. They can therefore help companies approach such challenging issues as political engagement and diversity, equity, and inclusion.

Human rights stand at the nexus of corporate responsibility and geopolitics. Unlike ESG, human rights frameworks don't envisage companies enacting good works in a world devoid of other actors, power dynamics, and political pressures—or doing it only when there's a business case for them. The framework explicitly considers the relative positions and responsibilities of business and government in society.

Human rights are aligned with our aspirations. Popular unrest over the negative impacts of business isn't about to go away. Global interest in human rights and freedoms is flourishing. In chapter 1, we explored the boom in popular protest, much of it demanding greater individual rights and opportunities.[15] Cultivating respect for human rights can help companies meet and anticipate emerging challenges.

Human rights align with regulatory attention. The EU is expanding its list of legally mandated human rights obligations, and the United States is taking action that pertains to trafficking and forced labor. Authorities in countries including the United States, the Philippines, and the Netherlands are laying the groundwork for class-action lawsuits on human impacts of climate change.[16] For example, in August 2023, a public interest law firm representing youths in Montana won a case establishing that the state laws incentivizing oil, gas, and coal production violated the state constitution, which says residents have a right to a healthy environment.[17] Overall, if you wish to anticipate and plan for future regulation on both social and environmental issues, a superb starting place is to survey your human rights impacts.[18]

Human rights consider trade-offs. While human rights are indivisible, complexities are inevitable. Some human rights appear to contradict one another—the rights to privacy and freedom of expression, for example. Robust guidance and a body of law weigh how to prioritize and negotiate them. These approaches are practical. BSR, for instance, made recommendations as to how Meta could better understand and address competing human rights pressures regarding end-to-end messaging encryption; notwithstanding clear trade-offs between the needs to protect user privacy and to protect users from child exploitation, human rights methodologies enabled a path forward.[19]

Human rights aren't corporate-centric. Because human rights frameworks require direct consultation with your stakeholders, they can act to counterbalance any tendency to place the company's interests at the center of the universe. At the same time, human rights frameworks provide a way to prioritize stakeholder demands by addressing impact and causation.

How to Assess Human Rights Impacts

According to the UNGPs, a good human rights assessment meets the following criteria. First, it's about your impact on human beings, rather than the risks you perceive. This is not about the centrality of the corporation's self interest, but the views, experiences, and concerns of those impacted by its activities. Second, you assess your impacts in the light of internationally recognized human rights rather than your company's judgment as to which impacts might be most relevant.

This means that the best place to begin any human rights impact assessment is with the principles we discussed in chapter 3 on how to build stakeholder trust. In the next section, I will describe a human rights impact assessment process. You can use this to populate the stakeholder axis of the corporate materiality assessment I describe in chapter 4.

The scope of your human rights assessment will vary according to your operations and business model. A corporate human rights impact assessment is a great starting point, though many complex global businesses aim to go further.[20] Diageo is a leading example of a company that has conducted human rights impact assessments in all of its markets. Diageo made its executive team responsible for human rights and included a commitment to human rights in its cost of conduct, including an explicit clause respecting its employees' right to join a union.[21] Locally, human rights risks are managed by risk management committees that, in turn, report to the company's global audit and risk committee. (I'll address questions of internal governance in part 3, "Leading and Shaping the Future.")

Many companies conduct human rights impact assessments for specific products or services, and enterprises with a strong on-the-ground presence might focus on a particular locality or country. Google, for example, did a human rights assessment of the interface for its celebrity recognition application program, and mining company Goldcorp assessed the human rights impacts of its Marlin mine in Guatemala during both operating life and closure.[22] To do this, companies commonly tap the expertise and credibility of independent NGOs.

On entering a market, assessing the status quo can enable you to comprehend the baseline conditions surrounding your prospective operation.

Bear in mind that your impacts—and the expectations of civil authorities and other stakeholders—may extend beyond the formal geographical limits of your operations. You must anticipate that your human rights issues will evolve; an infrastructure project, for instance, will wield highly varied impacts during construction, operation, and closure.

If you examine the national, regional, and local context for corruption, as discussed in chapter 4, it makes sense to assess human rights at the same time: corruption exacerbates risks to human rights.[23] Understanding formal and informal power dynamics in the political and regulatory realm will bring insights into leverage, influence, and appetites for change.

Once you've determined the scope of your assessment, you can proceed.

Step 1: Understand all relevant impacts

The first step is to gain a thorough understanding of the human rights relevant in your sector and location of concern. Starting with the rights described in the International Bill of Rights and ILO Core Conventions, establish which rights pertain to your operating context. Social media companies will impact privacy and freedom of expression. Oil and gas enterprises will affect security, freedom of movement, and the right to a clean environment. The right to health should inform assessments for makers of pharmaceuticals, tobacco, and sugary drinks. Freedom of assembly and protest will concern almost all companies.

In chapter 4, we discussed how to identify the landscape of environmental and social issues relevant to your business; reviewing that landscape can now help you identify applicable rights. The Business & Human Rights Resource Centre has for years produced industry assessments, and numerous taxonomies and resources are available to help you.[24]

Step 2: Consult the humans you affect

The second step is to consult your stakeholders ("rightsholders," in human rights terms) to find which human rights impacts they see as most significant and salient. This might involve interviews and focused group sessions with affected communities (a common approach in mining exploration), as well as discussions with independent experts. It will be important to speak with employees on the ground, not just senior decision-makers. As with a materiality assessment, a description of the impacts and rights in question should be provided to participants, and you must try to communicate clearly and respectfully. It might help to consider what rights apply to which stakeholders, or which of your activities or products might affect particular rights.

Step 3: Prioritize on the basis of impact, not risk

Once you've come to understand your impacts, start mulling over the difficult task of prioritization. The UNGPs advise that you consider *scope* (how many people will be affected), *scale* (the level and severity of harm presented; a minor pollution incident is less harmful than a lack of safety controls that put employees' lives at risk), and *remediability* (the degree to which the harm a victim experiences can be mitigated or reversed). For a new project or investment, you should also consider what the impact would be if you do nothing, and what your options are for taking action.[25]

Then consider your role in these impacts. This means thinking about whether your company's operations are *causing* the impact (the workers in your own factories aren't given proper safety equipment) or *contributing* to it (deadlines or cost pressures on your suppliers make safety violations likelier). And even though you may not directly be causing or contributing to a problem, you may still be linked to the impact via your operations, products, or services. (For example, you're doing your best to respect human rights in your supply chain factories, but the government in question is conducting aggressive surveillance and arbitrary detention of the local population, which is affecting your workers.[26])

Many other tools—innovations emerge constantly—can help you measure and quantify your environmental and social impact. To take just one example, prominent academics such as Harvard's George Serafeim are working to measure the cost of corporate externalities so they can be included in financial accounting.[27] Such measurement efforts fit well within business and human rights frameworks, and are becoming the focus of sustained attention.

Step 4: Manage your impacts

The UNGPs recommend "integration" of human rights across the company and incorporation of human rights management into specific functions and processes. The best way to achieve this is to acknowledge that human rights are integral to both your legal responsibilities and your environmental and social priorities. This is yet another reason why grounding values in human rights obligations can help reduce the natural tendency toward siloed, fragmented approaches. In addition to Diageo, Vestas Wind Systems provides an excellent example of a company grounding both its integrity and social responsibility efforts in a commitment to human rights that includes an explicit pledge to "ensure the integration of human rights in the energy transition."[28]

It's vitally important to be realistic about how much leverage your company has, especially when it comes to affecting governmental activities. Anticipate strong overlap with your degree of leverage regarding corruption. If you're a big player with an impeccable reputation working in a dominant sector, a government may respond to your concerns—or try to. But many situations pose a much starker choice between complicity and withdrawal.

In considering human rights exposure in Xinjiang, the applications of human rights principles would make it clear that a company's first obligation is to responsibly manage its own operations and protect workers from direct human rights abuses. Given the wider context of forced labor in China, invasive surveillance, and religious and cultural suppression of Muslim minorities in Xinjiang, there's no justification for maintaining operations or sourcing from the region. Western businesses lack meaningful leverage with China's government over these practices, and independent audits and due diligence can easily violate Chinese anti-espionage laws.[29]

Still, it is unrealistic to posit a broad withdrawal from China by Western businesses. And there's no clear case that large-scale divestment from China would lead to advances in human rights. While any business formally cooperating with China's government is *directly linked* to rights abuses in Xinjiang, there are many independent businesses (in the healthcare sector, for instance) that might improve livelihoods and human rights in China.

As for the US Supreme Court's nullification of *Roe v. Wade*, human rights principles suggest that the right to health is paramount, with reproductive rights a key element. Making reproductive health care equally available to all employees and contract workers across the United States (including travel) is a critical response in addressing the decision's negative human rights impacts. (Note that none of this entails "speaking up" on abortion rights; I'll discuss speaking up in chapter 12.)

The most astute corporate responses respect the principles of privacy and freedom of choice. They do not require employees to discuss their choices with HR departments but provide funds and medical coverage that can be accessed without involving the employer. So long as there exists no effort to force such health care on women who oppose abortion, it aligns with human rights principles to provide the same access to every staffer, anywhere in the United States. The rights of employees with values-based objections to reproductive care are not violated by this provision of care to colleagues. Companies that fund candidates and organizations seeking to restrict this right are contributing to negative human rights impacts, however, and such contributions should cease.

Outstanding Challenges

Human rights principles are robust, coherent, and defensible. They make the greatest sense for serving as a foundation for corporate values and should not be treated as yet another exercise in risk and compliance. A bureaucratic response of that legacy nature would emphasize certifying and auditing external actors while striving to manage legal risk and avert negative publicity.

This mindset still tends to overwhelm good-faith efforts to tackle systemic challenges and at times might even make things worse. "As EU legislation ramps up, many companies will be tempted to use their supply contracts to shift the responsibility for carrying out, and paying for, due diligence onto their suppliers," Sarah Dadush, a professor at Rutgers, tells me. "When bad things happen—perhaps because of the buyer's own purchasing practices, like imposing too-low prices or too-tight deadlines—the supplier will take the contractual fall and may even have to pay damages to the buyer. This obviously does not do much to improve human rights. We need a radically different approach, one that sets aside responsibility-shifting practices and operationalizes the shared-responsibility principles enshrined in the UNGPs, including in contracts."

Struggles in the cocoa industry illustrate how difficult it is to counter reputational pressure with meaningful action. According to a 2021 report from the US Labor Department, more than 1.5 million children engage in dangerous labor in cocoa-growing regions in West Africa.[30] Kids as young as ten are trafficked to Côte d'Ivoire from neighboring countries to work on cocoa farms. About half of the children interviewed in a *Washington Post* article said they were not allowed to return home and may face threats or physical violence when working.[31] Working conditions are dangerous and include harmful agrichemicals, heavy lifting, burning fields, and use of sharp tools. Deforestation is an equally devastating impact: roughly a quarter of Côte d'Ivoire's forest loss since 1970 has been tied to the expansion of cocoa production. One report found that as the human rights movement was growing to maturity, deforestation and child labor continued to increase.[32]

Why has it been so difficult to make progress? Much of the world's cocoa is grown in Ghana and Côte d'Ivoire, so attention can readily focus on West Africa, where the root problem manifests. The cocoa industry's manufacturers and traders are relatively concentrated. Governments have cooperated to develop regulations and agency oversight. If there were any industry in which we could expect to have addressed human rights issues, it's cocoa. Yet, after twenty years of effort, problems persist.

In 2019, I watched as Stephen Badger, the chairman of Mars, acknowledged the limits of a single company's action in a conference speech.[33] In making a stirring commitment to reduce poverty in global supply chains, he told the audience: "What makes this so difficult is that it's outside our direct control. . . . The only way to make progress is through collaboration with others and using our influence to drive action."

I followed up on Badger's points with an expert who has worked on human rights in the cocoa industry for decades and lived for a time in

West Africa. She did not wish to be identified, but still holds a human rights role at a large confectionery manufacturer. She explains:

> A focus on monitoring alone will not change the root causes of the situation on the ground. . . . In the end, it's really about changing behaviors in a context of endemic poverty. Farmers want their children to work on their farms so they can learn how to farm, because they will inherit the farms and have to maintain them. This is very different from slavery. Then there is also an overall context of poor infrastructure, weak law enforcement, and insufficient government capacity and prioritization. It's not enough to say children should be in school if that's not an option. These things aren't really the responsibility of businesses, but we are sourcing cocoa from those communities, so it could make sense to contribute to improving community infrastructure where needed.

She argues for the expansion of programs her company has funded to create the equivalent of village savings and loans associations: "We have around eighty thousand members who get entrepreneurial support to grow their businesses and get access to finance, which is otherwise hard to get. This has proven to be a very empowering approach, and it's giving people agency—a route out of poverty."

Such efforts tend to be treated as low priorities, she says, compared to countering media criticism with transparency and traceability: "Traceability is expensive and onerous, and doesn't tackle the root-cause problem. But it is difficult to talk about these underlying behavioral drivers without sounding like you are condoning child labor and other practices seen as unacceptable in the West."

Indeed, there are numerous contexts in which businesses have striven to meet human rights commitments, only to achieve negative outcomes for many people. Take the large-scale corporate divestment from Myanmar in the wake of the country's 2021 military coup: many Western businesses ended up in the hands of unethical investors, and unemployment among women skyrocketed.[34]

Some efforts simply fall short, in keeping with corporate scope and inclination. Moves in the United States to protect the reproductive rights of female employees did not aid contract workers who lack robust health-care benefits (as most do) or the unemployed. These are the female workers likeliest to be affected negatively by the restrictions.[35]

This raises complex questions. Should US companies lobby for universal health care? Should they take stands against Supreme Court decisions restricting abortion rights? The UNGPs' advice that companies should use leverage over governments with regard to human rights implies that it would be legitimate for business to exercise political influence in this context.

What about other contexts? I'll turn to them in chapter 7.

STEPS TO HIGHER GROUND

Neither ESG nor legal compliance frameworks provide clear guidance helping companies move beyond instrumental self-interest to rigorously consider their ethical obligations to wider society. Values and agendas are contentious, and generic commitments to integrity are of little help in the face of mounting stakeholder expectations and political pressures.

Consideration of human rights offers a path out of this thicket because they are universal and non-ideological. Human rights obligations can provide a solid basis for ethical commitments in your code of conduct that go beyond legal compliance. Basing your purpose, values, and supporting ethical commitments on your impact on human beings is likely to prove robust and defensible over the long term.

A further key advantage of human rights frameworks for business is that they are grounded in international law while *also* offering a methodology to consider corporate impacts on wider society. They center on core corporate responsibilities—specifically a baseline commitment that you will make as much effort as possible to do no harm. This is in line with traditional notions of corporate responsibility and with our expectations of how businesses should behave.

Human rights can also enable you to design and set guardrails (including prohibitions, but also guidance to help teams evaluate investments and projects) that shape your environmental and social strategy and incentives. Finally, your human rights obligations can help you to make connections among imperatives in legal compliance and social responsibility. I'll return to these critical questions of internal governance in part 3.

Human rights cannot solve all systemic challenges. They raise important questions about the legitimacy (and limitations) of any corporate effort to exert political influence.

7

Getting Serious about Corporate Political Responsibility

n October 2022, the former CEO of Unilever, Paul Polman, wrote that business should "step in" to back legislation aimed at abolishing the death penalty in Ohio. He suggested companies "have a clear interest in supporting criminal justice systems that heal our societies, rather than divide and destabilize them," adding that the death penalty is "fiscally irresponsible." Polman justified his advice on the grounds of our rising expectations for CEOs: "Society increasingly expects its corporate leaders to take a stand on big, touchstone issues that speak to their company's values, and to promote basic standards of dignity and justice."[1]

An immediate issue here is that you won't find the death penalty on any credible materiality assessment. Although aspects of the US criminal justice system bear clear human rights implications, your business is not causing or contributing to them unless it runs private prisons or manufactures drugs or equipment used in executions. Finally, the death penalty is a contentious, partisan issue.

Polman's arguments raise important questions about how and when business should get involved in public policy issues. We've already noted the raging appetite to place any environmental, social, political, or leadership concern—from cybersecurity to criminal justice, from migration to public health—into an undifferentiated bucket of "ESG issues" that corporations should be doing something about. Even country risk is included: in March 2022, Philippe Zaouati, CEO of Mirova, the $30 billion sustainable investing division of Nataxis Asset Management, described Russia's invasion of Ukraine as "one of the most important ESG issues we've ever had."[2]

In this chapter, I will consider what a business should and shouldn't do when it comes to public policy questions that pertain to its environmental and social priorities and impacts. If climate change appears as a top priority in your materiality assessment, what does this imply for your company's position on climate change regulations? If you need to prioritize diversity and inclusion but your recruitment pipeline is not diverse, should you invest in the education system to improve it? When your employees (or other important stakeholders) ask you to take a stand on a hot political question, how should you weigh and shape your response?

In spring 2022, thousands of Salesforce employees signed an open letter urging co-CEOs Marc Benioff and Bret Taylor to bar the NRA from marketing and fundraising on its platform after a school massacre in Texas.[3] Like Starbucks and Unilever, Salesforce is regarded as a sustainability leader.[4] Benioff is an outspoken advocate for gun control who once told CNBC that corporate leaders "need to take direct action" on social issues such as gun safety and abortion rights.[5] The co-CEOs responded, however, by pointing to previous decisions banning the sale of automatic (and some semiautomatic) firearms on the platform. Salesforce, they said, would not bar specific customers from using their software.[6]

In addition to *how* a company executes commitments in its operations, it must also determine *which* of society's problems to seek to address, if any. Consistency and clarity here are a big challenge. It's important to consult stakeholders on the social impact of your products, services, and decisions so you can set coherent internal policies and processes to address harm. But purporting to represent stakeholder views in the policy arena raises big questions about the extent of your reach and responsibility, not to mention your purpose. Stakeholder capitalism frameworks do not set clear limits on these responsibilities. This raises both normative and practical problems.

In seeking to fulfill the imperative to consider your impacts, you need to think about how your goals affect—and are affected by—public policy and regulation. This chapter will necessarily focus on the unique political context of the United States, where these questions are particularly contentious, important, and potentially influential elsewhere.

Corporate Political Irresponsibility

Numerous surveys suggest a growing public appetite for CEOs to assume leadership roles in society. The prominent Edelman Trust Barometer found in 2021 that six in ten respondents selected their employers in keeping with their personal beliefs.[7] A year later, 81 percent agreed that CEOs should be personally visible when discussing public policy issues; 60 percent expected CEOs to speak out publicly on controversial social issues.[8] (The survey didn't ask about CEOs taking public positions that *conflict* with respondents' personal values.)

The combination of employee pressure and media messaging is hard for leaders to resist. We saw in chapter 1 that CEOs appreciate opportunities to seize brand advantage by linking corporate values to popular positions. In 2017, for instance, almost four hundred CEOs, mostly in technology, signed on to a campaign urging President Donald Trump not to cancel the Obama-era DACA program, which prevented the deportation of undocumented immigrants who'd been brought to the United States as children.[9] The CEOs might more effectively have supported staff human rights by providing immigration support to the tiny proportion of employees who were directly affected. But behind-the-scenes activity was of little interest. The CEOs spoke out on this heated, divisive issue to meet the emerging expectation that business should take a stand on important questions.

By suggesting their values gave them a role to play in pushing popular causes, however, leaders unwittingly extended the range of potential declarations and interventions far beyond that of shareholder value. Now, whether it concerns a military invasion, reproductive rights, racial equity, gender identity, the environment, or a specific item of legislation, prominent brands are expected to issue opinions. (All this has transformed "speaking up," a topic we'll return to in chapter 12.)

Even riskier for many companies, it's only a matter of time before people start asking if you meant what you said. Judd Legum's *Popular Information* newsletter has avidly tracked the discrepancies between corporate statements and actions, as have such organizations as the Center for Political Accountability and InfluenceMap.[10] At BSR's annual conference in 2018, Anand Giridharadas warned hundreds of sustainability leaders in attendance: "You may have lobbyist colleagues in DC that wear nice suits and cancel out your work." Then the January 6, 2021, invasion of the US Capitol highlighted the contradictions between stated support for democracy and political financing of election deniers.

When a US Supreme Court ruling in 2015 rendered same-sex marriage legal nationally, some states pushed back. North Carolina passed a law banning transgender people from using preferred bathrooms and blocked local governments from enacting laws against discrimination (and establishing minimum wage levels). More than two hundred CEOs signed a letter opposing the state's transgender bathroom ban.[11] But at least forty-five of the companies signing the protest bore some responsibility for the law via prior financing of the Republican State Leadership Committee, which helped elect legislators that passed it.[12]

This split-screen approach between corporate speech and spending is commonplace. Reports by the Center for Political Accountability cite companies opposing racial discrimination while supporting racially inspired gerrymandering, corporations speaking up on climate change while lobbying against climate-disclosure standards, and even contraceptive makers helping elect congressional candidates who seek to defund Planned Parenthood.[13]

When an environmental or social issue is material to your business, supporting policies to help achieve your interest would seem a no-brainer. That so few companies have managed to align speech and spending supports the case that corporate leaders persist in viewing environmental and social responsibility as a matter of public relations. With top-down initiatives morphing into bottom-up pressure campaigns, companies find themselves at the painful intersection of employee activism and political risk.[14]

The money in question is plentiful. While many nations limit corporate political spending and lobbying, the US Supreme Court's *Citizens United* decision freed corporations to spend unbounded sums of "shareholder" money on political influence.[15] The ruling enabled the creation of political action committees (PACs) with unlimited budgets. For the most part, political funding has since stemmed from billionaire mega donors. But subsequent rulings loosened disclosure rules to let corporations donate to "dark money" PACs, so their actual contributions are shrouded from public view.[16]

This is difficult to justify from either the perspective of shareholder value or stakeholder capitalism. Milton Friedman's original vision was that companies should maximize shareholder value while respecting the law—and what he called "ethical custom," which he didn't discuss much. Shareholders, Friedman said, should be protected from managerial discretion, on the basis that other company stakeholders already have direct leverage: employees are given wages, lenders get interest, and customers can take their business elsewhere.[17]

Friedman saw limiting government power as the best way to manage the risk that corporations might seek to influence the political system in order to increase shareholder value.[18] Today's corporations don't just accept the rules of the market, they intervene to make them more conducive to their interests. Former Federal Reserve governor Alan Blinder has shown that regulation typically involves serving corporations by watering down provisions intended to protect the general public.[19]

Examples of this continue to mount, enraging the public. After Boeing faced a legal reckoning for safety failures, internal emails showed staff describing the 737 MAX airplane as "designed by clowns who are in turn supervised by monkeys" and boasting about how they "just jedi mind tricked [regulators] . . . I save this company a sick amount of $$$$."[20] After one of its trains exploded in Ohio and enveloped local communities in fumes from burning vinyl chloride, it emerged that rail company Norfolk Southern and its peers had lobbied against more stringent safety regulations.[21]

If you view shareholder value as the superordinate goal, you might defend corporate political spending to reduce regulatory burdens or boost competitive influence, especially if everyone else is doing it. In reality, though, financial returns from politicking are hardly assured amid frequent and dramatic electoral reversals.[22] As for their vaunted rights, shareholders generally have little visibility or say over political spending.

It's also important to note that not *every* investor gains when companies pursue parochial self-interest at society's expense. An enterprise could shape a compelling business case against accountability for its carbon emissions, the mental health effects of its algorithms, or the harm to public health from sugar in its products. There's a business case for tax avoidance—and even for a higher death rate.[23]

However, there comes a point at which corporate efforts to externalize costs start to undermine a society's foundational systems. In a 2019 study of global public markets, asset manager Schroders found that in a single year, listed companies around the world earned $4.1 trillion in profits while creating net social and environmental costs of $2.2 trillion.[24] Even if your business can avoid causing fires and floods, climate change is rendering some regions too hot for gainful function in large stretches of the year, and wildfire smoke can travel thousands of miles.[25] Damage to the Amazon basin will eventually cause it to emit more carbon than it absorbs, affecting everyone.[26]

Such prominent advocates of shareholder activism as Rick Alexander of the Shareholder Commons point out that a "universal owner"—someone with assets so broad they essentially own a chunk of the world—can find great business cases for tackling climate change and sustaining healthy, functional democracy and social services.[27] Corporate political activities can thereby put companies in conflict with some of their biggest, most influential investors, particularly pension funds.[28]

As for stakeholder capitalism, a corporation is not a democracy and stakeholders aren't an electorate. Companies have neither grounds nor governance mechanisms to gather stakeholder (or even employee) perspectives in a fair, democratic way.[29] This plays out in one of three ways. In the first mode, the C-suite makes top-down decisions about where to spend money, often reflecting its biases and proclivities and overriding those of workers.[30] In the second, the top brass responds to the loudest stakeholders, worsening polarization. In the third and worst case, executives aim to fulfill their own agendas via behind-the-scenes political influence while seeking to placate employees and the public with a cover story.

Meanwhile, both left and right press for more political exposure: the left favors standing up for causes, while the right advocates behind-the-scenes spending. What the general public wants is for CEOs to steer clear

of politics: a survey from JUST Capital in the wake of the January 6 tu-
mult suggested that most people in both major US parties want companies to *limit* political involvement while being *more transparent* about
any political contributions they make.[31]

Managing Political Exposure

Corporate political exposure takes many forms. Here are the most prominent, from highest to lowest risk:

> *Campaign finance:* Most US companies maintain PACs. They
> draw the most scrutiny—which you can try to duck by donating
> to super PACs. The latter aren't allowed to donate directly to cam-
> paigns but can spend unlimited sums on such activities as adver-
> tising for a candidate (or against an opponent). Super PACs are far
> less transparent and are regarded as much less ethical. Companies
> also fund campaigns indirectly via trade associations.[32] These
> forms of spending tend to be grouped together by critics.[33]
>
> *Astroturfing:* This is a corporate marketing campaign designed to
> exercise political influence but misrepresented as grassroots pres-
> sure from the public or community.
>
> *Political speech:* Until around 2014, most large US corporations
> focused on positioning themselves as politically neutral. Many now
> display far more appetite for controversial political speech, usually
> justified on the ground that stakeholders demand it.
>
> *Lobbying and advocacy:* Companies pursue their interests by
> trying to influence political or regulatory decision-makers. There's
> a place for ethical lobbying in a healthy democracy; politicians
> can learn much from business inputs on regulatory legislation and
> rulemaking.[34] But lobbying can be used for unethical purposes
> and is frequently derided as influence peddling. Reforms focus on
> bringing greater transparency and integrity to the process.
>
> *Trade associations:* Many companies value trade group member-
> ships, but conflicts between association policies and the stated

positions of member corporations on particular questions feed perceptions of hypocrisy.

Government advisory roles: Companies often provide executive support to government task forces and advisory bodies. It is generally not seen as unethical if disclosed.

What can a corporate leader do to ethically navigate this troubling realm without undermining the business? Help is emerging fast. Useful guidance for the US context can be found in the Erb Institute Principles for Corporate Political Responsibility and the CPA-Wharton Zicklin Model Code of Conduct.[35]

Give your board oversight of political spending

The board of directors should oversee political spending and engagement. This is a core issue in corporate governance, not least because of the potential for misalignment among managers, boards, shareholders, and stakeholders. The Erb Institute suggests formal agreement that "any political activities using company resources or management authority reflect the company's views, not those of the individual manager or officer"; and "companies do not pressure or coerce employees, shareholders or other stakeholders when engaging in political activities."

Leo Strine Jr., former chancellor of the Delaware Court of Chancery and chief justice of Delaware's Supreme Court, suggests that *both* directors and shareholders vote on corporate political spending.[36] He contends that board and shareholder approval should be secured for any divestment from particular countries or states/provinces on the grounds of poor political oversight, retaliation, expropriation, or unfeasible operating conditions.

Disclose your political activity

Consider the Erb Institute's recommendation to disclose all political activity. It's becoming critical to review the totality of your political exposure—and set guardrails.

Advice to embrace fuller disclosure might seem counterintuitive, given the advance of dark money since the *Citizens United* ruling. But trends, including a surge in shareholder resolutions, point to greater transparency. PR guru Richard Levick warned: "Most corporate political contributions are no longer opaque. . . . There is a 100% chance you will be exposed for contributions inconsistent with publicly expressed corporate views as there are now publications and NGOs that study these political contribution records and make them public."[37]

Leadership in this area remains scarce, and most companies insist they need to be at the table. Some recognize mounting pressure for corporate political responsibility and see an opportunity to set a better tone, particularly if they have undertaken a substantive commitment to transparency in funding. Early adopters of this move to greater transparency included Ford and First Energy.[38] (The latter underwent a reputational crisis and CEO resignation over bribing lobbyists in Ohio.[39]) Edison International pledged a stance that entails a commitment to healthy democracy.[40]

Ensure that your spending does not undermine your stated priorities

Even if you choose not to opt for full disclosure, it's getting riskier to indulge in direct or indirect corporate political spending that isn't aligned with your sustainability strategy and public positions. Perfect consistency at all times is impossible for a dynamic, global business, but that's no excuse for unforced errors. If you enthusiastically speak up on climate action, women's rights, or diversity, it's hard to justify funding candidates, trade associations, or other organizations that resist or undermine progress in those areas.

Companies tend to counter that their political funding reflects consideration of the totality of candidates' positions, making some misalignment inevitable.[41] The critiques are naive, they say. But business's history of providing support across the spectrum to maintain friends on all sides has hit a wall in polarization. Positions on such issues as climate change and transgender rights have diverged so radically that corporate throat clearing has turned thunderous. Companies must pick sides.

The Erb Institute recommends that enterprises "strive for alignment" between their political activities (including those via trade associations) and their "commitments to purpose, values, stated goals and stakeholders."[42]

Microsoft has been particularly ambitious in stating it will engage on policy questions that affect its customers, employees, or the core business.[43] The company's candor in reporting its missed climate targets in 2021 was criticized, but this effectively heightened media scrutiny of other companies' avowed goals and of Microsoft's efforts to support climate-disclosure legislation.[44] Its approach demonstrated a good grasp of pressure for transparency (our focus in chapter 8) and an understanding that adopting an effective stance on policy would help the company go further, faster. Melanie Nakagawa, corporate vice president and chief sustainability officer at Microsoft, explains:

> Being transparent regarding both progress and challenges is essential to building trust in our company's sustainability commitments and activities. Addressing climate change is difficult work, and it can take many months or even years for efforts to bear fruit. Additionally, no single government, company, NGO, or other stakeholder group is going to be able to do this alone, which is why Microsoft puts significant effort into sustainability-focused policy advocacy and collaboration across a diverse set of partners. For example, meeting our company's carbon negative commitment is intricately interdependent on the world transitioning to clean energy infrastructure—and this is not unique to Microsoft. When companies can be more transparent around a challenge that we *all* face, we can also come together to reach solutions faster.

Trade associations and business groups pose a particular problem in channeling corporate contributions to specific candidates at their own discretion. Microsoft continues to face questions about trade association memberships in light of its advocacy commitments.[45] Leaders at most companies say they must stay involved in these organizations and do not directly oversee the groups' political strategies. Nakagawa agrees: "Given the breadth of our policy agenda, it's unlikely we'll agree on every issue, but we've learned that engagement—even when organizations or individuals hold different positions—is an essential part of achieving progress. We also regularly evaluate our trade association and business group memberships." To avert the inevitable accusations of corporate hypocrisy, the wisest path may be to remain in such groups while stipulating that your company's fees not be deployed in support of specific candidates.

When an association's agenda aligns poorly with your company's public statements, there's little justification for staying involved.[46] Responsible investors such as Boston Common Asset Management have long focused on political misalignment. The firm scored a notable success in 2013, for instance, when it secured Visa's withdrawal from the American Legislative Exchange Council after arguing that ALEC was misaligned with Visa's values.[47] Boston Common subsequently pressed Netflix to be more transparent about its lobbying practices.[48]

Given the particularly high risks they face, extractives companies with climate commitments have reappraised some memberships. BP withdrew from three trade associations whose positions it deemed inconsistent with its pledges.[49] Royal Dutch Shell and Total have reviewed industry memberships, as have mining majors.

Withdrawal

Few leaders may agree at this time, but halting direct political contributions would be a smart, forward-looking move. Your company would remain free to lobby ethically and provide expertise in helping craft effective public policy.

To support this position, consider how questionable the financial returns from political spending have become. A review by Michael Hadani and Douglas A. Schuler in 2013 found: "Our research strongly suggests that [corporate political investment] is not profitable, and indeed may be detrimental to firm performance. We find that firms' political investments are significantly and negatively related to market valuation."[50]

Through its long history, IBM has maintained a policy of not contributing directly to candidates. It has no employee political action committee, and it prevents its membership funds in trade associations from being channeled directly to candidates. "I don't believe it puts us at a disadvantage," CEO Arvind Krishna told the *New York Times* in 2021. "I think it's actually done us a service" by keeping the company from being perceived as partisan or interested in purchasing influence.[51] IBM's position is ethically justifiable and saves money. The company stands on higher ground while others get mired in controversy—or worse.

Anti-corruption

We've seen in chapter 5 that an effective anti-corruption approach necessitates consideration of your wider political systems and relationships, not least because they make you vulnerable to political retaliation.

An additional point applies here, particularly for companies assessing their political exposure in the developed world. Whether their sources of wealth are legitimate or not, global elites rely on the complicity of respected financial institutions, lawyers, and accountants to tuck much of it out of sight of tax inspectors and regulators. In June 2021, tax returns leaked to investigative website ProPublica showed that the wealthiest people in the United States pay virtually no income tax.[52]

In this century, the anti-corruption community has been zeroing in on the pernicious impacts of the gatekeepers of corruption, especially the role of lawyers and accountants in facilitating illicit financial flows and blocking keener oversight of their professions.[53] Following Russia's invasion of Ukraine, the role of UK lawyers and advisers in enabling oligarchs to shift money into London's property market came under particular scrutiny. The *Economist* commented that British lawyers were a "gaggle of flunkies" serving oligarchs and kleptocrats.[54] Robert Barrington wrote in the *Law Society Gazette* that the legal industry is "close to moral bankruptcy" and called for more voluntary and governmental oversight.[55]

Together with persistent large-scale leaks from offshore jurisdictions, the furor about "Londongrad" suggests that the next phase of anti-corruption activity will focus on practices that are both legal and commonly pursued by almost all multinational businesses. It's all the more reason to adopt clear and defensible public engagement principles—sooner rather than later.

Expanding Your Ambitions

Without making a foundational commitment to political responsibility, business has no justification for taking a stand on the broader policy questions around inequality, democracy, voting rights, criminal justice, and immigration. The best way for your company to support such improvements is to protect the human rights of your direct and indirect workforce and to manage your negative externalities, including any resulting from undemocratic influence you may have exercised over the political system.

Speaking up for democracy is less important than withdrawing funding from candidates who show authoritarian leanings; supporting effective antitrust efforts is more important than speaking up for small business. Corporate responsibility works best when companies prioritize tackling issues under their direct control (a further reason why a commitment to human rights can help). Business ethics scholar Muel Kaptein suggests companies should be much more explicit in their codes of conduct by stating what they will *not* seek to address.[56]

It's become common to suggest that advocating for social justice is a way to meet stakeholder expectations. In 2018, Oxfam America decried the "co-mingling trends of a more outspoken corporate landscape alongside what seems like an unending concentration of corporate power." A paragraph later, the NGO hailed the idea that companies speak up and take action on behalf of "social justice."[57]

If by "social justice" we mean redistributive policies to drive more equitable social outcomes, that describes a progressive political agenda that involves trade-offs. It is not universally agreed that this is an appropriate brief for corporations. This means that while some vocal stakeholders might be pressuring you to do something in this vein, it isn't accurate to frame such an effort as part of a stakeholder agenda. Even with the best intentions, your actions might generate a political or popular backlash that could undermine progress on the very problem you've been called on to solve. It's very hard to anticipate all the consequences of a corporate intervention, especially when important stakeholder groups disagree. If you start to indicate that you can tackle public policy questions of this kind, you'll invite problems to be dumped in your lap.

In spring 2022, I watched a speaker from a sustainability branding firm discuss how Gen Z consumers regard brand activism. He showed us several videos of young people expressing deep fears over climate change, racism, human rights, and the future of democracy. In one, a nineteen-year-old said she'd sometimes boycott a brand "even if it's inconvenient."

Such perspectives, said the presenter, proved a pressing need to build "more caring and authentic brands."

As the discussion progressed, I grew ever more disturbed. It didn't seem that the young people in the video had ever looked into the root causes of the problems that concerned them. I could understand why they had concluded that pressuring brands (or their employers) to take action would be a more productive route to achieving political goals than voting or engaging in civic activity; corporations often respond to pressure more quickly and effectively than governments. But bigger questions about the authority and accountability of corporations weren't just being left unresolved, they were becoming murkier and more contentious by the day.

We've all begun to expect action on the issues of the day from brands we patronize. We cannot possibly keep track of all the issues and corporate stances, let alone consistently and effectively reward or punish companies via our spending, or in statements we post on social media. This illusory process has lured us down a side trail of unrealistic expectations. It redirects valuable energy that's needed to run businesses and responsibly manage operational impacts. It distracts the public from pursuing healthy political endeavors.

It might not bring much short-term brand advantage, but emphasizing the value of individual democratic engagement and pointing out that your business shouldn't exercise undemocratic political influence will better sustain your company's long-term health.

Indeed, corporations invite scapegoating when they take positions on policy issues not directly related to their operations and whose solutions are elusive. We lack good fixes for such ESG issues as the ethics of AI, big refugee crises, systemic racism, and environmental irresponsibility. Private-sector innovation can play key roles in addressing them. But public policy and grounded corporate values commitments are needed, too.

ESG's Polarization Problem

Controversial positions can come from all sides. They can even claim the same virtues. In the United States, whether you support or oppose ESG, you're likely to frame your position as rational capitalism—and that of the other side as misguided and antidemocratic. Michael Bloomberg asserted that "Republicans need a crash course in capitalism," and Mike Pence said, "ESG is a pernicious strategy, because it allows the left to accomplish what it could never hope to achieve at the ballot box or through competition in the free market."[58]

Critics of ESG lumped concerns such as climate change, diversity, and transgender rights into an old civil rights term with a peculiar name: "woke issues."[59] They contended that corporations should *not* adjust their business practices to advocate for causes, address shifting societal dynamics, or even account for the rising costs and risks of climate change. Republican leaders in 2022 targeted large investment firms, most prominently BlackRock, for supporting an ESG strategy. Later that year, five US senators warned dozens of big law firms—many of which had developed ESG practices in response to growing demand (and booming litigation risks)—that ESG is a collusive "scheme" to restrict the supply of coal, oil, and gas.[60]

In reality, ESG frameworks largely ignore political spending and influence. But soaring corporate rhetoric has invited political pageantry, grandstanding, and retaliation. Given how hard it has become to ignore ESG, widening state-by-state inconsistencies—in favor of and opposing consideration of ESG issues (as well as employee reproductive rights)—have made life grueling for companies and investors. Action to thwart climate change can be penalized. So can inaction. These trends necessitate a rethink of internal governance, a topic we'll explore in part 3.

I've focused on the uniquely fraught US context in this chapter. But before we proceed, it's worth noting that ESG issues and political risk are converging everywhere. Luiz Gustavo Gouvea, general secretary of corporate governance at Brazil's Vale, sees this as a further reason to ensure that your approach is sharply focused and strategic: "Institutional and government relations are intrinsic aspects of our business. Mines, railroads, and ports are government concessions. Vale used to be a state company until 1997, and the pension fund of Banco do Brasil is Vale's second-largest shareholder. This brings challenges and pressure to our business. For example, there have been recent media discussions about replacing Vale's CEO and questioning our tax benefits. The way we try to respond is to embed the whole thing in our strategy and business."

Nowhere can these risks be entirely avoided. If you opt for continued political engagement (as most companies will), there's no business case for lobbying or donating *against* your business interests (although, as we've seen, many companies do just that). There might, however, be a business case for supporting shrewd regulation to level the playing field, including emissions disclosure, campaign finance reform, effective market watch-dogs, tax transparency, voting rights, and meaningful enforcement of anti-corruption laws.

The Erb Institute suggests it's good strategy to engage on any issue that threatens your company's foundational systems *and* for which you possess relevant expertise. It's worth emphasizing again that advocacy efforts focused on supporting foundational systems should *never* come at the expense of good-faith efforts to manage your direct business impacts.

The measures outlined in this chapter should protect you from political turbulence and from any inclination to respond reflexively to stakeholder pressure. It's harder for critics to label you and your company as partisan tools if you don't support any candidates. Such forbearance also makes it easier for you to contend that your professed environmental and social priorities are unmotivated by political bias. It's always wise to mull where public opinion, investor pressure, activism, and media coverage are heading on these issues. How, where, and why business and politics intersect will remain controversial for the foreseeable future—sometimes explosively so.

We're almost ready to turn our lens inside the organization, but first, we need to talk about transparency. Often ballyhooed as a panacea for most of society's ills, the realities of transparency are vastly more complex than its enthusiasts claim, as we'll see in chapter 8.

STEPS TO HIGHER GROUND

Corporations have exponentially expanded their positions on contentious political issues in response to pressure from employees, the public, and even investors. The consequence is that the activism shines an unforgiving light on one of the most vulnerable flanks in corporate ethics: political spending and influence.

There's little justification for corporations to influence the political sphere from the perspectives of shareholder value or stakeholder capitalism. Nonetheless, some countries, particularly the United States, have exacerbated the practice by loosening regulations governing campaign finance. Amid insistent scrutiny, smart leaders have begun preparing for a new era in corporate political responsibility.

Public engagement and responsible lobbying by companies can be justified on the grounds of their expertise and legitimate interests. It's much harder to justify funding political candidates and trade associations that undermine your stated values and environmental and social priorities. At the very least, oversight and disclosure are vital imperatives to ensure alignment with your stated values.

Engagement to ensure that legal, political, environmental, and social systems remain functional might be justified on the grounds of relevant expertise and support for core human rights commitments. First, it's vital to ensure that your actions don't undermine these systems. Prioritize doing no harm in your own operations before attempting to influence the policy agenda.

8

Being Transparent without Making Everything Worse

F or a long time, nondisclosure and non-disparagement agreements (NDAs) with forced arbitration clauses made it impossible to speak up about harassment at work.[1] Then, in the wake of the #MeToo movement, a 2022 US law invalidated NDAs in instances of sexual harassment.[2] Former Fox News anchor Gretchen Carlson, who backed the bill, explained that it could transform culture by allowing women to share their experiences: "The point of NDAs is to cover up behavior, but it's also to stop the women from being able to coalesce together. . . . You don't know that maybe ten other people at your same firm are being treated in the same way."[3]

As I noted in the beginning of this book, a pressing reason to reimagine organizations as open social systems is the unstoppable increase of transparency in corporate life. Late in 2022, New York City followed Colorado and California in mandating disclosure of salary ranges in job listings.[4] In the EU, new due diligence requirements on human rights are likely to shed much more light on opaque corporate supply chains.[5] The US Securities and Exchange Commission is poised to force big companies to disclose more data about their carbon emissions.[6] The Corporate Transparency Act of 2020 requires companies to disclose their beneficial ownership, whose importance we discussed in chapter 5 on the anti-corruption fight.[7] In the *Financial Times*, Rana Foroohar warned that corporations must stop being "black boxes."[8] In reality, they haven't much choice: the boundaries separating organizations from society are ever weaker and more porous.

If a single concept drives today's businesses, regulators, journalists, and NGO activists, it's that transparency is the route to accountability. More of it—together with more consistent sharing of data—is seen as the best way to incentivize companies to improve their ESG performance. Conversely, when a lack of transparency is observed and reported, this comes as an accusation. It sounds corrupt, dirty, ominous.

Transparency is difficult to define. Its meaning varies depending on whether you're discussing economics or architecture, leadership or corruption. It suggests openness and permeability, not just to information but to arguments and ideas. Corporate transparency is commonly understood as a principle allowing stakeholders (who might include employees) to gain information about the operations and decisions of an organization.[9] It is both a means and an end: disclosure of information is often equated with transparency.

Transparency has both external and internal dimensions. So far, this book has focused on the role of corporations in society, but as I review transparency pressures, I'll start pivoting to a focus on organizational culture, management, and governance. Part 3 will explore these issues in detail, beginning in chapter 9.

Our enthusiasm for disclosure as a solution to corporate misconduct surged in the late twentieth century after a spate of corporate ethics scandals.[10] In 2003, a book called *The Naked Corporation* declared that we had entered a new "extraordinary age of transparency" where "if you are going to be naked you had better be buff."[11] In 2006, Christopher Hood wrote: "We might almost say that 'more-transparent-than-thou' has become the secular equivalent of 'holier than thou' in modern debates over matters of organization and governance."[12]

The twenty-first century has since brought vast increases in access to information. From official corporate reporting to employee leaks, activist exposés, and posts on social media, we've never had so much information about the business of business. Since humans cannot solve problems they don't understand, this offers some unquestionable benefits. As a vice president at BSR, Dunstan Allison-Hope has been involved in corporate sustainability reporting since early efforts in the late 1990s. He tells me: "I remember a time when transparency was so poor that you couldn't find out anything. The advances we have seen are a huge improvement, no question, and have driven far more understanding of what responsible business really takes."

One might think that by now we'd have moved on from mere disclosure to taking action. Despite the vast increase in available data about corporate responsibility efforts, there's no clear indication that corporate behavior has improved or that trust in business has risen.

In chapter 1, we discussed how heightened transparency has forced corporations into a much more interactive and dynamic relationship with their stakeholders. And in chapter 3, we saw that trying to manage and manipulate your reputation with defensive impression management has become an increasingly risky exercise. Now we need to talk honestly about how to negotiate this unsettling information environment.

The Trouble with Transparency

The mythical status that transparency has acquired makes it extremely hard to discuss its challenges candidly. Ethics leaders privately agree with me that blanket demands for transparency are no panacea, but they're universally reluctant to say this publicly. A senior ethics executive at a major multinational tells me: "If you are sitting on a podium, saying you have concerns about full transparency, you are already dead, right? You can't say this. But if you don't have a protected place where you can exchange and discuss and talk openly about dilemmas, you will never come to a good decision. Of course, publicly listed companies already must meet rigorous transparency standards, and I'm a big fan of transparency over beneficial ownership, for example. But after that, you must figure out what transparency means to you—and where it can be helpful."

Let's review the most common challenges resulting from calls for transparency.

Transparency demands underplay the role of interpretation

We often claim that transparency will lead to accountability without having first delved into the role of the information *receiver*.[13] Most discourse on transparency implicitly presumes that corporate disclosures provide objective data that's easy to find and interpret; that audiences have the time, energy, and interest to do so; and that recipients will react rationally and predictably. None of these assumptions stand up in the real world.

Even when human beings take in simple information, our responses are driven by entrenched cognitive biases and existing beliefs, selection, framing, ambiguity, and inconsistency.[14] But business disclosures are bound to be technical, complex, and confusing, *even when a company is not deliberately obfuscating.* Corporate financial information requires expert auditors and accountants—backed by attorneys—to act as interpreters and translators. As corporate reports have grown more voluminous and comprehensive in recent years, fewer outsiders are equipped to assess their claims, and that task is getting harder, not easier.

While financial accounting is complex, responsible business metrics are exponentially more so. Potentially thousands of qualitative and quantitative metrics might be relevant. All need to be developed using specialist expertise, placed in the appropriate context, and then evaluated for progress over time. Judgment and interpretation are as important as raw data. To complicate things, such qualitative issues as trust, dignity, culture, and purpose all resist quantification. This does not render them unimportant.

Let's hear again from Ken Pucker about his efforts as COO of Timberland from 2000 to 2007. He describes how difficult it is to gather accurate information, let alone drive change:

> When it came to the environmental agenda, Timberland committed to reduce carbon emissions by double digits each year—which we did, while the company doubled in size. You may think, "Wow, that's impressive." But, if one were to look at the footnotes in our responsibility report, it noted that our emissions reductions were limited to scope 1 and scope 2 emissions only; scope 3 emissions [emissions from the value chain, including from suppliers] were not included. To measure scope 3 emissions, Timberland needed to gather data for more than fifty thousand data points for our footwear line every six months. We didn't have useful software capability, nor did we have the ability to mandate data collection from

our suppliers. Even today, way less than half of public companies report their scope 3 emissions.

If you've ever gotten exhausted in the supermarket, trying to decide between oat milk or soy, organic or local vegetables, shade grown or fair trade, corporate responsibility reporting is all that, on steroids. It is not reasonable to think that an informed member of the public (or even an activist, employee, or investor) can review disclosures and successfully ascertain whether a company is making its best effort to be a responsible business.

Whether we're looking at ESG or financial metrics, it's no surprise that most corporations will try to manage reputational and financial exposure by disclosing information that shows them in the best light possible. Demands for transparency elicit accounts that conform to official rules for openness and responsibility in order to gain our social approval, *not to inform us or help us identify problems.*

Transparency can become a substitute for action

The issue of climate change shows how companies get stuck at disclosure and never seem ready to proceed with practical moves. The nonprofit Carbon Disclosure Project (CDP) was founded in 2000 to press for corporate reporting on climate emissions; the reasoning was that "investors would use their authority over corporations to encourage disclosure, leading to insight and action on climate change."[15] Backed by a prominent group of investors that control more than US$100 trillion in assets, the CDP laid out a framework for corporate climate disclosure.[16]

Among its familiar arguments supporting disclosure are "What gets measured gets managed" and "Sunlight is the best disinfectant." More transparency will generate trust, leading in turn to better reputation management. Even better, transparency boosts your competitive advantage by enhancing your access to capital. You can benchmark performance, identify risks and opportunities you might have missed, and get ahead of regulation. Disclosure, concludes CDP, is an essential first step toward environmental action.[17]

It's telling that decades after CDP was founded, we remain embroiled in debates over precisely what companies should have to report—and to whom. All the while, corporate carbon emissions have risen. As a 2021 review in *Nature Climate Change* pointed out: "The main risk to the disclosure narrative is the implicit exemption of the finance sector itself from the need for more radical actions beyond transparency."[18]

This is not how transparency was supposed to unfold. In the aftermath of the 2008 financial crisis, *Wired* commented: "We should tap into the massive parallel processing power of people around the world by giving everyone the tools to track, analyze, and publicize financial machinations. The result would be a wave of decentralized innovation that can allow the market to regulate itself."[19]

Transparency, in other words, was to become a means to make the recipients of your information responsible for policing your subsequent behavior. Instead, disclosure wound up letting companies avoid *either* policing their own activities or bowing to oversight by a formal authority. This was in line with a 2005 paper by Daylian M. Cain, George Lowenstein, and Don A. Moore, who found that when salespeople disclosed their conflicts of interest, they became likelier to engage in unethical behavior.[20]

Transparency generates paranoia

At the start of chapter 3, I noted that reputational risk is laden with twentieth-century baggage and that defensive PR no longer protects companies. Rather than thinking freshly about how to proceed through unpredictable, dangerous terrain, many companies are knee-deep in a defensive mode, spending more and more time and money on efforts that don't address critical issues and generate little more than cynicism. For example, the Alliance to End Plastic Waste, which has seventy-seven corporate members, has been dubbed little more than a greenwashing scheme after meeting only 0.2 percent of its targets.[21]

In 2012, Charles Fombrun, Naomi A. Gardberg, and Michael Barnett posited that the *entire point* of corporate responsibility programs is reputation risk management: "A company's reputational capital is therefore the value of the company that is 'at risk' in everyday interaction with stakeholders."[22] Similarly, in a critique of corporate responsibility efforts, Peter Fleming and Marc T. Jones argued: "The instrumental goal of CSR is to protect and enhance the corporate and brand reputation."[23]

The notion that reputation can be accumulated and banked, like money, has taken on a life of its own. Rather than focus on setting clear, ethical priorities for corporate behavior, leaders maintain teams that monitor social media in search of threats with the obsessive insecurity of teenagers. Doug Pinkham of the Public Affairs Council tells me of the consequences:

> Every big company has a social media–monitoring service. And it's like if you get a whole-body x-ray and they find a benign tumor somewhere in your body that you would never have known about: you could die at ninety-five, and that would never be anything. But they find it, and then you have to decide whether to remove it. Social media–monitoring services are like that in that every time a company gets criticized, the head of communications gets a report of today's criticisms. And of course, the CEO gets a digest, and they say, "Oh my God, people are upset with us."

A common tendency is for separate teams to focus on political risk, consumer perceptions, NGO activism, and internal employee engagement. These teams don't so much shape strategy as play internal Chicken Littles. They raise alarms about criticism the company will need to counter—usually by building ever more sophisticated defenses. This is a particular problem because CEOs tend to be closely flanked by lawyers and communications professionals. Both disciplines encourage paranoia even as they proffer conflicting advice on how to counter it.[24]

The unrelenting pressure can tempt companies into pursuing grossly unethical behavior that worsens whatever vulnerabilities it was intended to address. Astroturfing—the creation of shell organizations or agencies designed to appear independent but dedicated to promoting a company's agenda—has been thriving. Edelman helped run Exxon's Exxchange, a platform created in response to the Democratic Party's growing prowess after the 2018 elections; Exxchange has falsely portrayed itself as an independent "community bringing together energy supporters to take action on issues affecting the energy industry and everyday lives."[25] In 2020, global consulting firm FTI was found to have designed, staffed, and run websites funded by energy companies to falsely project grassroots support for fossil fuels.[26] FTI also created fake Facebook personas and tracked and targeted activists.

There's no benefit to society—or to companies—in this endless game of cat and mouse over ever more sophisticated forms of manipulative PR. Time and effort devoted to distracting the public diverts corporate attention from the efforts needed to build genuine trust.

Transparency is often weaponized

The business case for transparency can be boiled down to the idea that releasing more information than is legally required can bring social and financial value. But even positive disclosures can be weaponized—a risk that's rising. It leaves well-intentioned leaders struggling over whether and how to disclose problems whose solutions are unclear or do not yet exist.

I realized this when I was approached by a reputable London law firm that wished to build a class-action lawsuit against British apparel retailers for their exposure to forced labor in Xinjiang, China. The lawyer I spoke with explained that the first target of the investigation would be a retailer that had disclosed its primary suppliers, rather than companies that had declined to do so: "Knowing who their suppliers are makes it easier to build a case," I was told. The retailer making a good-faith effort to be responsible and accountable was to be first in line for denunciation and punishment. Laggards could remain comfortably below the radar.

This was no isolated case. In December 2019, a group of Congolese plaintiffs filed a class-action lawsuit under the US Trafficking Victims Protection Reauthorization Act alleging that a number of technology and auto companies had knowingly benefited from child labor in their cobalt supply chains. They pointed to the companies' own disclosures in human rights commitments to claim that the defendants had thereafter shown a lack of due diligence and risk management.[27] (This is an example of litigation aiming to hold parent companies responsible for human rights abuses in their global supply chains.) Such cases have signaled companies that the more effort they might make to understand, disclose, and address a problem, the higher their potential vulnerability to litigation.

If the lesson from these examples might seem that it's best to sweep problems under the rug, that's no solution. In 2023, the SEC secured US\$35 million in penalties from Activision Blizzard after the company failed to track and manage instances of workplace misconduct, despite the clear financial risks this issue posed to its business.[28]

Human rights lawyer Jonathan Drimmer explains the situation to me: "Disclosure is the tip of the iceberg. The body of the iceberg is how all that information gets aggregated, compiled, and substantiated so it can be reported. Companies are making disclosures that avoid buzzwords that might get you into trouble, but whether they can really back up what they are saying is a different question. We have all this pressure on companies to be transparent, and then we use those disclosures against companies in litigation. We don't incentivize companies to be honest and fulsome—and give them the benefit of the doubt when they are."

Transparency is both internal and external, and there's a feedback loop

Much literature on organizational reputation distinguishes external perception, or "image," from internal perception, or "identity."[29] But as we've seen, the line between internal and external perceptions is blurry, and employee activism can create a feedback loop between them. A consequence is that as external demands for transparency increase, so do leaders' efforts to surveil and control employees.

Internal transparency is usually portrayed as a powerful tool to improve organizational productivity and worker performance. Many operational innovations in factories are designed to allow perfect observation of what every worker is doing at all times. For example, a core principle of the Toyota Way is to "use visual control so no problems are hidden."[30] The idea that so much transparency might invite problems or unintended consequences is hard to acknowledge and discuss.

Ethan Bernstein, a professor at Harvard Business School, conducted detailed studies of workers in Chinese technology factories whose managers felt that being able to minutely observe each worker was essential for performance. By embedding students in factories, Bernstein learned that workers knew many tricks to heighten efficiency and productivity, but the moves were banned by management and needed to be concealed. His embeds were told by their peers to perform the task as instructed while being watched, and to use the productivity hacks when managers were absent or distracted.

In the second phase of his experiment, Bernstein put a curtain around a particular team to ensure privacy. The team behind the curtain managed to innovate far more effectively. Bernstein described this as the transparency paradox: "Observability may reduce performance by inducing those being observed to conceal their activities through codes and other costly means; conversely, creating zones of privacy may, under certain conditions, increase performance." Bernstein cited an enormous body of literature showing that privacy enables experimentation, the maintenance of expertise, the capacity to trust, and the development of long-term relationships. The factory workers themselves described this as "the privacy we need to get our work done."[31]

The US Congress provides another revealing case study of the negative unintended consequences of greater transparency. Before 1971, its operations were opaque to external observers. Then a series of popular reforms mandated reporting of how members voted and introduced a requirement for open committee meetings. In *Foreign Affairs* in 2019, James D'Angelo and Brent Ranalli described how openness and debate were damaged, exposing the legislative process to special interests and undermining collaboration: "The reforms also deprived members of Congress of the privacy they once relied on to forge compromises with political opponents behind closed doors, and they encouraged them to bring useless amendments to the floor for the sole purpose of political theater."[32]

This is a salutary tale for business. Corporations expend vast amounts of energy and effort on corporate responsibility theater. It's time to refocus on more realistic, constructive activities.

For instance, rather than focusing on speaking up, motivation, and commitment, many companies are now involved in energetically attempting to control and channel employee voice to corporate advantage, often by giving rewards for supportive social media posts. To wit: "Dell's employee advocacy program incentivized employees to share brand-related content online in exchange for certification as a 'social media and community professional.'"[33]

What Good Transparency Looks Like

In practice, transparency provides a linear path to neither accountability nor responsibility. It is a double-edged concept that presents considerable risks—and opportunities.

As philosopher Byung-Chul Han commented in his illuminating book, *The Transparency Society*, "Where transparency prevails, no room for trust exists. Instead of affirming that 'transparency creates trust' one should instead say, 'transparency dismantles trust.' The demand for transparency grows loud precisely when trust no longer prevails."[34]

In the social context of diminished trust, then, how can companies better meet valid demands for greater transparency regarding their activities?

Get ahead of the curve on emerging pressures

I've provided examples in this chapter of how disclosure is used as a substitute for change, not to drive it. I've pointed out that there's little incentive to disclose negative information because it will often bring punishment, not reward. This means that the most useful forms of transparency are either forced on companies or are volunteered as prescient moves to get ahead of emerging pressures. How can companies that comprehend the realities of diminished societal trust map a constructive way forward?

Forced transparency is how we usually learn about corporate human rights abuses, corruption, and poor leadership. Advances in transparency often occur in the aftermath of scandal, when companies have little more to lose.

In December 2014, an Associated Press investigation using US customs records found that many food companies were indirectly using slave labor in their shrimp supply chains.[35] The *Guardian* published dozens of articles on this subject from 2014 to 2016, followed by class-action lawsuits citing a number of international brands. In response, Nestlé funded a yearlong investigation by nonprofit Verité, which interviewed more than a hundred people and issued a public report.[36] In conjunction with the government of Thailand and in line with good human rights practice, many brands joined voluntary collective action initiatives to help promote good labor standards.

In 2022, Rio Tinto revealed the unflattering conclusions of a workplace culture audit conducted by Australia's former sex discrimination commissioner as the company was trying to recover from having overseen the destruction of two sacred forty-six-thousand-year-old Aboriginal shelters.[37] An internal survey completed by ten thousand employees showed that 30 percent of the women and 7 percent of the men had been sexually harassed at work. Nearly half the respondents said they'd been bullied, and there were many complaints of racism. The company's open, comprehensive approach seems to have reassured employees, half of whom said they were confident the issues would now be tackled. The *Economist* rated the company's approach as "ahead of its time."[38] While the survey did little to counter damage from the caves' destruction, it was essential to Rio Tinto's internal reset and was broadly appreciated.

In 2019, after CEO Travis Kalanick was fired for a range of ethical missteps, Uber moved to voluntarily disclose the rates for injuries, fatalities, sexual harassment, and misconduct in its branded vehicles. I was impressed as I watched a thoughtful young woman explain how the company had carefully classified and evaluated the data, notwithstanding its dispiriting content. Uber also formed a partnership with the National Sexual Violence Resource Center and the Urban Institute to develop a new data taxonomy to comprehend the reality of unwanted sexual experiences. The report and this taxonomy were the first of their kind and have been made available for use by other companies and organizations.[39]

Uber certainly faced more scrutiny after its disclosures. The company was hit by several lawsuits, including one in which California's Public Utilities Commission sought further details on the assaults and Uber refused. Still, by working with the CPUC and nonprofit partners, Uber got a fine slashed from US$59 million to US$150,000.[40] Such companies as Lyft and Microsoft have since disclosed harassment data, and Bloomberg reported that many more businesses felt pressure to do so.[41] You may not be able to shield yourself from litigation risk, but you can effect wider systemic change with well-timed disclosures.

Even better, get ahead of the curve by anticipating these pressures. Here, too, the useful approach is less about curating an appealing story and more about taking a first-mover position that encourages your peers to adopt emerging good practice.

Take Google's 2010 decision to publish its first "transparency report," a public account of its relations with law enforcement.[42] This was not the result of a specific scandal but an effort to correct widespread misunderstandings about the relationship between technology companies and law enforcement. Google made a sensible decision to be candid about what elements it can influence and which are out of its hands. The move was announced in a private meeting. It took other companies by surprise and left them scrambling to react.

There are many positive reasons for technology companies to share data with law enforcement, including efforts to tackle trafficking, child abuse, and money laundering. Companies need to balance such requests against users' privacy rights. They also face requests from governments that may aim to pursue users in ways that undermine human rights. BSR's Dunstan Allison-Hope provided several examples in a 2019 article: "Motel 6 was fined over US$7 million for sharing guest lists with U.S. immigration authorities. Bloomberg News reported that 7-Eleven Inc. had shared information with U.S. immigration that led to raids in over 100 of the company's franchises. And in China, the Associated Press revealed that more than 200 automotive manufacturers . . . are sharing location information and other important data to government-backed monitoring centers."[43]

This is a complicated topic. It's easy to misunderstand both the scope and the limits of a company's choices. In order to try to enhance understanding and improve debate, Google chose to report on when and how these requests occurred—and what it did about them. Its farsighted move has since been emulated by more than seventy technology companies.[44]

Google perceived advantage in being ahead of the curve, and broadening the discussion about technology and law enforcement brought positive consequences. Reporting raised awareness and understanding and consequently improved public policy proposals. It gave NGOs ammunition to expose privacy violations by governments. It also increased technology companies' accountability on human rights in general; many now disclose their content-moderation decisions. Whether the state of human rights and technology has actually improved is difficult to say, but parameters for what to do became clearer, and the challenges much better understood. This is significant because privacy breaches carry implications far beyond the technology sector.

Avoid governance by social media

Obsessively monitoring social media is unhealthy for people and even less healthy for companies. While an impulse to react to calls to speak up on every hot issue is understandable, it's best to resist. For many reasons we've discussed, it won't protect you from further demands. It can enable you to be scapegoated over issues you can't control, provide ammunition for you to be portrayed as two-faced, and distract you from running the business.

The good news is that a reputational barrage might not last long; another should soon grab our attention. The bad news is that you can't just ignore public perception. A passing furor can be excited by (or incite) employees, and it can prefigure a genuine need to take substantive action on an emerging issue.

This is yet another area in which your materiality and human-rights-impact assessments can help set clear parameters. When your business activities aren't involved and cannot be leveraged to make a difference, there should be no need to take action at all. Nor must you have the loudest voice or take the boldest actions compared with other organizations: standing out is often punished. Still, as we just saw with Uber and Google, it's important to note when the tide is turning in an area that's material—and useful to jump at the right moment.

The leaders I interviewed for this book offer some strategic advice. They recommend asking where your company's voice will have the greatest effect. If you've identified worthy impacts or changes you can encourage, proceed. The only responses you need to make public are to highlight actions you have *already* taken.

Think through public goals and targets, and be clear about misses

Public expectations often conflict with reality. They make it difficult to determine the best course of action. The push for transparency brings impatient calls for an issue to be addressed instantly; sustained change generally requires time. Avowing long-term, ambitious goals can quickly be derided as empty virtue signaling; conversely, securing minor, short-term achievements can be dismissed as pointless incrementalism.

In June 2022, David Wallace-Wells commented in the *New York Times* that a "basic phenomenon, in which powerful people make climate pledges that turn out to wildly outrace their genuine commitments, has now become so pervasive that it begins to look less like venality by any one person or institution and more like a new political grammar. The era of climate denial has been replaced with one plagued by climate promises that no one seems prepared to keep."[45]

I spent five years speaking with responsible investors about sustainability reports. They told me again and again how much they—and the companies—would benefit from a less-varnished assessment of activities. Silvia Garrigo, who has held many senior corporate sustainability roles in large companies, tells me: "A report that is dedicated solely to saying 'Look at all the wonderful things we are doing' is a bad approach. It's not authentic."

A report on the net-zero commitments of the world's twenty-five biggest businesses found that nearly half had never made a specific commitment; the rest had made commitments amounting to only 40 percent of their emissions, not the net-zero result suggested by the use of the term.[46] The exaggeration regarding net-zero achievements generated skeptical scrutiny. Companies that had avoided making such claims generally went unscathed.

With suspicion about greenwashing rising, and with glossy corporate responsibility reports generating little more than eye rolls, the prevailing mood has become less ambitious and much more cautious. Still, there are many opportunities for differentiation, and they need not involve dialing back on commitments.

Setting sustainability goals is getting tougher. For one thing, observers want to see fast progress on challenges that will take time to address. It's wise to start with the effective conclusion you desire and then set forth a clear path to get from A to B. Think through how you intend to measure and determine impact. A good approach involves setting an ambitious long-term direction whose fulfillment may require collaboration and partnerships, accompanied by shorter-term, achievable milestones.[47] It's important to be honest about barriers to progress that you encounter along the way.

For example, Australian tech company Atlassian issued a practical guide for companies on getting to net zero in 2023, using the striking title

"Don't F&*! the Planet."[48] The company warned of growing blowback over the use of carbon offsets and explained its own efforts to directly cut emissions by 90 percent while making it clear that this would be impossible without pursuing ruthless priorities and collective, combined action from corporations and the government. Atlassian's 2022 sustainability report led with a discussion of where the company fell short on its goals and what it planned to do about this: "[W]hile we strive for transparency, it is more important to us that we do the work, rather than checking every box on a framework just to say we did."[49]

Finally, look to provide perspective and act in accordance with what is realistic. Separate long-term goals from short-term ones. If your eventual objective is to double the number of female employees in a specific job role, publicize that long-term goal as well as a shorter-term achievable goal (e.g., an increase of 20 percent). For example, mining major BHP has been able to outperform its goal of creating a 50 percent female workforce by seeking partnerships and publicizing a stretch goal.[50]

Focus on trust, agency, and healthy culture—not control

Intrusive tools to monitor employees abound. They are sold aggressively to companies under the guise of increased transparency and accountability. In 2019, the *Wall Street Journal* detailed advances in workplace surveillance techniques and said personnel have become "workforce data generators."[51] This approach flourished during the Covid-19 pandemic and the abrupt shift to remote work. In 2021, Gartner found that the number of employers using surveillance tools, including facial recognition, doubled to 60 percent during the pandemic. It predicted further growth.[52]

Just as with reflexive responses to external pressure, the urge to substitute control for trust bears negative, unintended consequences both for workers and for corporate performance. Transparency develops into what philosopher Michel Foucault called a "disciplinary technology."

J. S. Nelson, an associate professor at Villanova Law School, has raised pressing ethical concerns about arguments that favor employee surveillance on the basis of perceived needs for productivity and enterprise control. Her 2020 paper, "Management Culture and Surveillance," cited numerous examples of companies that installed surveillance systems to ensure productivity and then used them to track employee health, interpersonal relationships, conversations, and travel—even to manage and manipulate employees' emotional responses at and away from work.[53] She warned: "[I]t is a particularly dangerous combination for workers that surveillance may both satisfy regulators and feed a psychological need for managers concerned about control."

A more effective and ethical response would be to focus on the elements of a healthy culture: employee agency, motivation, dignity, respect, and effective, proportionate oversight. As with all the topics we've discussed so far, that's easier said than done.

We've now completed our review of how to evaluate and respond to environmental and societal pressures. We've seen that many ideas presented as shortcuts ensnare us in quagmires or route us back to where we came from. We've seen that focused energy and effort provide the firmest route to higher ground. The time has come to turn our lens inside the organization.

In part 3, I'll discuss how to build cultures that are more ethical and effective. We will start with a broad review of how organizational culture is transforming—and why this suggests that ethics efforts must transform, too. Then we'll zoom in on the four most important dimensions of this effort: leadership, compliance, speaking up, and organizational purpose. Let's keep going, onward and upward.

STEPS TO HIGHER GROUND

In the twenty-first century, it became common to frame transparency as a catchall solution to almost every imaginable challenge in corporate ethics. It is widely held that enhanced transparency and consistency of data will incentivize companies to be more ethical and accountable. By contrast, saying that a company shows a lack of transparency amounts to an accusation. It sounds ominous, nefarious.

Transparency can be a powerful and positive force. It drives a more interactive, dynamic relationship between companies and stakeholders.

But for corporations, it's a nuanced, double-edged concept. Top-down transparency lets leaders better observe their subordinates to spur performance and reduce fraud. Inside-out transparency efforts enable organizations to scan the outside world for risks and to identify potential innovations. Outside-in transparency invites the external world to peer inside the corporation and makes leaders uncomfortable. Bottom-up transparency, which allows employees to observe and judge leaders, can mire enterprises in conflict and inefficiency.[54]

We tend to equate disclosure with accountability, though we often get stuck at the disclosure stage. There is excessive faith in the power of metrics to shape understanding and behavior—and abundant risk of teaching to the test or gaming the metrics.

In response to all these pressures, companies have two options. They can focus on carefully curated messaging to project an unrealistic level of consistency, or they can engage in good-faith dialogue regarding how they intend to address stakeholder expectations.

The best transparency efforts are honest and focused. They can help set new standards and expectations for entire sectors, which can bring competitive advantage. Leading companies are helping to raise awareness of best-practice efforts, highlight the limitations of voluntary corporate action, and galvanize the powerful coalitions needed to solve our biggest challenges. In a world of empty pledges, authenticity stands out, even when the truth is uncomfortable.

PART III

LEADING AND SHAPING THE FUTURE

Rethinking Ethical Culture

C ould drinking a beer help fight corruption and protect human rights? Punk beer brand BrewDog shouted yes. At the start of the Qatar World Cup in 2022, the Scottish brewer sought to draw attention to its sustainability credentials with a brash marketing statement: "Football was dragged through the mud, before a single ball was even kicked. Let's be honest: Qatar won it through bribery. On an industrial scale. Football is meant to be for everyone. But in Qatar, homosexuality is illegal, flogging is an accepted form of punishment, and it's OK for 6,500 workers to die building your stadium."[1] To prove this wasn't just empty talk, Brew-Dog added that it would donate the profits from sales of its Lost Lager during the tournament to fight human rights abuses. A few days later, the company was forced to clarify that it had just signed an agreement to sell its beer in the Gulf via a distributor and would continue to broadcast World Cup matches in its pubs.[2]

Media coverage zeroed in on BrewDog's colorful history of disingenuous rhetoric rather than the human rights issues it was hoping to highlight. Journalists reminded readers that only a year after the fast-growing brewer had obtained vaunted B Corporation certification as a responsible business, employees had issued an open letter alleging a toxic and misogynistic "culture of fear" at the company, where they said they'd been bullied and "treated like objects." Just weeks after the Qatar campaign launched, all that funding from impact investors, an "equity for punks" crowdfunding round, and BrewDog's proclaimed efforts to decrease deforestation, manage waste, and reduce carbon emissions crashed into a wall of questions—and renewed interest in a BBC documentary critiquing the company's workplace culture.[3] When BrewDog's board proved unable to satisfy a request for "additional measures" from the administrators, it lost its B Corp certification.[4]

At the very least, the sudsy saga shows that if you wish to prove your company has values, you cannot treat how you impact your employees (who are members of society) as a separate concern from how you impact the world. The legacy approach treats organizational culture as a separate practical concern from sustainability or compliance: the human resources department "owns" culture and employee engagement while compliance manages the rules and processes meant to prevent wrongdoing.

We are regularly told that sustainability commitments enhance employee motivation and loyalty.[5] The case of BrewDog illustrates how much more is required than external messaging and enunciated goals. Maintaining an integrated organizational culture has never been more important, and standard approaches never more anachronistic.

A further big barrier to progress is that "ethical culture" sounds fluffy and amorphous, while regulatory requirements are clear and specific. It's temptingly easy to focus on processes and rules and to delegate their enforcement to compliance and HR teams rather than ask uncomfortable questions about how leadership, oversight, norms, and decision-making need to evolve. Enacting meaningful change takes time and effort. It's so much easier—and quicker—to degrade a culture than to build a better one.

According to influential scholar Edgar H. Schein, culture is "the way we do things around here."[6] Culture comprises formal systems and processes as well as "work climate"—the set of informal behavioral norms and values in an organization. A good corporate culture needs purpose as well as profit, role models as well as rules, followers as well as leaders, participation as well as direction, and incentives as well as prohibitions. This has always been true, but heightened transparency makes it easier to peer into the inner workings of today's organizations. Barely a week passes without news of the latest botched redundancy, contentious town hall meeting, Slack channel drama, or management misstep.[7] We're all armchair culture auditors now.

As we saw in chapter 1, companies can no longer rely on the timeworn expectation that internal matters will be kept confidential. But reduced control of information is just one dimension of how porous and contested organizational boundaries have become. The shift to intangible value registers in where and when we work, how we lead and manage, how we set and implement strategy, and how we exert influence and are influenced in return.

As the *Economist* wrote in 2020: "CEOs' mechanism for exercising control over their vast enterprises is failing, and where and why firms operate is in flux. . . . [T]he boundaries of the firm, and the CEO's authority, are blurring. Uber's 4m drivers are not employees and neither are the millions of workers in Apple's supply chain, but they are mission-critical. . . . Factories and offices have billions of sensors pumping sensitive information to suppliers and customers. Middle-managers talk business on social media."[8]

So far, we've been talking about how to deal with shifting suppositions about the role of business in society. The impact of these shifts on internal culture is just as significant—and we're no less confused about what to do next.

Even as the boundaries around companies blur and dissolve, we find it hard to let go of metaphors that describe an organization as an inert barrel: all we need to do to keep it healthy is remove the bad apples. Let's start by exploring where these ideas come from, why they persist, and why we need to move on.

Bad Apples and Rotten Barrels

When ethics scandals hit the headlines, we tend to be served comforting explanations that the problems stem from a few "bad apples," who will now be swiftly separated from the good ones. In his 2016 Senate testimony, then-CEO John Stumpf emphasized that Wells Fargo's problems reflected the activities of a mere 1 percent of its workforce.[9] Martin Winterkorn, then chairman of Volkswagen Group's board of management, initially dismissed the manipulation of emissions data at VW in a video statement as "the terrible mistakes of a few people," whom he did not identify, before resigning in "shock" that misconduct had occurred on a grand scale.[10]

This argument is simple and seductive. It conveniently absolves leaders of personal responsibility for wrongdoing on their watch. And it suggests that CEOs need only find and remove malignant employees—a straightforward task they can delegate while focusing on more important activities. These appealing arguments are buttressed by a legal system bent on finding and punishing a wrongful mind.

The bad-apple idiom originated in the Middle Ages to explain how rot spreads in organizations. In Geoffrey Chaucer's *The Cook's Tale*, an apprentice chef is fired before his unsavory behavior can infect everyone else. Benjamin Franklin warned that rotten apples would spoil their companions, and the metaphor became commonplace in nineteenth-century sermons. A century later, though, its meaning morphed 180 degrees. We now talk about bad apples as shorthand to suggest that expelling a few scapegoats is all it takes to build and preserve a healthy organization.

The present-day interpretation is much more than a metaphor. It illustrates how the legal system frames the challenge of business ethics as a matter of individual cognition rather than social conditions. As we saw in chapter 2, commercial law is strongly inclined to view business ethics as a principal-agent problem. The law sees the corporation as a precious, if fragile, type of fictional person: the "corporate principal." Like a real person, the corporate principal has rights, goals, and a legal identity. Like a deity, it relies on human agents—employees—to fulfill its goals.

That directors and employees have a fiduciary duty to protect the value of the corporate principal at (almost) all costs is an article of faith in corporate life. Since the US Federal Sentencing Guidelines were introduced in the early 1990s, the government has heavily incentivized companies to police themselves. Realistically, enterprises cannot eliminate the risk that the human beings they employ will break the law. But if the government agrees that a company has made its best effort to thwart wrongdoing, the bad apples it coughs up will face legal penalties; the corporation will not. Consequently, corporate ethics efforts have historically emphasized protecting the corporate principal from rogue employees. (The principal has no values or conscience and is motivated solely by economic self-interest.)

Compliance units exist to find and remove rule breakers before their behavior can threaten corporate value. This approach implies that the first imperative of an ethical organization is to keep out bad people, and the second is to make the costs of wrongdoing outweigh any of its benefits. While this is challenging work to execute, the approach is straightforward. Companies impose policies and rules, mandate training to enforce them, listen to employees who speak up, and investigate wrongdoing.

(Before we proceed, let me be clear: without a compliance function that has authority, and without meaningful sanctions for wrongdoing, you won't get far. Policies, rules, training, speaking up, and investigating wrongdoing are all *critically important elements of an ethical culture.*)

My concern about how all this plays out is twofold. One issue is that these foundational efforts suck up the vast majority of the energy and discussion, even though they can, at best, be necessary but insufficient. The second concern is that compliance programs are often designed to deflect regulators while paying little attention to how rules and processes impact human cognition and behavior. Dicta and deterrents are far less effective at influencing us than we like to imagine; incentives and norms are far more potent than we think. We've known this for a long time. A groundbreaking article by Lynn Paine in 1994 laid out why instilling ethics requires holistic effort, not a rules-based process. Pointing out that a punitive stance toward legal compliance can backfire, she emphasized that managers should be held responsible for the values and aspirations—and staff conduct—on their watch.[11]

We'll explore the question of what better compliance looks like in chapter 11. For now, let's look at the bigger picture. What do we miss when we view the cause of business ethics problems narrowly, through the lens of bad apples that threaten the value of the precious corporate principal?

This lens gives us a simple, clear, and ultimately unhelpful picture of how organizations become unethical. It prevents us from focusing on how structures, processes, and norms impact human behavior. It encourages us to see organizations as black boxes or inert containers that exist only to safeguard their self-interest in the narrowest terms. And it suggests we can wall companies off from huge social shifts on issues of inclusion, impact, and values. By reimagining organizations as the open social systems they actually are, we can start to comprehend and resolve our emerging challenges.

No Ethics Scandal Has a Single Cause

Leo Tolstoy wrote that "all happy families are alike; each unhappy family is unhappy in its own way." When it comes to organizational culture, the opposite is true. It's hard to generalize about ethical culture, less because morality is subjective than because culture is unique and idiosyncratic. Conversely, unethical cultures have a lot in common. That's because they reflect *absences*. In unethical organizations, you'll find an absence of perspective, an absence of purpose (beyond making money and defeating competitors), and an absence of awareness.

The uncomfortable truth is that we can't explain what happened at VW, Wells Fargo, Purdue Pharma, or Facebook, to name a few, as a problem of rogue employees undermining corporate value. Rather, we find an obsession with securing or maintaining competitive advantage, reinforced by direction from the top, widespread willful blindness, toxic incentives, and narrowly conceived oversight. Such cultural conditions can persist and metastasize, even if leaders are removed. Wells Fargo went through four CEOs in the eight years after its fake accounts scandal broke in 2014. Boeing had three in the three years following the grounding of the 737 MAX. Both companies continued to appear in headlines for all the wrong reasons.

If your company is heading into an ethics scandal, this will frequently show up in its culture long before the problem is discovered. The issue isn't so much that concerns aren't visible; often, no one is looking.[12] In a study I conducted in 2015, the twenty-three experts I interviewed agreed that unethical cultures have much in common:

- The ends justify the means, and there's an urge to seek market dominance at any cost.

- Autocratic command-and-control leaders make employees fearful and reluctant to share concerns—which also provides leaders plausible deniability.

- A lack of individual accountability diffuses personal responsibility at the top.

- Incentives are designed without market conditions in mind, and employees are judged by whether they hit targets, not how they do it.

- Cultures of urgency and necessity undermine stated values and are complemented by powerful in-group dynamics.[13]

These challenges can be addressed only via holistic, contextual thinking. Hiltrud Dorothea Werner, who was called in to redesign VW's ethical culture after its emissions scandal, tells me what she found and what she did: "No scandal has just one cause. So we looked at processes, we looked at systems, we looked at people. Corporate culture is very unstable; if you aren't taking care of it, it's deteriorating. You can't think in a siloed way, and you need to identify and tackle root causes. We had to put in place new rules and regulations in many areas. We had to change the decision-making process. We had to change promotions and management evaluations. We had to tackle the lack of dynamism—which led to silos—and overconfidence in management."

Her perspective highlights a recurring challenge: Companies tend to conduct budgeting and planning in isolated units while neglecting to consider the relationships within and among teams.[14] When we understand that an organization is a system, the importance of group dynamics becomes much clearer.

"Companies don't usually look seriously at their culture until after the fact, and then it's too late," Werner says. "We needed to bring all the changes together and think through the relationship between risk management, governance, HR, and compliance. Otherwise, the business will get five unrelated requests and miss the bigger picture."

Brazilian mining company Vale is seeking to recover from two disasters that killed hundreds in just four years.[15] The company's general secretary of corporate governance emphasizes the overwhelming importance of culture: "You have the technical part, the three levels of defense, and we have adopted the new global industry standard on tailings management," Luiz Gustavo Gouvea tells me. "But the more work we do, the more we understand that if people take decisions by themselves and don't have core business impacts front of mind, problems will happen again and again. So cultural transformation is one of the key levers in our strategic plan. Our CEO states that his main legacy will not be a new huge mine or a new railroad. It will be a company with a new culture."

While our legal system is geared to seek out a wrongful mind, employees in an unethical organization frequently don't feel that they are doing anything immoral. Almost all humans think they're more ethical than the average person—just as we all like to imagine we are better-than-average drivers. Ethical scandals do not kick off simply because a hitherto honest individual woke up one day and decided—out of the blue and of their own volition—that this would be a good day to bribe someone.

A renowned study in 2004 discussed how unethical practices become normalized in organizations. It cited three mutually reinforcing processes that lead to normalization: institutionalization (a corrupt decision or act becomes embedded in structures and processes), rationalization (self-serving ideologies develop to justify the behavior), and socialization (new employees are induced to view corruption as permissible).[16] Plenty of research supports the argument that unethical cultures develop gradually, along a slippery slope of degrading norms. Questionable conduct by auditors, for example, can begin as minor moves and escalate into substantial violations over time.[17] In 2009, Bernie Madoff told *Vanity Fair*: "It starts out with you taking a little bit, maybe a few hundred, a few thousand. You get comfortable with that, and before you know it, it snowballs into something big."[18]

Unethical behavior can flourish as a top-down, companywide phenomenon. It can occur in particular teams, functions, or countries. Cases in which it can truly be traced to a rogue employee are far less common than is customarily suggested. Much more frequently, an unethical leader shapes a culture in which rogue employees thrive. Soon everyone's doing it. Any group is more than the sum of its members, and this includes companies. We all behave differently in a team, crowd, or mob.

Any effort to build an ethical culture must focus on how organizational conditions *impact employees*. This means looking at power, resources, incentives, and norms. How they're structured and designed will reflect how leaders view the company in its wider environment—often referred to as its "purpose." How a company makes money and accounts for its impacts has come to be as important as the rigor of its legal controls. The crucial questions are: What behavior does the organization reward, and what does it punish?

After years of grappling with what it takes to build an ethical culture, Markus Jüttner tells me of the mindset he brought to his work when he was vice president of group compliance at E.ON, an electric utility based in Germany: "It's one of the fundamental mistakes in the compliance industry just to look at the individual and not at the system itself. We need to distinguish types of misbehavior. But first of all, there's misbehavior between people. Then we have misbehavior against the company. And then we have misbehavior in favor of the company. This is key: the responsibility to prevent, detect, and respond to misbehavior *in favor of the company*."

A frequent trigger for unethical behavior is a sense that the organization's survival is imperiled. The most common rationale among staff is a keen sense of peril from a competitive threat, often backed by a perception that any unethical conduct would constitute a victimless crime. VW engineers didn't cheat on emissions tests for kicks; they were following incentives from leaders who were determined to dominate the North American market for diesel vehicles.[19] After a global corruption scandal emerged at Siemens, a key executive involved in the behavior explained it by saying: "We thought we had to do it. Otherwise, we'd ruin the company."[20]

Insufficient internal pressure to account for—and address—a business's negative impacts is a vulnerability. The failings at Boeing over safety, Purdue Pharma over opioid marketing, Johnson & Johnson over product liability, and many, many more corporate scandals tell a similar story. They weren't *primarily* deficiencies in compliance. They reflected a business model that prioritized commercial success over consequential costs to society. In other words, one explanation for these scandals is the reluctance of these companies to account for their impacts upon the world as they pursued profit.

Organizational Boundaries Are Dissolving, Along with Our Defenses

In chapter 8, on transparency, I discussed how the line between internal and external factors has blurred. Time, space, power, and strategic boundaries are all in flux. A consequence of our more transparent, intangible world is that it has become far less effective to implicitly view business ethics as a matter of creating defenses to deflect regulatory and reputational risk. (See figure 9-1.)

FIGURE 9-1

We are in the era of the intangible company

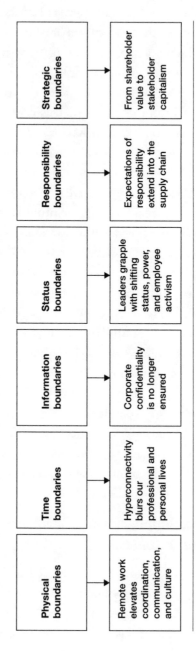

Office hours no longer limit our working days

Corporate life was already growing less material before Covid-19 sharply hastened the change. One estimate suggested that nearly two-thirds of the US workforce did some remote work in 2019, before the pandemic.[21] In placing a premium on coordination and communication, remote work transforms the nature of both.

Some leaders issued edicts to get people to return to the office, but most companies have compromised to some degree. Still, working days no longer end for many of us when we physically leave the office; the boundaries of time and space around our working lives have dissolved. Research by Microsoft found that about a third of white-collar workers now have a "third peak" of productivity late in the evening, as registered in keyboard activity; its CEO, Satya Nadella, warned of the negative impact on our mental health.[22] Discussions of burnout pervade the business media.

One significance of office social ties stands out in data showing that whistleblowing increased significantly during the pandemic surge in 2020. As Bloomberg noted, "People feel emboldened to speak out when managers and co-workers aren't peering over their shoulders."[23] A corollary is that retaliation against employees who report wrongdoing has also increased, according to a survey by the Ethics and Compliance Institute.[24] Those weak social ties don't just make it easier to report wrongdoing; they make it easier to punish those who try to speak up. The relationship between remote work and unethical behavior appears to be anything but predictable.[25]

Remote work offers individuals a powerful opportunity for greater flexibility and control. An organization aiming to be more inclusive could start by granting more latitude to employees who have achieved good results so they can better manage familial and personal commitments. But group dynamics remain important. Preexisting tensions over in-groups and out-groups at an office can be exacerbated (or reduced) by a turn to remote work.

Traditional ideas about power and authority are losing steam

Notions of hierarchy and authority have shifted. In a 2022 TikTok video, a young woman offered a hilarious monologue on what office life is *really* for: "So, a lot of people are confused about what an office actually is. Some people have this misconception that offices actually, like, 'function' or produce something. That's a misconception. They're actually religious buildings. There's this religion called professionalism, and one of its core tenets is hierarchy, so an office is just a shrine to hierarchy."[26] She proceeded to say that C-suite leaders "don't really do anything, their purpose is to just physically be there. The temple is just a place for them to waft around. . . . Their immediate servants are called managers, and their job is to kind of observe the lower ranks and make sure they are doing their jobs. The thing is, the managers don't know how to do any of those jobs."

In chapter 1, we noted a rising focus on the intersection of social identity and power in organizations. While this was exemplified by the #MeToo and #BlackLivesMatter movements, they're the tip of a big iceberg. I regularly hear of young employees who feel empowered to question leaders in ways that seem striking—and reckless—to older colleagues. Managers tell me of interns challenging CEOs over a deficiency of diversity at the C-level at town hall meetings. In choosing among jobs and roles, my students pay close heed to whether they are likely to be heard and empowered.

Leading today is far less a matter of setting direction and telling people what needs to be done, and far more about creating conditions in which decisions can be made and action taken promptly. An article in 2020 asked whether it is "time to retire the title of manager" now that team leaders are expected to act more as coaches and influencers.[27] In practice, leadership can no longer function mainly as a means of control and delegation, but must experiment and adapt to constant change.

This brings us to ethical decision-making. Employees are taking matters into their own hands, frequently because they feel that the compliance, HR, and ESG functions lack answers to their questions. They want leaders to examine and manage their companies' impacts on the world. This calls for rethinking oversight and speaking up, topics we'll explore in chapters 11 and 12.

Companies now need to consider impacts beyond their direct control

The final example of how the line between internal and external realms is blurring is the most significant: corporations are now perceived as responsible for impacts on individuals they do not employ, and on organizations they neither own nor control.

The gig economy exemplifies how institutional boundaries are fraying. In many companies, a glaring fault line has opened between full-time employees, who are granted sick leave, vacation, and pensions, and contract workers with few or none of these privileges. Gig workers are neither employees nor third-party players. They sit on organizational boundaries filling ambiguous roles, often with access to a lot of information and without a fiduciary duty of loyalty. Leaker Edward Snowden, for instance, was a contract worker at the US National Security Agency.

The lower status accorded tiers of contract employees tends to be visible, and the corporate caste system can have a toxic effect on organizational culture. I began this book by highlighting how white-collar employees at Starbucks supported baristas in an open letter. At Google, too, staffers have been willing to deploy their voice and power on behalf of contractor rights.[28] Before Covid-19, the gig economy's growth was often framed in terms of the benefits it provided workers: flexibility, ownership, freedom, the joys of a portfolio career. These arguments grew untenable amid a public health crisis that placed many of them on the front lines and put the corporation's responsibility for an individual's well-being back into focus.

The pandemic also revealed that in supply chain management we have prioritized efficiency and cost over resilience and continuity, and this has led to a broader reckoning over supply chain risk and responsibility.

As we saw in chapter 6's discussion of human rights, leaders are increasingly held accountable for the impact of their products and for what goes on in their supply chains. Several factors—not least, the exponential expansion of access to mobile phones—have endowed the human rights movement with the ability to instantaneously gather and share evidence when labor rights or environmental standards have been violated. This has forced companies to at least try to peer into the darker reaches of their supply chains.[29]

Growing interest in scope 3 emissions (those produced by contributors in a supply chain) suggests that the company should be responsible for operational carbon emissions across its entire value chain, including from customers and supplier operations it does not control.[30] Tackling this is far from straightforward. Unilever's Alan Jope confessed that he has "no idea" how the company is to meet its scope 3 net-zero targets because this would require radical changes in behavior by the end user: consumers.[31]

The wider questions these efforts raise remain unresolved. Who, after all, is responsible for a plastic water bottle floating in the sea? The person who discarded it? The bottled water vendor? The company that extracted the oil to make the plastic? Our focus on allocating blame often stymies the sense of shared responsibility that we need in order to solve systemic challenges. Conceptualizing their organizations as an open system can help companies evaluate where they can act, where they need to collaborate, and where other institutions need to step in.

Pressure over Inclusion Isn't Going Away

Soaring interest in more diverse, equitable, and inclusive organizations best illustrates how emerging ethics challenges are not principal-agent problems in need of legalistic solutions but multidimensional issues that are fast transforming organizational culture.

Today's imperative for companies to become far more inclusive poses conflicting pressures. Globalization implies the breaking down of geographical boundaries and cultural differences, and vigilance against hypocrisy presses organizations to be more consistent in their practices. Companies face a countervailing need, however, to honor a variety of cultural norms and values. That's difficult enough to manage in itself before we add the external pressure for companies to act on social issues. How does an organization celebrate LGBTQ people while operating in locales where their lifestyles are punished? How does a company balance internal pressure to speak up on controversial issues against the prospect that it might foster unrealistic expectations and trigger retaliation?

A particular challenge regarding pressures for diversity, equity, and inclusion is that they come with distinctive dimensions for individuals, teams, organizations, society, and political change. Employees increasingly claim such characteristics as age, values, race, and gender as important factors in their identities and what can be expected of them. Now factor in soaring political polarization and partisan tensions.

These intersectional identities weigh heavily on perceptions of fairness and satisfaction at work. The expectation that an organization should adapt to individual needs is growing. Advice abounds on how to realize personal values at work.[32] Having matured among the echo chambers of social media, many young people come into the workplace with an inclination to discuss political and social issues and the expectation that this will bring positive attention. Meanwhile, plenty of other employees remain reluctant to share their thoughts openly. Notwithstanding views expressed by a vocal minority, it's critically important for you to avoid thinking that any consensus exists in the workforce. Well-intentioned advice to align your corporate giving with "employee values," for instance, can make employees feel pressured by a boss to donate to a popular cause they quietly oppose.[33]

As discussed in chapter 1, there's no neat, comprehensive solution.[34] Companies recruit heads of diversity and charge them with transforming the organization, but they frequently lack sufficient budget and authority to drive the effort. Another problem is that employee expectations seem to be growing so exponentially that slow and steady progress on issues of inclusion and responsibility can feel more like backsliding. Where inequities are recognized, there is agreement on erasing them, but views differ markedly as to an acceptable timeline and how drastic remedial measures need to be.

It makes good sense to regard diversity, equity, inclusion, and belonging in a human rights framework, which emphasizes that everyone deserves dignity and respect. Managing backlash over controversial questions on vaccines, reproductive rights, sexual identity, and so forth becomes easier once you recognize that each person deserves freedom of expression and bodily autonomy but has no right to impose beliefs on others.

The Culture Imperative

That bad-apple myth is hard to shake off. It's reinforced by the legal system and by long-standing power dynamics. It made more sense in the twentieth century. So what can you do differently with your company—a dynamic, adaptable social system—in this new world of work?

Instilling or creating an ethical culture means institutionalizing a conscious focus on fairness, awareness, efficacy, empathy, and decision-making.[35] If you intend to create and sustain a healthy, ethical culture, the most important factors to pay attention to are leadership, oversight, speaking up, and organizational purpose. Each merits a chapter in its own right, and we'll focus on them for the remainder of part 3.

I'll close this chapter by arguing that there is concrete value in rigorously measuring and evaluating culture. It's no second-rank "nice to have." Although many companies survey their cultures, they often limit inquiries to pulse surveys on engagement or compliance-driven benchmarks that score their culture against others in the sector. The last thing you should do is approach ethical culture as a competitive sport or presume that what worked in one company will succeed—or even suffice—in another. Each company is a unique system.

This is where behavioral science can help. The business world has been discovering the power of social and cognitive psychology in such bestselling books as Richard H. Thaler and Cass R. Sunstein's *Nudge*; Chip Heath and Dan Heath's *Switch*, and Max H. Bazerman and Ann E. Tenbrunsel's *Blind Spots*. But while leaders are enthusiastic about using behavioral science to sell products, too many ignore its insights when it comes to considering their cultures. Change is afoot.

The most obvious way to measure culture is via a well-designed survey. (In today's low-trust environment, never assume that employees will be completely candid.) Analyzing information from whistleblowers can be very useful, but it's vital to identify any pockets of organizational silence in which employees have determined that speaking up may be futile or dangerous. A further option is to peruse Glassdoor or a comparable website on which employee grievances proliferate, so long as you bear in mind that comments and anecdotes you encounter may not accurately represent organizational realities.

If you wish to conduct interviews or stage focus groups, it might help to retain independent consultants, who will respect psychological safety and maintain confidentiality. It's important to explore what drives people in your organization, how they assess success, what kinds of behavior get rewarded, and the stories about the company that spring to mind. Any reluctance to answer questions can reveal anxiety about being blamed for complaining. What you essentially need to learn is the degree to which your employees feel valued, included, and respected at work. Do they feel they can say what they think?

If you measure your culture, it becomes possible to design behavioral experiments to improve it and then rigorously log the results. With many elements of organizational culture undergoing such profound shifts, experimenting carries much more promise than trying to project certainty. Pioneering companies such as Novartis and GSK staff behavioral science specialists in their compliance teams, and "conduct risk" has become a specialized function in many banks.[36]

STEPS TO HIGHER GROUND

In today's organizations, the sharp boundaries separating working lives from personal lives, leaders from followers, and internal versus external interests have all become blurred, porous, contested. Internal culture is in full view as never before.

The result is that we can no longer view business ethics as synonymous with efforts to protect the corporate principal from the presence of bad apples. We need to focus on how to adapt to these new conditions and think about leadership, oversight, voice, and purpose in radically new ways.

Legacy programs no longer suffice. Treating culture as a siloed HR concern isn't effective. Nor is framing ethics efforts solely as matters of regulatory compliance or a purported business case. Culture, or the "way we do things around here," is a consequence of how organizational structures, processes, and norms impact employees, who then make decisions that impact other stakeholders.

Addressing the culture imperative is a key element of a broader shift away from twentieth-century thinking that envisaged companies as self-interested entities operating in a vacuum. It recognizes that culture needs more than principles. The good news for leaders is that maintaining a healthy organizational culture has never been a better source of strategic advantage.

Today's senior business leaders will find a premium placed on their ability to balance competing interests, come to terms with hyper-transparency, and align the organization's stated values with its culture—all in the context of sharply reduced top-down control. Organizational leadership will become more a matter of influencing diffuse networks than of directing human and financial resources.

Instead of building stronger defenses, we need to experiment and measure and then analyze the results to create more dynamic organizational systems. We need to replace certainty with curiosity.

10

Leading in the Mid-Twenty-First Century

hese are the best and worst of times for ethical leadership. In February 2022, as Russia launched its unprovoked invasion, all eyes turned to Volodymyr Zelensky, Ukraine's inexperienced president. Zelensky hadn't been anyone's idea of an ethical leader. A comic who had once played a fictional Ukrainian president on TV, his track record as a real president was mixed. But despite being the most obvious target in the country for state-sponsored murder by Russia, Zelensky dismissed offers of evacuation to the US: "The fight is here. I need ammunition, not a ride," he was widely reported to have told a US intelligence officer.[1]

Zelensky's courage was all the more compelling because contemporary examples of moral leadership are so scarce. My thoughts instantly turned to my home country, where then–Prime Minister Boris Johnson was consumed with his latest unconvincing attempt to explain to UK citizens why he hadn't followed the rules he'd set for them.

The adulatory reaction to Zelensky's stark words unveiled a deep global hunger for inspirational leadership. As Howard Gardner's classic analysis showed, what we want from our leaders is a narrative about our shared identity—who we are and where we are going.[2] You cannot do this with stories alone. Leaders must embody the idea that we're all in it together.

Around the world, political leaders who consider themselves exempt from rules that apply to everyone else have become the norm. A 2020 survey of twenty-nine thousand people in twenty-seven countries by the Milken Institute and Harris Polling found that 70 percent felt their nations stood at the lowest point in history; two-thirds said their leaders were out of touch or "don't really care what happens" to citizens. Some 61 percent said that business had played a bigger role than the authorities in "keeping my country running."[3]

With political frustration mounting in the 2010s, we gradually began expecting business leaders to take on more overtly sociopolitical roles. Aaron K. Chatterji and Michael W. Toffel's 2018 piece on the emergence of "The New CEO Activists" quoted a contention by Brian Moynihan, Bank of America's chairman and CEO, that the CEO's role includes "taking action on what we think is right." He named Apple's Tim Cook, Salesforce's Marc Benioff, and Starbucks's Howard Schultz as inspiring examples.[4] (Schultz went on to launch a short-lived bid for the US presidency.)

Then, after Covid-19 struck, some CEOs embraced the opportunity to tout their achievements, framing themselves as societal saviors. In 2021, for example, Benioff attested at Davos that "in the pandemic, it was CEOs in many, many cases all over the world who were the heroes. They're the ones who stepped forward with their financial resources, their corporate resources, their employees, their factories, and pivoted rapidly—not for profit, but to save the world."[5]

Benioff spearheaded a US$25 million effort to secure medical equipment, and Salesforce boasts an excellent track record in sustainability and social activism.[6] But philanthropy is no long-term solution for intractable societal problems such as rising inequality or tax avoidance.[7] CEO pay packages keep growing more extreme, even in companies that trumpet corporate social responsibility.[8] Tim Cook's US$99 million 2021 pay package at Apple drew shareholder ire—criticism he countered by reiterating a pledge to bequeath most of his fortune to philanthropic causes.[9]

An intriguing study at Stanford found that companies with more narcissistic CEOs tend to earn higher ESG scores. As well as displaying one of the weaknesses in ESG-scoring mechanisms, it renders leaders' avowals of passionate devotion to society less reassuring.[10]

Some CEOs are charting a more promising path. A quieter leadership cohort seems to reject the Silicon Valley god/emperor model in favor of collaboration and humility. Early in 2022, the *Financial Times* and *Quartz* each declared the onset of an era of empathetic CEOs. Satya Nadella at Microsoft and Sundar Pichai at Google have come to epitomize these traits. Heidrick & Struggles has found that the new generation of senior executives is more likely to be female, come from nations other than where the company is headquartered, have cross-border experience, and hold advanced degrees. An increasing number of incoming CEOs are neither former COOs nor CFOs and bring more diverse experience to the role.[11]

Even in their recruitment, CEOs are being called on to care more about the welfare of their stakeholders. An academic study published in 2021 after seventeen years of research showed that listening, empathy, and persuasiveness have become far more valued qualifications in C-suite job descriptions and recruiter checklists.[12] These traits are particularly prized at the very companies where intangible value and network influence first became paramount: big, information-intensive enterprises with firsthand experience of the limitations of hierarchical management. In an era of soft corporate boundaries and intangible value, an ability to tap into and leverage influence has become indispensable. So have familiarity with— and competence at handling—pressures regarding social responsibility and diversity, equity, and inclusion.

Even more important, leaders are increasingly being forced out for behavior considered unethical, even if it's legal. In 2019, Steve Easterbrook lost the top job at McDonald's for having consensual affairs with colleagues, and in 2020, Jean-Sébastien Jacques was toppled from running Rio Tinto after he authorized the destruction of ancient Aboriginal caves.[13] In 2022, a senior executive was fired from Estée Lauder after making a racist Instagram post.[14]

Given that our expectations about the role corporate leaders play in society have become so complex and contradictory, confusion is inevitable. In *Reimagining Capitalism in a World on Fire*, Rebecca Henderson wrote that "the successful purpose-driven leaders I know are almost schizophrenic in their ability to switch from a ruthless focus on the bottom line to passionately advocating for the greater good."[15]

To describe an ideal leader as "schizophrenic" indicates that we now prize traits that rarely coexist in a single human being.[16] What it all really means is that we need to move on from legacy top-down control and build in organizational checks and balances from above and below. Today's businesses are so global and diffuse, and the challenges they face so complex and unpredictable, that no CEO—no matter how personally impressive—should make judgment calls in isolation. An organization that wishes to demonstrate and maintain ethical leadership must build robust systems to check and balance *any* leader's personal judgments.

In this chapter, I will be looking at leadership as a vital dimension of corporate culture—specifically relationships among the board, executive leadership, and the rest of the organization. In chapter 11, I'll examine how leading companies are rethinking rules and processes to prevent wrongdoing.

Ethical Leadership in the C-Suite

"Integrity starts at the top" is a cliché with legs. Ethics executives I've spoken with while researching this book tell me again and again that their achievements wouldn't be possible without wholehearted support from their CEOs. I've repeatedly seen commitments to ethics and corporate responsibility crumble when an engaged CEO is replaced. Not surprisingly, most ethics professionals agree that success relies on their sitting at the table among the senior leadership team—and even better, having a direct line to the company's board.

Leaders *are* powerful role models. People watch and evaluate what their boss does in order to see what behavior is rewarded, so leaders need not be personally aware of wrongdoing to bear some responsibility for any that occurs on their watch. But it's never sufficient for a leader to be a good person. In a company of size, few employees will regularly observe the CEO's personal conduct, but all will experience the outcomes of decisions made regarding rules, processes, goals, incentives, and norms. Unless you opt to proactively emphasize ethics—or a crisis forces you to choose publicly between exploiting a financial advantage and embracing an ethical imperative—it's likely that staff will perceive your leadership as ethically neutral, at best.[17]

Hence, behavioral ethicists agree that while leading by example is important, it's crucial to focus on building employee capacity for ethical decision-making.[18] An ethical leader takes oversight seriously, aims to build wider capacity for moral decision-making, and focuses on instilling trust and psychological safety throughout the organization.

Companies should never neglect the basics of compliance, which I'll discuss in the next chapter. But they must also manage the full spectrum of ethical commitments in practical ways. This poses particular challenges when you're dealing with an increasingly vocal yet divided workforce. Many companies appreciate the scale and scope of these new challenges; compliance and sustainability executives are increasingly quartered in the C-suite.[19] While this reflects how important it has become to bring their expertise into decisions on strategy and capital allocation, cross-functional integration is critical.

Notwithstanding dramatic shifts in how the broader world views business ethics, silos and incoherence persist in many companies. Sustainability was originally focused on going "beyond compliance" via such voluntary initiatives as reducing waste or energy use and organizing volunteer employee efforts. Much advice on how to build an effective corporate sustainability strategy implies—or flatly states—that legal compliance is merely a basic functional requirement.[20] An array of pressures, from the regulation and professionalization of ESG reporting to employee activism and political backlash, suggest we need to go further. Some organizations are embracing a more holistic view of ethics, one designed for use by thinking, breathing human beings.

Hui Chen is a former prosecutor who became the first in-house compliance counsel expert in the US Department of Justice, where she advised federal prosecutors in evaluating corporate compliance programs. What she tells me mirrors my career experience: "I've been baffled by the complete lack of interaction between the ethics and compliance community and the ESG community, because to me they're really the same thing." BSR's Dunstan Allison-Hope agrees: "I've been wondering about the internal disconnect between ethics and sustainability since 1999."

In conducting a research study for the World Economic Forum in 2021, my colleagues and I found greater alignment among the critical functions that shape ethical commitments and practices.[21] These include compliance and sustainability and can encompass risk, internal audit, HR, government affairs, and corporate affairs. Some companies drive alignment via committees or dotted-line reporting. In an article I wrote with Robert Eccles for *Harvard Business Review* in June 2023, we argued: "Compliance and sustainability teams should have clearly defined roles but tight coordination. The sustainability team can help differentiate between the material issues that drive innovation and value creation and those that present risks and require ethical guardrails (such as human rights impacts). Compliance teams can help ensure rigorous, legally defensible disclosures with regard to material risks. Close alignment is also necessary over the commitments companies make in their codes of conduct and values statements, especially as litigation over greenwashing starts to mount."[22]

Some companies have found it best to appoint a single executive leader to oversee these teams and ensure a coherent and strategic approach: Unilever has a chief business integrity officer, while companies including SNC-Lavalin, Lockheed Martin, and Tenneco have combined the oversight of ESG and integrity issues.

Klaus Moosmayer is the chief ethics, risk, and compliance officer at Novartis, as well as a member of its executive team. Since the pharmaceutical industry is constantly exposed to ethical dilemmas, Moosmayer says, ethical considerations must be integrated with risk management: "At Novartis, we want to become a holistic assurance model that brings together ethical considerations to enterprise risk management, as well as our compliance systems. Compliance does not own ethics in Novartis."

Moosmayer tells me that pressure to proceed comes from varied sources: "Investors are relevant, of course, but our own employees and associates also play a role. We are competing for the best scientists and chemists in the industry, and increasingly they want to work in environments that champion ESG." Novartis crowdsourced its new code of ethics with direct input from thousands of staff members. The company also conducted an ethical culture survey of its 150,000 employees—which it developed with its internal team of behavioral scientists—and has incorporated the consideration of ethical dilemmas into recruitment.[23]

The changes have positively affected how his role is perceived, Moosmayer says: "In most corporations, ethics and compliance is sitting in a certain corner, maybe respected and feared, but in a silo. The big opportunity is to get a holistic view that can improve both culture and risk management. If you don't connect the ethical debates and dilemmas and discussions to your company, they stay somehow artificial and siloed. So our ambition is to bring ethical considerations, pragmatic enterprise risk management, and a compliance management system together in one structure—knowing that this still isn't 'owning ethics.' We are still on this journey."

When he led compliance at AB InBev, Matt Galvin's counterpart in sustainability belonged to the procurement team. Galvin witnessed how many connections there were among ethics and compliance, sustainability goals in agriculture, and human rights. "I was the first person at a senior level to have ethics in their title, and at first I was skeptical," he tells me. "But as I developed the program, I focused on gathering data that could be useful to the business as a whole and that helps the business see the costs of unethical behavior far more clearly. And that bought me the trust in the business that I need to get things done."[24]

Adapting to the new ethics landscape is far from easy. But companies can become exponentially more effective by taking simple steps to avoid mixed messaging on one hand and one-size-fits-all thinking on the other. Effectiveness isn't about throwing more resources at the problem. It's about putting firm foundations in place.

Beyond Tone at the Top: Checks and Balances from Above

Traditional definitions of corporate governance focus on the tension between shareholders (ownership) and management (control)—again, based on agency theory. Shareholders have little direct leverage; they elect board members and auditors charged with ensuring that the leadership and its management team do not undermine shareholder interests. The relationship between the board and the management team is traditionally framed as adversarial: just as compliance polices the organization, the board polices senior management. But board effectiveness is questionable. After any corporate scandal, a predictable chorus cries out, "Where on earth was the board?" Too often, the answer is: "Who knows?"

After Enron collapsed, US stock exchanges mandated the use of audit, compensation, and nomination committees, limiting membership in them to independent directors. The Sarbanes-Oxley and Dodd-Frank acts both focused on strengthening the independence of directors, enhancing requirements for financial expertise, and so forth.[25]

In a trajectory similar to that of compliance, the structural reforms aimed at increasing board effectiveness flopped. Explanations range from overly narrow definitions of fiduciary duty to the need to pair structural changes with a focus on process. While there's much to these arguments, it's far simpler to look to group dynamics.

Nell Minow, one of the leading corporate governance specialists in the United States, describes herself as an "anthropologist of the boardroom." Drawing on decades of directly observing board dynamics, she has this to tell me:

> I often think about what went wrong at Enron because it illustrates a lot of problems with decision-making at the top. One of the board members was asked: "When the board was asked to waive the company's conflict-of-interest rules, that should have been a red flag to you. Why did you go along with it?" And his response was, "Well, no one else said anything." That's the last kind of person you wanted on the board. But that is the kind of person we have on boards.
>
> We take these people of extraordinary ability and achievement. We put them in a boardroom, and there they suddenly become totally incompetent. Why is that? My answer is that these are people who have a genius for sizing up the norms of the room and adapting to them. And that's a fabulous quality to have. But unfortunately, you've got eleven people like that—and one very visionary, dynamic leader who controls their information, their access to other people in the organization, and even their tenure and their compensation. That's not a good system.

Our adversarial notions of corporate governance don't bear much resemblance to real life, where there's often a cozy relationship between the CEO and the board. In a detailed study, J. Robert Brown Jr. concluded in 2015 that substantive qualifications, while of some relevance, are secondary to the board members being "reliable" from a CEO's point of view.

Commented Brown: "Directors are selected primarily because of their willingness to support the policies of incumbent management."[26]

Board selection criteria vary, but while efforts have been made to increase the independence of board members, personal and social connections still predominate. Many studies demonstrate that members tend to have similar backgrounds, political affiliations, and even religious beliefs.[27] Bonding on the golf course remains a hallowed professional practice.

A 2021 survey by PwC of the C-suite's view of the board reflects a mixed and contradictory picture of this relationship. Most respondents felt that the independence and risk awareness of the board was positive, but 89 percent of executives felt one (or more) member should be replaced; 70 percent felt the board lacked ESG expertise.[28]

Board committees don't necessarily perform better. An EY study in 2022 found that oversight of human resources issues was concentrated in the compensation committee, and environmental issues were mostly overseen in the governance and nominating committee. Both committees already had full dockets and were unlikely to give serious, focused consideration to these issues.[29]

Expertise in handling emerging societal and environmental pressures remains in relatively short supply on the board. A 2021 study from NYU's Stern Center for Sustainable Business explored a shortage of relevant expertise in material ESG issues among directors of US public companies.[30] The greatest level of proficiency was found on social issues, mostly diversity, but the study described a dearth of prowess on such core governance topics as transparency and anti-corruption. (The study did find that health-care company boards usually include some expertise on public health.)

With all these challenges in mind, what might we do differently that could actually work?

Diversify (really)

When my MBA students assess where they want to work, they look closely at the composition of the board and C-suite as indicators of how much inclusion and opportunity a company is likely to offer them. It's getting much harder to justify a board whose membership fails to resemble the company's employee profile or customer base. Dasle Hong, who works in software, summarizes for me the evaluations many young people now conduct: "When I was searching for my next job, I looked at the board of directors, I looked at the C-suite. There's diverse representation. That convinced me."

Amid evidence of growing diversification in senior leadership, there are numerous signs of continued misunderstanding and resistance. Shareholder pressure to diversify boards and augment board skills has mounted significantly, as has scrutiny of board conduct. In 2021, women and people of color were appointed in a surge to board roles at S&P 500 companies. Recruiters described roaring demand to diversify.[31] These changes came in response to demands from employees, investors, and the public.[32]

"A small group of White men controlled everything. I was directed to 'Call this person, say you know me, and they will help.' So much of this happened quietly, behind the scenes. That is a great deal of power in the hands of a few," Alice Korngold, who works to diversify nonprofit boards, tells me. "Now there is a greater expectation that these networks and relationships be opened up to be more transparent and inclusive. Communities, employees, and consumers expect greater accountability, and boards are having to step up."

Nonetheless, greater demographic diversity does not automatically bring heterogeneity of perspective, experience, and opinion—which is what companies need for effective leadership. There's telling evidence that in the S&P 500 from 2008 to 2020, political partisanship among executive teams grew by almost 8 percent, a result partly driven by a 9 percent growth in C-suite dominance by Republicans. A 2021 paper found "an increasing matching of executives with politically like-minded individuals."[33]

How is it that as companies diversified in such areas as gender and race, they ended up with narrower, more homogeneous political perspectives? "Meta-analyses of rigorous, peer-reviewed studies found no significant relationships—causal or otherwise—between board gender diversity and company performance," wrote Robin J. Ely and David A. Thomas. "Having people from various identity groups 'at the table' is no guarantee that anything will get better; in fact, research shows that things often get worse, because increasing diversity can increase tensions and conflict."[34]

Although it might alleviate criticism, adding a few diverse candidates won't bring meaningful change in itself. No single social identity characteristic can explain a person's worldview or experience. There's certainly a relationship between demographic and cognitive diversity, but it's neither straightforward nor predictable.[35]

"The conversation on diversity and inclusion is, of course, the locus of the discussion on how power and authority need to shift from barking orders to creating conditions," Megan Reitz, a management expert at Hult International Business School, where her work includes a focus on employee activism and speaking truth to power, tells me. "But we are still uncomfortable, so we tend to reduce diversity to targets and numbers and whether you have enough people of a certain social identity type. This all utterly misses the point, which is to find different perspectives that reduce our blind spots."

Diversity is a valuable way to bring fresh views into stale boardrooms or the C-level. "When you walk into a room and everyone has a different background, then you might have to do some convincing," Mary-Hunter McDonnell of Wharton tells me. "You deliberate more during the meeting, and—because of that deeper deliberation—factual inaccuracies are more likely to surface, and potential pitfalls are more likely to be discussed."

Karina Litvack belonged to the board of directors at Italian oil and gas giant Eni for several years. "A big part of healthy board dynamics is the question of who's going to speak out when something troubling is happening, who's going to just stay quiet, and who's going to join in to back up the person offering a dissenting view, or even just asking an awkward question. When two new independent-minded people joined," she tells me, "we didn't necessarily need to agree on every specific point, but we knew we had allies who, as a matter of principle, stood up for each other's right to speak up and would either back us up or improve on our contribution. That's when the tenor of our board discussions changed markedly. It doesn't have to be confrontational."

Improved deliberation is certainly an asset, but a healthy group dynamic is needed to achieve the greatest advantage. Curiosity, critical thinking, and willingness to challenge an accepted perspective—particularly a monolithic one—is where diversity and inclusion imperatives really drive more considered and ethical decision-making.

Prioritize knowledge of relevant material issues

As enterprises become more active on social and political issues, boards are being called on to weigh in on political spending, speak up on controversial topics, and divest from certain countries or projects due to ethical concerns. These high-stakes questions carry powerful second- and third-order consequences, and it's very difficult to know what specific proficiencies might be needed to address a given question. That's how we wind up with calls for boards to hire "ESG expertise" and provide "ESG training" so they can create an "ESG committee."

Such moves are commonly ineffective. A PwC board survey of directors in 2022 showed that while 86 percent of respondents had confidence in the overall ESG strategy, 55 percent saw no link between ESG and the bottom line. Just 11 percent of directors said environmental or sustainability expertise is very important for their board.[36] This chasm between available expertise and assurance suggests that a few training sessions on climate change are hardly what's needed.

Now we come to one of those elephants that no one seems to see in the boardroom: apart from a handful of luminaries that pioneered the earliest investor moves, there is no such thing as an "ESG expert." ESG comprises too complex an array of topics. Some people have broad general knowledge of the landscape, the most contentious issues, and reporting requirements. Others are specialists in particular areas such as waste, water, human rights, community engagement, corruption, biodiversity, and so forth. Anyone with deep expertise in one or more of these areas will necessarily lack breadth, and vice versa.

Finally, as we've discussed, the tendency to lump ESG issues into a single category blurs the actual imperative—which is to clearly differentiate between commercial opportunities and negative impacts so as to better manage both. At the board level, risk management and ethical guardrails matter most. Seeing the rise of ESG as just another fad or reporting challenge is how you tick the box and miss the point.

ESG topics are extremely broad and keep expanding. You can secure the senior expertise you need only if you're focused and clear about existential ESG risks and opportunities you face. An apparel company doesn't need an ESG reporting expert as much as it needs someone with a background in supply chain resilience. Missteps in the mining industry partly resulted from treating community relations as a domain of corporate affairs rather than securing deep expertise in human rights.[37] Accessing people with experience in *relevant* ESG risks and ethical considerations is your key to success.

All these considerations significantly buttress the case for the stakeholder advisory boards we discussed in chapter 3. A group of well-informed, critically minded colleagues on speed dial can advise the board and senior leadership team without the company needing to employ experts in a vast range of technical disciplines.

Plan for the long term

Changes in society usually outpace board turnover, which is part of the point in having one. Boards provide long-term continuity and ought to outlast CEOs.

Corporate governance expert Nicole Bigby tells me: "Centuries ago, before you had written contracts, your word was bond. That whole concept is now so fragmented and dispersed through corporate structures, and subsidiaries, and reporting lines, and all the rest of it. We've forgotten the basic fundamentals: a business should be ethical and treat people fairly. And if as a business, you don't get that—well, then, you have got a fundamental issue."

Ultimately, the board's job is to ensure that the company is managing for the long term, which means it strives to address any negative impacts on society and shows dignity and respect for workers. This isn't about written principles or technical ESG expertise. What the organization needs is practical recognition that new imperatives necessitate a conceptual shift. When the company takes positions or sets environmental and social targets, the board must grasp what these commitments entail: what they mean for capital expenditures, what they mean for the workforce, what they mean for product development to satisfy evolving customer demands. The board's role is to ensure that the company has appropriate strategy and risk management systems in place to manage these commitments over the long term.

Mary-Hunter McDonnell is optimistic that this conceptual shift is taking place. "What is happening is a tremendous recasting of what corporate governance means," she tells me. "I think that the board's role has moved toward more of a team model of leadership, and they're supposed to work more alongside managers instead of necessarily policing them."

While securing a broader skill set at the top is vital, it's no less important to build checks and balances into the organization from below.

Beyond Tone at the Top: Checks and Balances from Below

How can companies think more creatively about how to correct blind spots in leadership? The question has become more urgent, with employees ever more inclined to take ethical issues into their own hands. I'll explore this in depth in chapter 11.

Jessica Kennedy's research has shed further light on Nell Minow's observations about how boards often seem ineffective when it comes to ethical oversight. Before Kennedy became a professor in management at Vanderbilt University, her work as an investment banker exposed her to numerous dysfunctional hierarchies.[38]

After opting to study psychology, Kennedy conducted a number of studies to explore what she had repeatedly witnessed: greater seniority leads to higher identification with your group. Ethical issues in particular cause cognitive dissonance, leading people to rationalize or minimize problems. This means that the more senior you are, the more likely you are to justify what the group is already doing—for better or worse. Her study of eleven thousand employees across US government agencies found that senior leadership was almost 64 percent less likely to speak up against unethical practices than the most junior employees were.[39]

Even if leaders created the very systems they oversee, they become products of them over time. This means that good leaders should be on guard that power will directly affect their judgment and moral compass; they should strive to build strong ethical structures from the start. It also means that making efforts to solicit dissenting views from more junior employees should be deemed a priority, not a risky move best postponed or avoided. One useful mechanism to consider: give a group of younger employees and executives an assignment to innovate and challenge the existing board.

How does Megan Reitz perceive the shift in conversation around the role of leadership? "Our view of how you respond in an agile way has had to shift from the traditional notion of someone at the top making all key decisions. Now we can't afford these structures because they slow us down too much. We also need reminding that a leader's perspective really is not the truth, because we all think that how we see the world is the way it is. You need to do more than you realize, and you need to do more than just invite speaking up."

At mining giant Vale, Luiz Gustavo Gouvea sees enabling everyone to raise concerns as central to the company's effort to transform. "We have to create a culture where anyone can say, 'Hey, it's not working with my manager; I need to go all the way up to the board,'" he tells me. "We have had a huge revision of our leadership team, and we have made sure we have people inside the company spreading this positive message. We're strengthening psychological safety in the Vale production system."

In this era of the intangible company, it's far beyond the capacity of any individual to ensure strategic ethical leadership. A single team can't do it. Organizations don't just need tone at the top; they need to solicit and support awareness, accountability, and voice at all levels.

There are signs of a shift toward broader, more responsive notions of governance, but the pace of change at senior levels is plainly insufficient. Giving employees ethical agency is easier said than done—and remains vitally important as corporations emerge as open social systems.

STEPS TO HIGHER GROUND

Our notions of what good corporate leadership should look like are evolving. There's a powerful thirst for heroic role models to fill gaps left by political leaders. That many corporate leaders say they want to save the world does not in itself signify an ethical, healthy culture. Messianic dreams can indicate the opposite.

We've grown more likely to value empathy, collaboration, and humility in CEOs, and this is a more promising path. To build and ensure ethical leadership capacity, organizations need to start from the premise that all leaders, no matter how personally impressive, have blind spots. Companies must install checks and balances *above and below* the C-suite.

As the realm of business ethics has evolved and expanded, so has the need for more conscious, active alignment among the functions that influence ethical conduct: compliance, risk, government affairs, HR, and sustainability. Leaders overseeing one or more of these functions can be more effective operating at the C-level. Better consideration and coordination among all these functions is essential for companies to address blind spots and develop a more strategic approach to ethics.

Boards, however, continue to lack the capacities, awareness, and resources they need. That's changing, but our expectations change faster. Tick-box demographic diversity will not suffice to instill more robust decision-making. Boards most need to improve capacity to challenge entrenched thinking, gather new perspectives, and plan for the long term. Oversight of risk and strategy is important, but the overall imperative is to understand and improve the business's impact on society.

Building voice and awareness from the bottom is just as important as instilling tone at the top, especially when workforces are more networked and ethically aware than ever.

11

Designing Rules for Humans

The compliance industry has grown exponentially over the past three decades, but ethics scandals remain depressingly frequent. An active compliance team, glowing press coverage, and best-practice awards are all unreliable proxies for ethical conduct at a company.[1] How can we explain this? The disturbing reality is that the corporate responses to regulatory imperatives aren't merely insufficient. At their worst, they lead to a narrow focus on removing bad apples—at the expense of focusing on how strategic goals, incentives, and hierarchical pressures shape behavior.

From 2015 to 2018, a slow-motion wreck unfolded at Wells Fargo. Evidence emerged that its retail banking employees had been pressured to open 3.5 million fraudulent accounts for customers, charge 800,000 people for unnecessary auto insurance, and falsify mortgage documents, driving some 274,000 customers into delinquency.[2] Where was the bank's compliance department? It was helping managers monitor whether staff was meeting sales quotas. In 2008, Wells Fargo employees were expected to sell eight products a day (an impossible target, given market size), for no reason other than the CEO's determination that "eight is great."[3] Employees were pressed to exceed targets, ranked on their performance, and given scorecards and "motivator reports." Even as problems began cropping up, the company dismissed them as ethical lapses by low-level, rogue employees; Wells Fargo fired 5,300 people from 2011 to 2016 for behavior it had pressed them to perform.[4]

A leadership obsession with hitting sales goals generally tends to trump compliance processes. In the 2022 trial of former Goldman Sachs banker Roger Ng for looting Malaysia's 1MBD fund, Ng testified about a company culture where, if you missed out on a business deal, you'd be hauled in front of senior management to account for it. He said the risk management "federation" of controllers and individuals in credit risk, market risk, and trading that Goldman had boasted about as exemplifying its institutional values could be easily circumvented.[5]

Oversight systems can be (and often are) co-opted by leaders who are obsessed with meeting unrealistic targets and who see ethics as an annoying constraint.[6] Compliance officers struggle with this because they've historically lacked a voice in core corporate strategy and incentive design. Moreover, trying to hold a member of the senior leadership team accountable can be (and often is) a career-ending move.

The relabeling of many departments as "Ethics and Compliance" suggests they've become responsible for more than just following the law. This is important, because ethics and compliance aren't necessarily synonymous. One expert summarizes the status quo for me: "There's been a lot of work creating documentation and designing processes—but not enough on influencing behavior and measuring effectiveness, because you don't learn that in law school."

Compliance officers quickly learn that if they want credit from regulators for running a good program, by far the safest approach is not to focus on effectiveness but to copy everyone else.[7] This results in one-size-fits-all programs that tend to inflict irrelevant processes on people who are already stressed and short of time. Weak oversight and limited resources are common consequences when compliance is viewed as a cost center. And risk is abundant when even a well-resourced team follows generic compliance guidance. Isomorphism (the subtle process by which disparate organizations converge over time) happens for three reasons: external coercion, professional standards, and imitation. The compliance industry has all three.

Notwithstanding its legacy issues, we need to rethink compliance, not do away with it. Companies need specialists to prevent, detect, and punish unethical behavior. At the same time, interdisciplinary thinking and tools need to be infused into compliance teams, which must learn to approach ethics through the lens of how human beings actually behave. In chapter 10, we showed why it's so important to have senior ethics specialists in the C-suite.

What else can we do to adapt ethical oversight for the mid-twenty-first century?

Good Oversight Begins with Firm Foundations

As pressures mount over environmental and social impact, it's easy to lose sight of the basics. The core goal of the compliance function is still to ensure that meaningful sanctions will follow bad behavior. Without imposing accountability for engaging in fraud, bribery, or harassment, any effort to build a more ethical business will be a Potemkin exercise. The quickest way to degrade organizational culture is to give leaders at any level impunity to ignore the rules and to retaliate against less powerful employees.

The best compliance programs focus on building what Ann E. Tenbrunsel and coauthors have called the "ethical infrastructure."[8] If you try to launch any effort that's more ambitious—such as a sustainability program—without having this core infrastructure in place, it will rest on shaky ground.

Your stated values need to be supported by a code of conduct outlining clear rules, including accountability for employees who violate those rules. These written expectations need to be clear about when staff should seek advice on gray areas—and where to get it. In other words, a compliance team needs both advisers (for preventive advice and support in navigating tricky dilemmas) and enforcers (for detection and removal).

Anna Romberg is a member of the executive management team at health-care company Getinge and has built ethics programs from scratch in a range of industries. "We both overestimate and underestimate the formal structures," she tells me. "We do great risk assessments, and we write the reports, and we put the policy framework in place. And we train people like crazy, and we do due diligence, and implement the whistleblowing hotline, and so on. You have to go through all the hard work to get that in place—that's the base."

"But as you put these formal structures in place, you challenge the status quo," she continues. "You start to build mechanisms of forcing management to see things in a new light. You get new information to the table. What happens then, and what do you do with this information? How do you treat that? You don't just have the program but enforce it via leadership practices and incentives, so ethics is part of the culture. That's when the hard work begins."

Values, Rules, and the Trouble with "Zero Tolerance"

Companies love "zero tolerance." It's a neat way to signal to regulators that you maintain an enthusiastic commitment to ethics and will tolerate no rule breaking. The term also sends a message to employees. But what does that message say?

"I've heard the phrase 'zero tolerance' so many times, and it's meaningless," Hui Chen, who wrote the guidance on evaluating corporate compliance for the US Justice Department's Fraud Section, tells me. "Everyone knows it's meaningless. I don't even know why people say it. I don't even know why they bother."

Let's look at this in detail. Behavioral economics has shown us that in real life, humans do not make rational calculations about the costs and benefits of their actions. In practice, social norms wield far more powerful effects than processes and oversight structures, even those backed by legal sanctions.

When companies emphasize rules, punishment, and surveillance, they signal distrust. This can sap employee morale and even diminish ethical behavior because it encourages blind rule-following at the expense of ethical judgment. A study by Todd Haugh mirrored findings from criminal law by showing that corporate deterrents are far less effective than we like to imagine.[9] If you try to design and enforce a regulation for every eventuality, too many rules will have negative outcomes: employees will either follow them literally, without exercising judgment or critical thinking, or they'll focus on evading the bureaucrats in the "business prevention department."

Maarten Hoekstra, who leads ethics at ABN Amro, tells me: "What I find very often is that when we're trying to fix an individual so they behave more ethically, I find out they don't even have time to do the right thing, for instance. Or they're never held accountable for doing the right thing, so it's much easier to do the wrong thing—and then of course, training will not help. That's very obvious. But companies still tend to take a reductionist approach."

Beware unintended consequences, warns Robert Mascola, who has held compliance leadership roles at several companies and overseen compliance programs at Fordham Law School: "Zero tolerance can easily force you into making decisions that are unfair. In a practical sense, what zero tolerance means is that if someone is involved in this behavior, they get fired. Let's look at an example: sexual harassment. If you say you have zero tolerance without distinguishing between gradations of sexual harassment, then there is one of two consequences. You either end up firing someone for a single inappropriate comment, or you find creative ways to take certain behavior and call it something other than sexual harassment."

While it's tough for companies to admit this for the record, even organizations with noble ethical intent must prioritize some values over others and some groups and individuals over others. Any decent compliance team knows the array of regulations it is subject to—itself a burdensome task, with national rules varying so much. And while a company must honor the laws of each jurisdiction in which it operates, potential violations of many statutes pose no meaningful risk or pertain to only a tiny proportion of employees. This necessitates choosing which rules to implement rigorously, which ones to honor formally, and which issues to manage with guiding principles, not rules. What's really needed are clearly stated *values*, backed with guidance, to help employees know where to get answers to practical questions, develop individual judgment, and speak up when they have concerns.

Instead of imposing generic rules, compliance experts agree that it makes sense to start by making a qualitative risk assessment of areas in which the company is vulnerable. The true risks a business faces might reflect such operational realities as where it operates or which industry it's in. Risks might stem from questions of incentives and power, which would entail identifying who interacts with government officials, who signs off on large expenditures, and who will win large bonuses if certain targets are met.

"The first thing you should do is to understand the risks that you face and structure your program accordingly," Chen tells me. "So you should look at your risks and then look at which functions are impacted by those risks. Let's take the example of an airline: the people that deal with landing permits face bribery risk—the baggage handlers, less so. This should be a very customized conversation."

To identify vulnerable areas, look at the external landscape—corruption and human rights assessments will add considerable depth to any review of market conditions and regulatory developments—as well as decision-making power, whistleblowing data, past incidents, and frequent scandals in your industry. A credible assessment of ethical culture will provide the greatest help, especially when combined with whistleblowing data. This can tell you which locations and teams account for frequent complaints. It can also identify pockets of silence in which employees might have concluded that speaking up is futile.

Once you've comprehended the root causes of your risks, you can identify where it will be useful to introduce clear rules (and whom they should apply to), and where an alternative approach might work better, such as adjusting incentive structures or performance criteria. It's also crucial to identify leaders who wield significant, unconstrained authority: Markus Jüttner, who led compliance at E.ON, focused on senior leaders with the biggest influence on commercial decisions.

A common vulnerability opens up when sales-based compensation schemes are set from afar with no concern for conditions in the local market. Richard Bistrong, who served fourteen months in prison for violating the US Foreign Corrupt Practices Act, describes such incentives as an "ethical and legal time bomb" and offers this question: "After bold forecasts have been achieved, does anyone ask, 'How did we get here?' Or is it all high fives in the C-suite and boardroom?"[10]

If you fail to give critical consideration to these questions, the result will be what Cass Sunstein calls "sludge": processes that are unnecessarily time consuming, frustrating, even humiliating.[11]

There may be times when it makes sense to introduce paperwork and approvals: to make people in the business think twice before acting for impulsive reasons, such as hiring a new third-party agent to help close a deal or agreeing to pay for an expensive client dinner. Using a tough approval process to add friction can help. Far more often, though, ethics and compliance teams create sludge to protect themselves and provide a paper trail for any investigation that might follow.

"My favorite example is from when I was in the [US DoJ] fraud section," Chen says. "A monitor came in, and one of the problems he had reported about the company was abuse of corporate credit cards. His solution was to propose a training for the entire company on corporate credit card usage. I just asked one question: 'How many people have corporate credit cards?' And it was about a hundred. I've seen this over and over again. Often, if the training did anything, it was to help people be more thoughtful and advanced in disguising their misconduct."

Regular, mandated compliance training that bears no relation to an employee's lived experience is one of the most pervasive examples of sludge. The result? Employees take the training during dull conference calls on Zoom. What might seem a cost-effective solution ends up wasting time and showing staff that an authority figure is being paid to make them waste time. The process leaves employees less likely to approach that annoying person with a genuine ethical dilemma.

What might work better? "The answer is to look at the substance of what you are being asked to do and dig into what is necessary and what is just compliance theater," Christian Hunt, who leads Human Risk, tells me. "If you treat irrelevant processes in a gold-plated manner, employees will think you are an idiot."

Finally, there's no substitute for insight from the people in the business who actually contend with its problems. Says Chen: "If the business will actually involve you, then you can come up with solutions. But you need to understand the business, and most compliance teams have not done enough to earn that trust."

Fairness and Consistency Are Crucial

If you intend to meaningfully sanction unethical practices, questions of fairness are central. All human beings care deeply about fairness. (There's evidence that animals do, too.[12]) Still, it's hard to agree on what's fair; the question often highlights differences in values and desired outcomes. For instance, whether you think it's more important that everyone has access to the same opportunities, or that policies be enacted to correct for historic inequities is likely to reflect your personal politics.[13]

Given their brief, compliance teams should focus on two forms of fairness. The first is procedural fairness: Are oversight processes and investigations run in a balanced, fair, and transparent manner, with the same rights accorded the most junior and most senior employees? The second form, interactional justice, addresses whether people are treated with respect and empathy through the process of speaking up and during any subsequent investigation.

Clearly, rules and sanctions must be overseen with a keen commitment to justice and fairness. This, however, raises tensions when it comes to the role and mandate of the compliance function. Can you really act as both enforcer and therapist?[14]

"If you talk to any ethics and compliance leader, you will hear the advice that to be effective you need to be a trusted adviser, understand the business, and come up with creative solutions," Mascola says. "At the same time, these ethics and compliance leaders are usually in charge of internal investigations. They will often say: 'I didn't want people to see me as the police.' But the fact remains that they are the corporate police! Striking the right balance between being a trusted adviser and credible investigator is one of the key challenges of ethics and compliance leaders."

The primary goal of a compliance officer is to manage violations that can harm the company, Mascola says, adding that the way to win trust is to conduct investigations fairly and professionally: "I compare all this to a police traffic stop, which is one of the most stressful situations you can be in, right? A study found that if police are trained to be respectful and transparent during these interactions, trust in the police significantly increases, even relative to those who have not been in a traffic stop."

The best way to build this trust is to ensure that concerns about politics and power cannot predominate, he says. "If there is an allegation against someone more senior than you, or the situation would impact your ability to conduct the investigation, then I think the onus is on you to step out and have someone external handle the investigation. Does this work 100 percent? Of course not, and that's why big enough companies have a separate investigations function. But that's not always possible in a smaller company."

Charles Paré now leads integrity efforts at the World Economic Forum, but was previously chief compliance officer at a number of companies, including CEVA Logistics. He agrees that questions of credibility and independence are critical: "To be useful to an employee, you need to be able to convince them that you have the authority, the goods, the strength to fix their problem. Junior compliance people may struggle to be convincing in that regard—their success will depend on the word of mouth around how much they could really drive change, fix people's problems, and actually have an impact. And you don't need to be friendly in the sense of being everybody's 'best buddy.' You just need to be polite."

Any compliance officer should think carefully about the tensions that lurk between advice and sanctions. Chen suggests you build an interdisciplinary team because former prosecutors with the procedural experience to conduct investigations often lack commercial experience, reducing their credibility among staff in the core business. Finally, behavioral and data scientists are invaluable at helping you traverse the sludge and identify where to focus.

Measuring Effectiveness Is a Huge Challenge

When it comes to ethics, how do you know the team is doing a good job? How can you tell if your company's ethical culture is improving? How will you know if misconduct is falling—or if miscreants simply aren't getting caught? As Chen and Eugene Soltes pointed out in a superb article, "Why Compliance Programs Fail—and How to Fix Them," a dearth of effective measurement is a big reason so many organizations waste so much time and effort on such meager outcomes.[15]

Most companies don't even try to measure the effectiveness of their ethics efforts. Those that do tend to emulate the drunk who looks for misplaced keys under the streetlamp because that's where the light is. They measure effort—training completion rates, calls to the hotline, and the number of investigations and resulting sanctions—not outcome.

Training completion rates tell us nothing about how appropriate or useful the training was. And how many calls to the hotline is a "good" number? You cannot answer that without an understanding of how the employees in the given team or region feel about the culture. Data on investigations and sanctions isn't useful unless you know how many employees breached rules but were not sanctioned—or whether there's been a disproportionate focus on punishing junior employees while letting managers off the hook. Raw data tells you little. Qualitative understanding is just as important.

Matt Galvin worked with film producers to create real-life gamified training based on integrity breaches that AB InBev had experienced—and for which there was no right answer. This creative approach bore fruit that greatly enhanced employees' willingness to discuss gray areas, and Galvin says it helped him work closely with business executives to draw the links between corruption and commercial advantage.

While culture measurement can help fill these gaps, designing the right metrics will always pose challenges. "Not everything that can be measured is worth measuring," Mascola says.

> I do not have a full solution. I once compiled a set of metrics that enable a fair and holistic evaluation of how leaders are using their position to advocate on behalf of a culture of integrity. But I was told it was too complex. People want simple metrics, but if you focus on one or two metrics, the picture gets distorted, and you end up promoting leader behaviors that don't really move the needle in fostering a culture of integrity—or worse, create the perception that it is just a paper exercise.
>
> So then I tried something much simpler, and I had each leader say to his subordinates that they should prepare to answer one question: How did you use your leadership position to advance ethics and compliance in your organization?

Mascola believes that while this approach isn't perfect, framing a question turned the issue into a priority. He argues that the ethics team can help by briefing a leader on the team's members, highlighting outstanding individuals, and providing relevant data in advance. "This can still become a tick-the-box exercise," he says. "Leaders can still bullshit their way through. But if it's conversation—and if the leader believes in ethics—I have seen this have a great impact."

Empower Employees to Make Ethical Decisions

Any company that aspires to maintain an ethical culture needs to help employees build moral reasoning and capacity. This empowers staff to navigate ethical dilemmas and reduces the need for the performative sludge that slows decision-making. But because most companies persist in blending ethics and compliance, these critical considerations can get buried under—and distorted by—legal anxieties.

Chen describes the challenge: "When you are talking about ethics, you are talking about values. And here, what we really need to do is learn to live with each other. This is the hardest thing. It's not an easy answer, and nobody wants to hear it. There are a lot of times that we're just going to have to struggle through issues with no answer. There are times we're going to come to compromises when nobody's happy. This takes diversity of thought and approach."

Ellen Hunt has fielded plenty of complaints as chief compliance officer for a number of companies. "I've had situations where people have come to me, and they certainly feel that something is very ethically and morally wrong," she says. "They're certainly entitled to that point of view, but if it doesn't violate our company's values, then you as the individual need to make a decision if this is the kind of company you want to keep working for."

Building capacity for ethical reasoning is a useful strategy in general, particularly in the face of rising employee and corporate activism. Businesses pioneering in this include a pair of Dutch banks that have moved deliberately to build thoughtful moral capacity.

Rabobank focuses on food and agribusiness. In 1998 it became the first global bank to form a standing committee to explore the ethical dimensions of its decisions. The Global Ethics Committee's leaders are Françoise Rost van Tonningen and Stefan Louwers. "It was intrinsically motivated," van Tonningen tells me.

> As Rabobank started to expand internationally, the managing board realized that we would be confronted with ethical dilemmas. It fulfills an independent role in the organization. It advises on cases (bottom up) and forward-looking themes (top down) based on the values of Rabobank and in line with Rabobank's

mission, "Growing a better world together." Every employee can raise a question or ethical dilemma. The committee deals with cases and themes with an ethical character in the "gray area." Often, there is not yet an internal policy or legislation or regulations in such dilemmas. The outcome of the dialogue can serve as a moral precedent for similar cases and/or contribute to internal policy making.

Explains Louwers: "The Global Ethics Committee consists presently of ten members, including the CEO, Legal, Sustainability, business representatives, and Rabobank Research. We are very aware that a senior perspective has its limitations, so one member represents Young Rabo, our network for younger employees. We try to name the elephant in the room and discuss sensitive topics. In the past, we've talked about solar panels from Xinjiang, responsible AI, and cryptocurrencies."

At ABN Amro, Maarten Hoekstra focuses on enhancing employees' capacity for ethical reflection by directly engaging them in shaping decisions. "We took a psychological approach where we really looked at the root causes of why people do the wrong thing sometimes, or what people need from the context to do the right thing. It's more realistic to fix the environment than try to fix the individual. We include three regular employees in our ethics committee, and we try to explore really tough questions. We also provide moral courage and ethical leadership training."

In Silicon Valley, companies are trying to cope with heightened staff concerns about the social impact of technologies such as AI. Notions of what constitutes ethical technology are complex and contested, and concern about legal risk and prospects for legal regulation are not the only business considerations. The tech companies have found that "doing ethics," in the traditional sense of pursuing compliance and policy commitments, helps little. In technology, corporate values need to be integrated into product development and performance, with checks and balances to ensure that users aren't harmed and the company isn't sued. The public will inevitably base judgments about how effective this is on outcome, not on a company's internal process. In other words, if Facebook is understood to have incited genocide, explanations about its procedures to identify hate speech won't suffice.[16]

After speaking with many tech employees, whom they describe as "ethics owners," Emanuel Moss and Jacob Metcalf published fascinating research in *Data & Society* in 2019. They discussed how employees (in such varied roles as safety, legal, data, policy, product design, and content moderation) who are operating amid the tensions between commercial and ethical imperatives find few tools and approaches to guide them. Moss and Metcalf saw an ongoing need to negotiate tensions between personal ethics and corporate duties. And they called for a greater focus on downside risks than on upside benefits. Staff, they said, must learn to consider how tools, products, and the business model of the company as a whole will impact human beings. (The human rights tools we discussed in chapter 6 can certainly help.) Employees need to be able to speak more openly about failures and to collaborate more effectively across functions.[17]

This is hardly a story of Sisyphean efforts by companies to impose moral considerations on employees. Moss tells me that many of the people he spoke with were self-taught on ethics issues and tended to see themselves as personally responsible for preventing negative impacts. As they tried to translate values into concrete practices, they experimented with different tools and approaches borrowed from safety, compliance, and crisis management. Many employees no longer see managing ethical pressures as the purview of one department, but as integral to success in a range of roles.

All employees need help in using their judgment, seeking advice, and knowing how to respond when they encounter gray areas. Recognizing that integrity is not clearly defined, Novartis developed an online, interactive ethical decision-making framework for staff. It does not replace conversation and consultation and does not give a definitive answer about what an employee should do. Rather, it guides users through fifteen questions to prompt deep reflection, exposes up to six potential biases, and suggests materials and resources for them to explore.

Novartis has also retained a team of behavioral scientists to support its ethics efforts. In an organization-wide study the team conducted into what makes employees more or less likely to speak up, a key finding was the need for a positive ratio of good to bad behavior, lest employees see raising concerns as futile.[18] Given the general human tendency to presume that coworkers and leaders are unethical, this discovery highlights the importance of circulating reports of disciplinary actions regarding un-ethical behavior—and, particularly, citing positive examples of ethical leadership in the organization.

STEPS TO HIGHER GROUND

Every company needs to build a compliance function to detect and punish unethical behavior. A well-resourced compliance program is no guarantee that you will avoid an ethics scandal. Ethical organizations need to look beyond rules to consider strategy, culture, and incentives. If elements of the business model—or specific products or services—are harmful, even best-practice compliance programs will struggle to address public concerns.

Be realistic about how senior leadership often overrides, co-opts, or neuters compliance functions. Common compliance pitfalls include unconvincing blanket declarations of zero tolerance and selective impunity for powerful leaders from rules that staff is expected to fol-low. Senior compliance leaders who have a role in shaping strategy, incentives, and performance metrics can help, as can more rigorous measurement of how specific policies and processes actually influence employees.

Focus on a few clear rules, build capacity for judgment, and estab-lish fair investigation and oversight. This means instituting procedural and interactional justice. You will also need to proactively manage speaking up, which I'll discuss in chapter 12.

Internal processes and structures must consider what is ethical as well as what is legal. A narrow focus on rules and processes to deflect regulatory scrutiny can reduce the beneficial role of human judgment. The best compliance programs consider and plan for the realities of how humans behave by taking social and situational pressures into account.

12

Speaking Up in an Era of Activism

S peaking up at work isn't what it used to be.

On March 17, 2022, Sofia Vashchenko, a web content manager at Nestlé based in Lviv, Ukraine, posted on LinkedIn that her eight years of dedicated loyalty to the company had come to an end after "speeches by top management" emphasized "that people of Russia also matter and Nestlé cares about them." Her post continued: "Nestlé obviously choses [sic] profits and funding war criminals above the people of Ukraine."

Vashchenko added that she had just spent three weeks "trying to support my team of 20 people mentally as well as ensuring the continuity of operations." She declared that her team was "mentally broken" after the Nestlé webcast, and she was leaving the company because "I want to show my integrity with my own values as a person and as a professional of my future employer."[1]

We know that a key foundation for an ethical culture is the perception of fairness. If it's absent, moral dissent will start to accumulate. And once this happens, employees' disengagement or resignations will be the least of a company's problems. Fraudulent practices will grow commonplace if breaking them for personal advantage is deemed justified. Another likely scenario is that employees will leverage damaging internal information by unleashing it in the public domain, forcing the company into what will invariably sound like an unconvincing defense.

Junior and mid-level employees have become ever likelier to blame senior leaders for what they see as ethical failings of their organization, and to seek to hold them to account in the court of public opinion. Even leaders make use of the new transparency weapons. In April 2022, a senior brand manager at Levi's published an article on a prominent blog and gave numerous media interviews describing how she turned down a large severance package so she could speak up over what she described as the company's aggressive efforts to stop her from commenting on Twitter against Covid-19 school closings.[2]

Employees are often much better positioned than investors or regulators to find and exploit a company's embarrassing secrets. Strategic leaks to investigative journalists (or directly onto social media) are now a primary source of reputational risk. This is not just about whistleblowers like Frances Haugen, a data scientist and engineer who worked as a product manager on Facebook's civic integrity team and dramatically leaked thousands of company documents to the *Wall Street Journal* and the US Securities and Exchange Commission after her team was shut down.[3] The *New York Times* relied on employee leaks of internal pitch documents, for example, to expose how certain McKinsey employees had simultaneously consulted for Purdue Pharma on opioid marketing and for the US Food and Drug Administration on pharmaceutical regulations.[4] And in the wake of Elon Musk's acquisition of Twitter, employees offered the media blow-by-blow accounts of internal announcements and decisions before gearing up to launch lawsuits.[5]

Organizations need new tools and fresh thinking to manage this dramatic transformation in employee voice. Traditional whistleblowing hotlines have always had limitations in that staff members need to trust that the lines are safe and anonymous. Even the best-run whistleblowing procedures place employees who speak up under considerable stress because any allegation needs to be investigated and resolved, and this can mean months of uncertainty and fear of retaliation.

Although the terms *whistleblowing* and *speaking up* are often confused, they're not synonymous. Because many employees now wish to give primary expression to their personal values, the communications system designed to help meet compliance obligations is no longer fit for purpose.

Nicole Diaz, Snap's global head of integrity, has friends who are actively pushing for change in companies, and friends who are on the receiving end of those demands. She tells me that employees are most effective when they accept that "there isn't going to be a fully consensus-based decision structure" and come to "recognize business demands." "If you can view employee voice as an asset and harness it," Diaz continues, "it certainly helps make better decisions. The most effective leaders are genuine in their engagement because canned responses can discourage employees from raising probing questions."

Harnessing the enthusiasm of younger employees can be a powerful, creative way for leaders to engage directly on the confounding complexities that face companies. Conversely, seeking to control and repress internal demands is unlikely to end well; when speaking up seems dangerous internally, it supercharges the possibility that staff concerns will play out on social media. And that would invite investors, customers, and the public to come to their own conclusions about how your organization handles debate and dissent.

I've already touched on examples of just how badly this can go, but the instance of Basecamp stands out because the company had made a selling point of its healthy, inclusive workplace. Founders Jason Fried and David Heinemeier Hansson coauthored five best-selling books on work culture; the most recent, *It Doesn't Have to Be Crazy at Work*, came out in 2018. It all backfired three years later when the two announced a "principled" policy of banning "societal and political" discussions on Basecamp's internal social media.

As the *Verge* came to detail, employees weren't tying up company time debating President Joe Biden's performance.[6] They were trying to stop a long-standing internal practice of collecting "funny sounding" customer names, which were frequently African or Asian in origin. After an employee suggested that such jokes constituted a gateway to more dangerous expressions of racial antipathy, Basecamp shut down the thread and disbanded an employee-led diversity and inclusion group.[7] One-third of the staff resigned in protest, and the incident became a meme.

The schadenfreude over Basecamp's troubles offered a salutary tale for leaders everywhere, but some weren't listening. Less than six months later,

Apple banned an internal Slack channel on pay equity because, while the topic was "aligned with Apple's commitment to pay equity," it didn't meet the internal requirements for topics allowable on Slack.[8] Discussion about Apple's track record on pay equity was soon raging on Twitter.

While banning internal debate is not a smart way to counter these forces, that doesn't mean you have to sign up for endlessly distracting, irresolvable conflict, or open up every decision to a staff vote. The intersection of personal and organizational activism is particularly troubled, given the fraying organizational boundaries we discussed in chapter 9.

Many leaders are uncertain about how to handle employee voice in this fraught context of shifting public opinion, heightened political risk, changing demographics, environmental and social concerns, diversity pressures, and so forth. In a polarized environment, nuanced and thoughtful responses often seem the most unpopular of all. What can you do about this?

Understanding the Demands of a Changing Workforce

Mary-Hunter McDonnell at Wharton observes that novel employee sensibilities strongly disconcert leaders who are accustomed to thinking that all they need do is set direction and incentivize performance. "As millennials and Gen Z are increasingly those buying products and company shares, I think that we'll see a lot more corporate engagement with various activist constituencies," she tells me. "But from watching activism take shape at the moment, employees are the most powerful agents of change because they have the easiest path to disruption. Young people really value working for companies who will give them a platform to make what they see as a positive change in the world."

The interviews I conducted for this book and the opinions I hear in the classroom both portray a workplace in the midst of sweeping transformation. I've already noted employees' rising focus on social identity and personal values, as well as their belief that an organization should adapt to individual needs and ambitions, rather than the reverse. This expectation applies to company stances on environmental and social concerns, along with such internal culture and performance issues as remote work and mental health. Businesses understandably find it impossible to please every employee when each one wants something different. Moreover, generational differences can make any decision seem biased toward one or another cohort.

When teaching undergraduates, I often hear the view that an employer should "step in" to protect employees' mental health. That the very topic is no longer taboo signifies stunning progress on diversity and inclusion, but this has brought little practical consensus on how to handle or accommodate mental health challenges in the workplace. A consequence I hear repeatedly from MBA students with managerial responsibilities is that they feel out of their depth and stressed about contradictory pressures to prioritize both well-being and performance.[9]

The varied forces troubling organizations aren't limited to the tensions over political speech and spending discussed in chapter 7. They include feelings of individual powerlessness and declining tolerance of divergent political views. Axios noted that "corporate America is finding itself trapped between society's progressive impulses, and the conservative backlash" after Kohl's, Anheuser-Busch, and Target cumulatively lost US$28.7 billion in market value in ten weeks during a conservative furor over LGBTQ-themed promotion efforts.[10]

Affective polarization has dramatically increased since 1994. Rather than accept differences in political thinking as inevitable or natural, many people now tend to feel profound dislike, even hostility, toward those on the other side.[11] As a natural corollary, political homophily—the tendency to seek out and form relationships with politically like-minded individuals—has grown, too. Some workplaces offer social venues in which people interact constructively across divides. But as I've noted, many others are becoming more partisan, in keeping with societal fault lines.[12]

In a research project we conducted in 2022 at Ethical Systems, interviewees agreed that most organizational cultures bear innate bias toward one perspective or another. People who had changed roles or industries during their careers told us that such partiality can differ markedly among companies and industries. Interviewees at most of the organizations we looked into suggested that while dominant viewpoints are celebrated—and reinforced by group dynamics—contrasting viewpoints are tolerated at best.[13]

This isn't new. Research in 2014 by Stanford's Adam Bonica effectively documented the political leanings in various industries.[14] But rising pressure on corporations to speak out has made the issue of workplace politics much more salient. Significantly, prevailing biases do not align neatly with demography or social identity. Technology and finance are both sectors dominated by men, yet their workforces respectively tend toward the political left and right. This can leave some employees without psychological safety and grant others far too much.

We've already discussed how to contend with political risk in chapter 7. It's time to delve into its impact on organizational culture. Numerous jobholders are motivated to advocate that their employer take certain political stances or actions and to resist organizational choices they deem harmful. Responding to their demands can effectively elevate the views of a vocal minority while making others in the organization feel silenced and resentful.

Even within factions that are generally aligned, there will be infighting. Progressive organizations are often beset with internal strife and "callout culture."[15] Generally like-minded people may agree that social justice should be an internal imperative, yet strongly disagree on how to meet it.

Finally, there's an expectation that work should provide a higher meaning and purpose for employees, as embodied in the expression "Bring your whole self to work." While this can boost motivation, it can foster unrealistic expectations, burnout, and exploitation. (See the conclusion for more on this.) Overall, when the line between work and personal life blurs, pressure increases on an organization to bring employees the wider social and political impacts they seek. If an employer seems to be supporting the "wrong" issue or failing to act on the "right" one, zealous employees might feel a strong sense of cognitive dissonance.

That the willingness of organizations to take stands on contentious issues prefigured the rise of employee activism suggests that a key driver is a perception by employees that values are now up for debate and should not be imposed by leaders. Instances include protests at Netflix over Dave Chappelle's views on gender and at Disney over Florida's so-called Don't Say Gay law. When Target faced a backlash from conservative customers and removed some of its LGBTQ merchandise, some employees felt betrayed while others appreciated the effort to prioritize their physical safety.[16] (A human rights approach would suggest you consult affected stakeholders on this issue to determine how to proceed—in this case, frontline employees and LGBTQ representatives.)

All of this demands a thoughtful approach to employee speech, organizational speech, and where they intersect.

The Promise and Perils of Employee Voice

Jonathan Drimmer, a partner at law firm Paul Hastings, tells me he sees speaking up as a top priority for any organization that aspires to be ethical: "I think people are increasingly recognizing the singular importance of confidence in speaking up as a measurement of corporate culture. It's a trust in management when you do raise something—that you won't be retaliated against. And that gets to procedural justice and fairness. So companies are focusing on it more and more."

Social media and the rise of remote work have transformed the nature and impact of speaking up. Social media–enabled collective action is one way to counter the hazard of retaliation from leaders. In 2018, Nike's human resources team didn't take action on allegations of harassment lodged against a number of male senior leaders. By crowdsourcing their experiences, women on staff confronted management with a powerful case, and some key male executives soon found themselves out of jobs.[17] Whistleblowing platform startups have even sprung up to marshal the power of collective voice by, for example, connecting employees who wish to raise similar allegations.[18]

The rise of internal channels like Slack has also helped employees to gather out of management's sight to share perspectives and plan collective action.[19] Sarah Repucci tells me she saw this every day in a senior role at Freedom House, a US-government funded nonprofit: "Public square accountability is real for young people. And those of us who are in power, we can't really keep up. They out-organize us really quickly. While I'm sitting on email with the other execs, they're on Slack, having massive conversations in channels I'm not in, spreading information and organizing—and then taking action."

James Detert and Amy Edmondson are among the many academics who have documented how vital bottom-up communication is to the success of contemporary organizations. Their research and that of many colleagues has been devoted to encouraging the speaking of truth to power and countering the chilling effects of hierarchy.[20] Only companies that take pains to offer psychological safety can expect employees to make evident the problems—and opportunities for organizational improvement—that leaders might otherwise miss.

The tricky question is how to encourage speaking up without supercharging internal conflict. Robert Cialdini's work has shown that people who publicly express opinions become likelier to act on them and find it harder to back down.[21] The tech-enabled boom in employee voice can propagate the combination of grandstanding and anonymity that characterizes some social media platforms.

This even happened to LinkedIn. Like most large US businesses, the Microsoft subsidiary faced a reckoning over systemic racism in the wake of George Floyd's murder in the summer 2020. LinkedIn held a company-wide town hall called "Standing Together" to discuss what had happened and how employees could support each other. In view of the sensitive subject matter and the imperative to ensure that people would feel safe speaking up, the company enabled anonymous comments and questions in the online chat that accompanied the meeting. What surfaced were comments challenging the meeting's very premise, questioning reverse discrimination, and even avowing racism.[22] Despite LinkedIn's best intentions, the process precisely replicated the toxic dynamics the company was trying to avoid.

What's a better approach?

Increase accountability. LinkedIn's experience reinforces lessons from social media about the need for ground rules to achieve healthy discourse. One takeaway is that if you want to find out what people really think, ask privately. Conversely, if you wish to invite an open, internal debate, it's unwise to guarantee anonymity. Cisco Systems faced a similar problem in 2020 when some employees made racist comments in the chat during a diversity forum. Because anonymity had not been allowed, leaders were able to quickly remove those employees, clearly signaling the leadership team's commitment to inclusion.[23]

It's constructive to help employees pause to think before they speak out. Harmon Brothers, a marketing startup in Utah, came up with a clever way to do this after finding staff increasingly prone to sharing partisan news on internal Slack channels. The company did not make Basecamp's mistake of banning "partisan speech." It set forth a rule that employees wanting to post an article must also post a video containing their own reflections about it; replies would need video posts, too.[24] This forced staff to reflect, dramatically reduced the number of posts, and took much heat out of debates.

Encourage healthy debate. The best nonpartisan approach for coping with escalating employee demands is to emphasize *individual* political engagement and choice, tolerance, and mutual respect, rather than implying that the organization can represent its employee's views on political questions. True inclusion means that someone should be able to hold an opinion, even if it's misaligned with the company's dominant culture, without being penalized or "canceled." Given the tense external environment, a very helpful requirement for promotion could be having compiled a track record of working successfully with people who hold very different values and opinions.

Allstate Insurance stands out for its creation of the Better Arguments Project, a civic collaboration with the Aspen Institute and Facing History and Ourselves. The project focuses not on stymieing debate but on making it healthier and more respectful.[25] Companies might also consider inviting a range of political speakers and promoting civic engagement by providing time off to vote. It's valid for organizations to match employee contributions to causes without embracing them. These approaches reflect the realities that personal values diverge and that employers should respect healthy, democratic discourse.

Set clear guidelines. These examples show how important it is to provide guidance on what employees will and won't be allowed to say at work. It's a good idea to define debates and opinions that cannot be entertained and which lines can't be crossed, but do so before a crisis, not during one. The line is best drawn at discriminatory behavior that could endanger psychological safety at work, such as the expression of racist sentiments. Only behavior that's relevant to the workplace should be considered; companies should not attempt to dictate what even senior employees say on social media about political or civic engagement outside the workplace.

Seek positive feedback. Some companies aim to encourage the internal sharing of views on all aspects of organizational culture—not just employee concerns—to build overall confidence and capacity for debate and discussion. At AB InBev, Matt Galvin worked on "trying to rebrand our helpline from one where people report unethical conduct to one where they also report examples of inspiring conduct and really rethink how they interact with the ethics team. Whistleblowing can have problematic connotations, but everyone wants to help the company build a more sustainable future."

Deciding When the Company Should Take a Stand

Leaders understandably have mixed feelings about the rise in employee activism. Megan Reitz and John Higgins described a spectrum of responses, from straight-up denial ("what activism?") through suppression and "façadism" (a kind of feigned empathy) to meaningful dialogue—and even efforts by some corporations to stimulate activism.[26] Despite all the caveats I've already laid out, there may be good reason to take an organizational position on an important social or environmental issue. This must be carefully considered from a range of angles. Leaders who encourage activism should not delude themselves into thinking they can retain top-down control over how it unfolds.

Re_Generation (formerly the Canadian Youth Business Council for Sustainable Development) produced a detailed toolkit to enable young workers to "help employees understand the difference between greenwashing and genuinely impactful sustainability efforts, and to hold employers accountable to their promises."[27] The report suggested: "All employee activists should . . . acquire a high degree of sustainability literacy in order to adequately assess their company's performance. The second stage of employee activism involves finding allies, organizing for change, and helping to spread the word through meetings, workshops, conferences, and informal channels such as internal message boards."

Organizations are emerging to facilitate and coordinate these efforts. After being Facebook's director of sustainability for six years, Bill Weihl left in 2017 to start ClimateVoice, a platform for coordinated employee activism on climate change in the tech sector. "I realized that the most important thing Facebook could do was to use its voice in the public policy battle on climate," he tells me. The problem Weihl perceived is that "many tech companies do the right thing in their own operations—and even keep expanding their sustainability goals—but are largely silent on public policy questions. Meanwhile, Big Oil uses every ounce of influence it has."

Weihl continues:

> We launched in early 2020 when federal action on climate was almost impossible, so we focused on state and regional action. For the first eighteen months, we focused on educating employees on the importance of lobbying and how to use voice for maximum impact. Many tech companies push propaganda on what they are doing inside their own operations, but this is less significant than their public policy positions, and we have educated young employees about these distinctions.
>
> Many companies could do more on climate but need a push, and we aim to provide that push. We helped align policies across companies and specifically tracked resistance to Build Back Better legislation via a simple scorecard. This led to coordinated questions from employees—and important policy shifts.

In light of these employee efforts, it's extremely risky to treat taking stands as a communications strategy that's divorced from internal priorities and spending. Today's employee activists aren't content to read management's supportive posts on Instagram. They're looking under the hood to ensure that corporate rhetoric and action on public policy are aligned. They expect the company to take political risks by standing up for its expressed organizational values. You can see where all this might leave a business that proclaims support for certain public policy positions while opposing them via its lobbying and contributions.

So how can organizations be more effective and less hypocritical regarding when and how they speak up? Organizational leaders can work actively to reduce divisiveness and promote pluralism and mutual respect, or they can choose to lean into increasing polarization and employee demands by taking more activist positions. Both routes feature pros and cons. Avowing neutrality won't solve all challenges, because silence is frequently interpreted as complicity. A more activist stance will alienate some potential employees and attract others, inviting difficult questions about overreach and representation. Any embrace of corporate activism must be based on rigorous, consistent criteria, not least because when you speak up on one question, you raise expectations that you will do so on the next, yet-unknown topic of keen interest.

Whatever your company's ultimate disposition, speaking up should never be divorced from questions of *values*, *culture*, or *environmental and social priorities*. (This is yet another reason why sharply focusing your priorities is such a good idea.) While leaders need to invite employee voice and participation, it's a bad idea to ask the workforce for a majority decision on every hot-button question. Not only is it likely to mire you in distracting conflict, you're running a business, not an electoral realm.

Values. An essential first step is to maintain clearly stated corporate values so job candidates and staff know your bright lines and commitments— and just as important, what they don't include. As we've discussed, these values are best grounded in the business's impact on its stakeholders. Still, you don't need to undergo an ESG materiality process to know that a commitment to inclusion is highly material to every company that employs human beings.

A prime complexity here is that fundamental human rights are politicized in many, if not most, countries. LGBTQ rights, health care, women's rights, racism, certain vaccines, dress codes, and gun safety all exemplify contentious topics that are both highly personal *and* fundamental to human rights commitments. Safeguarding the human rights of employees, contractors, and supply chain workers should be the first priority before your company attempts broader engagement.

A commitment to human rights isn't "woke" and doesn't need to be partisan. Conservative brand Chick-fil-A put forth a firm written commitment to "a culture of belonging."[28] Wanting to be treated with dignity and respect isn't ideological or partisan. Take the legal settlement by

Hertz, which falsely accused hundreds of customers of car theft, imprisoning one for thirty-seven days.[29] Or the revelation that some Amazon workers were forced to work all day alongside a human corpse.[30]

Culture. To learn whether employees feel insecure about their psychological safety, a good place to begin is with the advice furnished in chapter 9. Ask everyone in the organization to give anonymous feedback on your culture, including their level of comfort around speaking up. Training that addresses negotiation and respectful dialogue might be very helpful.

Environmental and social issues. As I discussed in chapter 4, it's a good idea to invite participation from the entire workforce on establishing environmental and social priorities. Once this process is complete and your strategic commitments are established, these stated priorities can be used for guidance on whether, when, and how your organization speaks up.

It's sensible to agree that the company won't speak up unless it has ensured that a proposed action will not undermine the broad social, political, and environmental systems we all rely on. The following questions might help:

- Is the issue central to your values, code of conduct, and/or other existing public commitments?

- Is the issue an environmental or social priority, according to a rigorous materiality assessment?

- Does the issue pertain to commitments you have made to your workforce, such as any to diversity and inclusion or human rights principles?

- Has your company already done all it can to ensure it isn't making the problem worse through its actions or business model?

- Does your company have relevant capacity and expertise to contribute to solutions for the issue?

- Is this a new issue that has a proximate relationship to the company's goals or operations?

- Is there a clear way your business can make a positive contribution in collaboration with others?

- Will acting on the issue support a positive operating environment for business in general? Would it support democratic participation, fair competition, equality of opportunity, and basic human rights?

- Can the company make a statement that's consistent with its values, prior actions, political spending, and environmental and social priorities?

A negative answer to any of these questions signifies that it would be unwise to proceed.

While some employees may demand speaking up, the second-order consequences of business engagement are unpredictable. Before you mount any public campaign, ensure that actions and spending are aligned and that you've taken concrete steps to protect stakeholders from human rights violations. (Most companies will find that further internal work awaits.) The worst possible approach is to view a public campaign as a way to compensate for—or distract from—a lack of meaningful action by your core business. In other words, don't speak up on the death penalty if your workers lack health-care support or a living wage.

For companies that decide to set forth a more contentious activist position, there are additional considerations. A dominant worldview among your employees may increase staff cohesion and help you attract and retain people who bring certain demographics and perspectives. But it will increase the prospect of political retaliation and can worsen polarization. It will also have the effect of discouraging the expression of internally divergent opinions and views.

If your corporation opts to embrace activism, it's important to commit fully after considering all the implications for how you intend to implement and signal your values. If your company chooses to embody distinctively partisan values, you need to decide whether employees—particularly the most visible members of the C-suite and board—will be allowed to dissent from those views, publicly or privately. It is equally important to note that prevailing political bias in an organization can lead to decisions driven by ideological leanings, rather than what might objectively be considered optimal for business success.

STEPS TO HIGHER GROUND

The realities of hierarchy have always made speaking up at work hazardous, with potential to end employment if not careers. While companies run whistleblowing lines to honor their compliance obligations, these conduits frequently lack visibility and trust, even when run well.

In recent years, both the substance and form of speaking up have transformed. Workers are using their voice to raise concerns over ethical priorities and environmental and social impacts, not just illegal activity by colleagues and bosses. Meanwhile, social media–enabled collective action is transforming power dynamics; the rise of strategic leaking means executives must assume that everything they say or do might become public knowledge. In an open social system, trying to control speech is a losing battle.

Much can be done to enable healthier speaking up and to take advantage of the insights that a more vocal and engaged workforce can offer. It's important to support psychological safety and empathy for all. Elevating some perspectives at the expense of others would make some feel silenced and resentful. It's also important to provide guidance as to what kinds of internal and public speech would cross the line.

Even improved conversation will prove insufficient if companies do not then engage on the substance of staff concerns. It's a good idea to establish clear values, measure culture, and set social and environmental priorities with full workforce involvement.

This will help companies establish principles to guide any policy decision to speak up or remain silent. Internal guidance as to when and how to use the organization's voice on an issue can be established so it isn't trapped in a reflexive mode. A stance that's either nonpartisan or more activist can be justified if the consequences are appreciated. Treating speech as empty PR will reflect hypocrisy, and great care should be taken to avoid this.

Purpose Starts with Impact

A s a child, Jo Alexander discovered a passion for nature and the determination to explore it. But after studying geology at university, she found youthful aspirations slamming into the cold realities of the job market. On realizing she was most qualified for a career in mineral exploration, Alexander chose BP because she admired its progressive CEO, John Browne, and the company's farsighted commitment to moving "beyond petroleum."

By 2015, after eleven years spent helping BP find fresh exploration opportunities, the company's Deepwater Horizon drilling rig disaster and an abrupt change in leadership left Alexander feeling she'd lost her way. "I was very worried about climate change, but it was more than that," she tells me. "The culture was not allowing me to flourish." She left BP and embraced outsider status to join ShareAction, an activist group that campaigns for responsible investment. She discovered a world of people who believed in transforming the financial system to drive positive impact. "At first, I felt like I had nothing to lose. I had so many self-limiting beliefs, like it wasn't my job to get involved in big ideas. But I managed to break those down, which was very freeing, and I became passionate about systems change."

Armed with fresh skills and confidence, Alexander showed up at BP's annual meeting in 2019 and publicly challenged the board, expressing disappointment at the company's direction. "I was quite emotional.

I explained who I was, why I left, and why I had lost motivation and ambition," she recalls.

> Then I posed a direct challenge to the leaders of BP: "When are you going to support loyal employees to help create the future?" At the end of the meeting, Bernard Looney found me and asked me to come and talk to him about my experiences. I didn't know he was going to become CEO, but a few months later he did. And he launched BP's new purpose—to reimagine energy for people and planet.
>
> Then I met with him, and I was very impressed by how he listened and asked questions and had such a clear vision for the company. It really resonated with what I thought we should all be doing. At the end of the meeting, I said I'd love to help, and he laughed and said OK, and I agreed to go back to BP. So now I'm the purpose expert at BP.

Alexander's career highlights how, in recent years, many companies have launched sustained campaigns to show us they have an intrinsic purpose. Calls for—and commitments to—"purpose" are becoming ubiquitous.[1] More than fifty years after Milton Friedman promoted share-price appreciation as the measure of good management, the purpose renaissance speaks volumes about today's pressures on business leaders.[2]

Purpose is a promising term because it offers a holistic response to those pressures. It encompasses reframing the role of business in society (our focus in part 2) and recognizes the central importance of culture and values in an individual corporation (our focus in part 3), and this implicitly acknowledges the feedback loop between internal culture and external impact. Purpose is unencumbered by the punitive, legalistic associations of ethics and compliance. In a single word, it conveys the notion that meaning, impact, and values can act in mutually reinforcing ways. Still, unless purpose can be grounded somewhere concrete and practical, it's at risk of becoming the latest iteration of confounding jargon about corporate responsibility.

Purpose was the focus of academic attention for decades before it entered mainstream business discourse. It has variously been defined as "an institutionalized ideal, a historical, value-based aspiration guiding strategic decision making and practices"; a clear, collective sense of a company's goals; "the reason for a corporation's existence and its starting point"; a company's "deep reflection on [its] corporate identity"; and a corporation's recognition of its "duty to society."[3]

In practical terms, an avowal of purpose can be considered a public declaration of a company's superordinate goal: why it deserves to exist. This goal should directly account for the company's impact on human beings. Making a profit is certainly essential to its survival, but a company does not exist solely to make a profit any more than humans exist only to serve as vehicles for our beating hearts.

There's no shortage of guidance on how to go about choosing or discovering a purpose. Much makes it sound like a magical elixir: flick a switch to unlock employee commitment, public trust, and brand value. Cambridge University interviewed leaders enthusiastic about purpose and found agreement that purpose does not involve trade-offs. One executive proclaimed that "it will be sustainable. It will be life-affirming and life-supporting. It will make a lot of money. A lot of money. More than we do now."[4] A larger survey by EY of 474 executives on the business case for purpose found near-universal agreement "about the value of purpose in driving performance."[5] Similarly, the new chief purpose officer of Deloitte advocated in 2021 that companies "authentically demonstrate a purpose beyond profit"—before swiftly insisting that "becoming purpose-driven is not about choosing purpose over profit."[6]

These pledges will persuade no one that companies mean what they say. Treating purpose as a rhetorical quick fix embodies legacy thinking. The paradox is that if you treat purpose as a performance, it will never drive performance.

Jo Alexander's view of these challenges has gradually sharpened. Like many leaders I spoke with, she frames corporate commitment to purpose as a driver of organizational change: "As we shift towards having to deliver on both profit and purpose, people are realizing that the complexity is increasing, and there are so many more things to consider. We have to figure out how to manage our processes without losing our minds."

Much discussion about how to shape a more responsible, ethical business suggests a mythical leader who makes top-down decisions with all the facts and trade-offs laid out before them. This is not real life. The future is difficult to predict, and we all carry self-serving biases. It's often impossible to objectively evaluate even the short-term, direct impact of business decisions, let alone longer-term, indirect ones.

Instead of suggesting you can neatly resolve this uncertainty, you must act in spite of it.

Purpose Isn't about Projecting Perfection

According to the illustrious British Academy, which consulted dozens of top business leaders to produce its guidance, a company has a purpose when it produces "profitable solutions for problems of people and planet."[7] Similarly, in his book *Grow the Pie*, Alex Edmans wrote that a purposeful company should pursue *only* business opportunities that also create social value.[8]

This seems a convincing counterpoint to the obsession with shareholder value. But it's why so many company leaders end up putting out a generic, rose-tinted reframe of how they make money. Factually accurate purpose statements such as "we make and sell shoes," "we drill for oil," or "we manufacture sugary beverages" aren't much in evidence. Coca-Cola's purpose is to "refresh people in both body and spirit. . . . [W]e have to lead, to be a force for progress and for good. We have an incredible opportunity ahead of us and wind in our sails."[9] Even more grandiose is Meta's fantastical vision to "give people the power to build community and bring the world closer together."[10]

Just as important, perceptions of good and harm vary according to your values. Amazon has addressed and further fueled consumer expectations for rapid delivery, provided employment for millions, and is consistently listed among America's most admired companies. Critics charge that it has undermined competition, snarled supply chains, and spurred the creation of armies of low-paid gig workers who spend their time delivering consumer goods and meals to the laptop class. "Would you work at Amazon?" is a question that sharply divides my MBA classrooms.[11]

While toxic, predatory business models exist, most companies generate *both* benefits (at minimum, employment and meeting customer needs) and negative impacts (at minimum, waste, pollution, and carbon emissions).

This isn't going to change anytime soon. Rather than seeking to put a positive spin on what you're up to in an effort to deflect reputational risk, you can head for higher ground by being focused and honest about what your business can actually achieve.

A good, unpretentious example of corporate purpose (supported by clearly stated values) comes from Australian tech company Atlassian: "Behind every great human achievement, there is a team. From medicine and space travel, to disaster response and pizza deliveries, our products help teams all over the planet advance humanity through the power of software. Our mission is to help unleash the potential of every team."[12]

Jess Hyman leads sustainability at Atlassian, where the idea of the corporation as an open social system is fundamental. She tells me:

> The founders at Atlassian give us permission to be honest. One of our values is "open company, no bullshit." So we always talk about both highlights and lowlights and where we are going next. And when I brief our founder, and I don't have enough lowlights, he asks me, "What's going on? Why aren't you telling me what is hard so I can help get rid of the roadblocks?" It's the same in our external disclosures: no one just wants to read about what's going well. They aren't going to believe us, and more broadly, this doesn't move the needle. We need a real version of the journey we are on—and the challenges we face—to make any progress.

Purpose Needs to Be Grounded in Values

It's no coincidence that the people most enthusiastic about purpose are branding consultants.[13] But the mere avowal of purpose is not a win-win. You must convince the human beings you impact that you mean what you say.

Rachel Ruttan is an assistant professor at Rotman School of Management whose work focuses on the myriad ways a company can misstep when seeking to appeal to higher values. As she examined reactions to George Floyd's murder in summer 2020, she noted how repetitive and empty the corporate statements were. She recalls that reading them made her feel cheapened. Ruttan has demonstrated just how much arguments for "doing well by doing good" can backfire by examining corporate messaging on the values people hold sacred, such as environmental protection, diversity, and patriotism.

When a person is *truly* committed to a value, they're unwilling to trade it off against other benefits, including money. As twentieth-century advertising guru Bill Bernbach put it: "A principle isn't a principle until it costs you something."[14] Over the course of seven studies, Ruttan showed that when a value is perceived as having been deployed for self-interested reasons, it signals a lack of genuine commitment.[15] So when leaders declare that they care about such issues as climate change or diversity because of the business case, they're tarnishing that value in the eyes of people who hold it sacred.

It's easy to wind up sounding as if you fear that the profit motive is fragile and needs to be protected from a terrifying onslaught of purpose. That's an understandable response to mounting, contradictory pressures, but it's no way to address society's concerns.

Having a purpose does not mean abandoning the profit imperative. It simply means you recognize that your *overall* goal should be positive. Just as important, it means your values should be grounded in reducing any negative impacts of your business on human beings. Basing your principles solely on the law or fear for your reputation is no route to higher ground.

Purpose Isn't about Imposing Meaning

Corporate commitments to become more purpose-driven are often tied to recommendations that employees "look within," craft personal meaning, and bring their "whole selves to work." The discussion directly links personal and organizational motivations. Hubert Joly, a Harvard Business School professor and former chairman and CEO of Best Buy, directly equated it with *ikigai*, a Japanese concept designed to help you find your personal purpose.[16] Saying that inspired, committed employees will be a company's best ambassadors, influential voices insist that today's jobs must provide more than a paycheck.

There's much value in this advice, and there's certainly an authentic appetite for more worthwhile and impactful work. Still, implementing these ideas is hard to get right. It's difficult not to notice how purpose statements proliferated just as many employees were questioning their life choices and finding better things to do elsewhere. Issuing an inspiring statement about how you make the world better doesn't necessarily reflect a healthy culture; it may even be a way of compensating for a bad one. Research from MIT suggests that toxic company culture was the primary driver of "the Great Resignation" of 2021.[17] Gallup's 2023 State of the Workplace report found that half the workers around the world are disengaged and suffering record levels of employee stress.[18]

Research examining potential sources of meaning at work shows that while nine of ten employees would take a pay cut to engage in more meaningful work, they regard personal development, social connection, and support as the most important factors.[19] When I ask my students what having impact at work means to them, they mostly describe being respected and listened to, and having a say in shaping the future of the company. This is best achieved with jobs that include autonomy and a sense of personal impact. Having work that's fulfilling does not compensate for a lack of economic security or dignity, though it may distract workers from seeking them.

Taking concrete steps to value and listen to your employees, and to provide rewards they care about, will prove far more effective than an aspirational rebrand or flagship sustainability commitment—particularly when data shows that 70 percent of employees regularly experience disrespect and rudeness at work.[20] If employees do not feel valued during the workday, any corporate commitment to higher purpose will be rooted in executive dreams. At best, you will generate cynical eye rolls; at worst, you'll provoke staff to wonder just how fulfilling their jobs are. They might quit or start venting on social media or at shareholder meetings.

Human beings *naturally* seek meaning and impact in our lives. We create and provide it. We don't wait for it to appear from above, and we don't necessarily need it from our job.[21] This means that if a company intends to redefine its purpose and suggest to employees that it will provide meaning, this cannot be imposed by a board decision or soaring public declaration.

What corporations can do is strive to build stakeholder trust. This entails recognizing that no one gets everything right—and engaging in practical dialogue about how to increase your positive impacts while addressing the negative ones.

Purpose Starts with Impact

I began this book with a discussion of the reputational risk facing Starbucks for its approach to labor rights. I pointed out that the company has regularly (and credibly) been cited as a sustainability leader. There's plentiful evidence of Starbucks's achievements and good-faith efforts in areas as varied as climate change, responsible sourcing, and yes, employee benefits. I do not doubt that many of the company's leaders do their absolute best to reach higher ground.

Yet, in the United States, Starbucks's anti-union stance has caused stakeholder agendas to align as overall trust in its intentions plunges. Reported Vox: "Communicating with other stores made employees realize that they have more similarities than differences. It has built an immense feeling of solidarity, so that these small shops, each with roughly 20–30 workers, feel like they're part of something much bigger."[22] That sense of shared meaning, of social connection, of feeling you have an impact on the world is exactly what the literature suggests is the value of purpose.[23] Starbucks's revised purpose statement, released in April 2023, spoke to this: "With every cup, with every conversation, with every community— we nurture the limitless possibilities of human connection."[24]

But as we see here, purpose cannot be imposed. All a company's leadership can do is create conditions for meaning to emerge. At Starbucks, this process is going poorly: internal dissent is accumulating, even though the company's anti-union activities are common practice in much of corporate America.[25] Media outlets were quick to share reports from workers in 2023 that Starbucks had told store and district managers in twenty-one states to take down Pride Month decorations, even though the company was not known to have received threats from conservatives, as some big retailers had. Starbucks denied this and accused unions of a "smear campaign"; once workers at various stores went on strike over the issue, Starbucks pledged to clarify its position on Pride decor.[26]

Several months earlier, in fact, a majority shareholder vote had forced Starbucks to agree to an independent review of its labor practices that would evaluate whether it had been meeting stated human rights commitments. Four significant shareholders wrote Starbucks to say it "should get input from workers themselves, as well as propose remedies if the review finds instances of harm done or policies that don't support labor rights."[27]

Jonas Kron is chief advocacy officer at Trillium Asset Management, a signatory to the letter and leader of shareholder engagement efforts with Starbucks, whose labor practices he sees as not notably worse than many companies. "We simply have generations and generations of managers in the US who don't have a sophisticated understanding of organized labor and have a knee-jerk reaction against it," Kron tells me, emphasizing that unionization is not the sole alternative. "There are ways workers can organize that don't need to involve unions and are useful and productive for everyone. We conducted a study on labor rights and ESG in 2022, and there is a real gap in knowledge—and need for an education process."[28]

The Starbucks board is a direct target.[29] "We want the board to take responsibility for the strategic vision of the company, including management's behavior," Kron says. "Not least, there are board members who know better: Microsoft CEO Satya Nadella and impact investor Mellody Hobson of Ariel Investments LLC. Microsoft has reached a constructive neutrality agreement with the CWA [Communications Workers of America] union, so there is expertise and helpful precedent."

What do these contradictions afflicting Starbucks tell us about how to run a good business in this transparent, turbulent world? They show that setting—even meeting—ESG goals in order to protect the value of a corporate black box won't make the grade, even if they're best in class. You will always be on firmer ground when you base your commitments and values on your impact. Starbucks "keeps wanting to tell us about all their benefit packages and all they do," says Kron, "and we aren't arguing those things. They are great. But if employees want to organize themselves, that's a human right that must be respected."

Starbucks's dilemma tells us that your employees are your most important stakeholders. What they think dramatically affects other stakeholder groups, including investors. Companies don't interact with stakeholders, but people interact with people, so even your finest programmatic achievements are less important than maintaining good-faith dialogue. This means you should engage only if you are prepared to act.

"This is about Starbucks adhering to its public commitments," says Kron. "We simply want the company to adhere to commitments it made of its own accord."

It also tells us that companies cannot wall themselves off from the dramatic shifts in social norms underway. Support for unions in the United States has climbed to its highest in decades. I witness sharply renewed interest in worker rights among MBAs in the classroom.[30] "We are trying to make the companies we invest in better, and to act as a kind of early warning system," Kron says of Trillium's approach. "We were engaging with companies on LGBTQ issues in the early 1990s, where there was little research on the value of an inclusive workplace, and many told us they didn't have any gay employees. But we were already clear that people shouldn't get fired or demoted for who they love. Of course, this, too, is a human rights issue."

Above all, Starbucks's predicament suggests that if we can learn to regard companies as the open systems they are, our priorities will change markedly. "People talk about separate political, economic, and social spheres. But they don't stay separate from each other. They all overlap, and the notion that they ever were separate was probably wrong," concludes Kron. "To try to think that you're going to continue to be able to separate them is a fool's errand."

In beginning this book, I argued that corporations are systems in constant motion, and that we shouldn't expect them to get everything right. Starbucks's good-faith efforts and achievements in sustainability are *not* negated by its failures on labor rights. However, the company's procedural, defensive response to challenges supports my argument that the best way to reach higher ground in this tumultuous, transparent world is by sharply focusing on your impact on human beings, and making your values and commitments more than words on a page.

What might that look like, in practice?

US food manufacturer Chobani was founded by Hamdi Ulukaya, a Turkish immigrant, in 2005. The company is clear on why it exists: "Our purpose is to make universal wellness happen sooner. We're totally and deeply committed to playing an active role in transforming our food system for the betterment of our planet, our people and our communities. Real change. Not just 'checking the box.'"[31]

Having used a US$800,000 Small Business Administration loan to buy an old Kraft yogurt plant, one of Ulukaya's next moves was to start an employee 401(k) plan encouraging workers to automatically allocate some pay into an investment account.[32] He also founded the Tent Partnership for Refugees, an NGO backed by hundreds of major businesses to help support employment and training for refugees. In 2016, two years after private equity funding valued Chobani at US$3 billion to US$5 billion, Ulukaya took the unusual step of awarding his two thousand workers an equity stake based on tenure; Silicon Valley startups tend to award equity stakes in their early years, not after a company's value has been so well established. Chobani called off an initial public offering in 2022 and subsequently questioned whether a public corporation can so readily focus on its purpose.[33]

I spoke with Nishant Roy, Chobani's chief communications and impact officer, about its culture and purpose. "We bring people into the business and invest in their upward mobility, alongside Chobani's. Our plants are in upstate New York and in Idaho. We wanted to not only hire people eager to go and work in plants in those rural communities but refugees who are resettling in these areas. We have over twenty languages spoken in our plants today," he tells me. "And then we include the ability for the hourly workers to participate in getting shares in the business. We broke records as a business and continued to thrive because of the people. As Hamdi says 'We built something; now we're sharing it.'"

Chobani partnered with Fair Trade USA to launch a certification program encompassing labor rights and standards for the dairy industry as part of an incremental mission to transform the food system.[34] "Our biggest commodities are milk and fruit, and in both cases the United States has a shortage of workers, which is a result of immigration policies. We raised the issue of undocumented labor, given the gap in the workforce needed to feed our country," says Roy. "In Chenango and Otsego counties in central New York, about ten thousand of the population is food insecure, and in Twin Falls around our plant in Idaho, it is eight thousand. We partner with food banks, pantries, shelters, and houses of worship to try to improve this. As a food business, let's behave as a food business and try to improve overall food access. We are one of the few food businesses in America that isn't part of a huge conglomerate."

Chobani operates in politically conservative locales where immigration is contentious. Hiring so many refugees might seem certain to bring backlash and dreaded reputational risk. Roy says: "It was the people of Idaho that stood up for us and said: 'I trust this brand, and I don't know these people as refugees. I think of them as the people in my community.' That was fascinating. I think the reason this all works is that we got to a human level of why people would want to support immigrants and refugees. These are people that have experienced extreme levels of adversity. In our workforce there's a clear path for progression, social connection, and feeling your impact."

Of course, Chobani doesn't have a perfect track record, and as a smaller, private company, it faces less risk and scrutiny than Starbucks. But its approach—and success—illustrates the value of a distinct purpose backed with consistent commitments. It respects the importance of focus: "We do not feel the need to be in the conversation on every issue that's out there. We're a purpose-driven food business that is in the fight to deliver natural food to the masses. We choose to stay disciplined about areas where we believe we can make a real impact," Roy says. Purpose can be a communicable condition, though: in June 2023, Adecco, Novartis, and dozens of companies pledged to offer training and support for 250,000 refugees in Europe in partnership with Ulukaya's Tent Partnership for Refugees.[35]

A View from Higher Ground

This book is about how to build a better business in the face of confusing and contradictory expectations and demands. I set out to write it because so many people—many with good intentions—appeared to be lost. It even seemed that we no longer shared a common language to discuss the challenges we face. I wanted to help cut through the noise and suggest a path forward, upward.

So how can *you* find higher ground?

Your purpose should be specific and grounded in your impact on the world. The reason your business exists can be as simple as to offer a good product or service that people want to buy. But let's be clear: you need to make your best effort to clean up any messes you make and to treat workers, customers, suppliers, and investors with honesty, dignity, and respect. With these fundamental commitments in place, your efforts will be firmly grounded.

Before promising to make the world better, do your very best to make your business better. Be focused and honest about how and where you seek to address your impacts and be mindful of the likely limitations of your efforts.

Respect the systems we all depend on. Your company isn't a self-contained, self-serving entity with a singular consciousness and agenda. It's an open social system that is highly complex. It influences and is influenced by wider social, political, and environmental systems. You should proceed with an awareness that unintended consequences loom when you seek to shape these external systems for your own ends, even with the best intentions.

You can't please all the people all the time. You won't build stakeholder trust by managing reputational risk. At the same time, your obligations aren't limitless. It's not your job to respond apologetically to every stakeholder demand, critique, or hashtag campaign. Focus closely on your real-world impact. Never solicit a stakeholder's opinion if you have no intention of making changes in response. You can achieve more via cooperation than competition.

Don't neglect the basics. Ensuring that your company and its employees do not break the law remains a core operating requirement. Still, it's a mistake to view legal compliance as the simple application of black-and-white rules; inconsistency and fragmentation are genuine challenges. Keep in mind that laws tend to lag behind shifts in norms and cannot be divorced from wider questions of social and political risk. Your impact on human beings is emerging as the basis for much new sustainability regulation, especially in the EU.

Basing your values on respect for human rights can bring conceptual discipline and prevent overreach. In this globalized, pluralistic world, values are constantly contested and contentious. Observing human rights principles won't solve all challenges or guarantee that you'll avoid controversy—far from it. But these principles are grounded in a body of international law and in dynamic thinking about the role of business, the function of government, and respect for individual rights and values. Making a meaningful commitment to honor human rights—backed by concrete effort—is incomparably more robust than issuing bland statements about integrity or trying to placate a cacophony of stakeholder voices.

In a world of ESG box ticking, a sharp focus is key to success. You should take the time to identify your environmental and social impacts, understand how they affect your risks and opportunities, and assess how it all might evolve. Strategy is the art of choosing what not to do, which means you should identify a few *existential* issues on which you need to act. Don't follow the herd by putting everything into an undifferentiated bucket of "ESG stuff."

Do not inadvertently undermine the functioning of political systems. The cumulative impact of corporate political influence is bigger than internal, operational efforts. If you undermine accountability mechanisms that level the playing field for everyone, external societal problems may wind up in your lap. Mind the fast-emerging imperatives of oversight and disclosure, and assume responsibility for your direct and indirect political spending. Once you have done all you can to address your own impacts, you may be able to contribute your company's influence and expertise to support positive policies.

This isn't about telling an appealing story. Pressure to be more transparent and open is potent and won't go away. Curated impression management is ever less effective. Time has run out for glossy brochures that hype the wonderful things you're doing. Genuinely ambitious, honest disclosure is still rare enough to be refreshing. Admitting to imperfection is less dangerous than you've been told; it can even bring competitive advantage and help drive fresh norms across entire sectors.

Culture is a source of strategic advantage. As value becomes more intangible and organizational boundaries dissolve, corporate culture is transforming.

Being dynamic, culture can be measured and improved with rigorous research. Bear in mind that no one knows all the answers in this new environment. Curiosity, humility, and experimentation offer the best paths to success.

Leadership isn't about barking orders from the top. What we want and expect from leaders is changing radically. Governance for the 2020s means bringing in more voices to shape decisions—and building in checks and balances from above and below. Meeting inclusion imperatives isn't about ticking social identity boxes; your business will benefit from considering the full range of perspectives before important decisions are made.

If you don't wish to be regarded as a hypocrite, think holistically. Because a corporation has no consciousness of its own, it's easy to look phony and dishonest if you don't coordinate your efforts. You need alignment among compliance, HR, government affairs, risk, and sustainability functions. Here again, your impact on human beings will offer the firmest conceptual ground for decisions on when to speak and act.

Rules only get you so far. Stop wasting staff time on one-size-fits-all compliance programs aimed at pleasing regulators. Consider the realities of human behavior and group dynamics. You might need to reflect on whether your strategy and business model imposes unacceptable situational and commercial pressures that encourage employees to break the rules. Build the capacity for ethical decision-making and reflection throughout the organization, because most dilemmas are not black and white.

If you offer to listen—or choose to speak—you'll need to act. Speaking up is a transformational process that's becoming more salient. Employee voice is an asset; it can help you identify and address organizational blind spots. But while you should invite participation in shaping priorities, values, and culture, you needn't open every decision to a democratic vote. Secure psychological safety for everyone, not just those who agree with your stances. Consider promoting people who display critical thinking and respect for the values of others.

You cannot impose meaning. You must work to create it. Involve your employees in shaping your organization's purpose and culture, and get clear about its role in society, its values, and how it creates value. Proclaiming an inspirational purpose is no substitute for instilling a culture of respect and inclusion, a sense of agency, and a commitment to personal dignity.

You can reach higher ground. Today, being a good business doesn't call for exaggeration, spin, or overreach. It's not about setting rules, pitching an appealing story, or listing your achievements. The time-honored approaches have lost potency. They're losing their grip. You'll need to imagine and then establish firm foundations in order to aim high.

. . .

Thank you for joining me on this journey. I hope this book helps you find your way to higher ground.

NOTES

Introduction

1. Motley Fool, "Starbucks (SBUX) Q2 2023 Earnings Call Transcript," May 2, 2023, https://www.fool.com/earnings/call-transcripts/2023/05/02/starbucks-sbux-q2-2023 -earnings-call-transcript/.

2. Ananya Bhattacharya, "Starbucks' Union-Busting Tactics Are Facing the Heat," Quartz, March 2, 2023, https://qz.com/starbucks-union-busting-ruling-remote-work -complaint-1850177425.

3. Josh Eidelson, "Starbucks Faces New Front in Its Labor Disputes: White-Collar Workers," Bloomberg, March 1, 2023, https://www.bloomberg.com/news/articles/2023 -03-01/starbucks-sbux-corporate-staff-slam-return-to-office-mandate-anti-union-push.

4. Noam Scheiber, "Starbucks Violated Labor Law in Buffalo Union Drive, Judge Rules," *New York Times*, March 1, 2023, https://www.nytimes.com/2023/03/01 /business/economy/starbucks-union-buffalo-ruling.html.

5. Danielle Wiener-Bronner, "Starbucks Shareholders Want More Information about the Company's Anti-Union Efforts," CNN, March 30, 2023, https://www.cnn .com/2023/03/30/business/starbucks-shareholder-proposal-unions/index.html.

6. Danielle Wiener-Bronner, "Bernie Sanders Confronts Former Starbucks CEO Howard Schultz on Company's Labor Practices," CNN, March 29, 2023, https://www .cnn.com/2023/03/29/business/howard-schultz-testimony-starbucks/index.html.

7. Greg Jaffe, "Lexi Rizzo Fought to Unionize Her Starbucks. Now, She's Out of a Job," *Washington Post*, June 17, 2023, https://www.washingtonpost.com/business /interactive/2023/starbucks-union-fired-worker/.

8. Josh Eidelson, "College Students Are Urging Their Schools Dump Starbucks Coffee over Shutdowns of Unionized Cafes," Bloomberg, May 11, 2023, https://www.bloomberg .com/news/articles/2023-05-11/students-urge-cornell-and-uc-dump-starbucks-coffee -over-union-busting-claims; Josh Eidelson, "Cornell to Stop Serving Starbucks Coffee after Company Shut Down Unionized Cafes," Bloomberg, August 16, 2023, https:// www.bloomberg.com/news/articles/2023-08-16/cornell-will-stop-serving-starbucks -coffee-after-shutdown-of-unionized-cafes?srnd=premium&sref=5w5OmZwT.

9. Greg Rosalsky, "You May Have Heard of the 'Union Boom.' The Numbers Tell a Different Story," NPR, February 28, 2023, https://www.npr.org/sections/money /2023/02/28/1159663461/you-may-have-heard-of-the-union-boom-the-numbers-tell-a -different-story.

10. JUST Capital, "Starbucks Corporation," accessed June 4, 2023, https:// justcapital.com/companies/starbucks-corporation.

11. Interviews were conducted for this book between June 2021 and August 2023. When no citation is provided, quotes are taken directly from these interviews.

12. Tim Bontemps, "MJ Stands Firm on 'Republicans Buy Sneakers' Quip," ESPN .com, May 4, 2020, https://www.espn.com/nba/story/_/id/29130478/michael-jordan -stands-firm-republicans-buy-sneakers-too-quote-says-was-made-jest.

13. Jemima McEvoy, "Every CEO and Leader That Stepped Down Since Black Lives Matter Protests Began," *Forbes*, July 1, 2020, https://www.forbes.com/sites /jemimamcevoy/2020/07/01/every-ceo-and-leader-that-stepped-down-since-black-lives -matter-protests-began/.

14. Milton Friedman, "A Friedman Doctrine—the Social Responsibility of Business Is to Increase Its Profits," *New York Times*, September 13, 1970, https://www.nytimes.com/1970/09/13/archives/a-friedman-doctrine-the-social-responsibility-of-business-is-to.html.

15. During the course of this book, I will cite examples of positive and negative practice, sometimes from the same company. I cannot provide a neat, holistic example of a company that gets everything right; I believe the expectation that this is possible is part of the problem.

16. Center for Political Accountability, "Collision Course Report," August 20, 2021, https://www.politicalaccountability.net/collision-course-report/.

17. Here is just one example: Scott Van Voorhis, "People Trust Business, but Expect CEOs to Drive Social Change," *HBS Working Knowledge*, October 21, 2022, http://hbswk.hbs.edu/item/people-trust-business-but-expect-ceos-to-drive-social-change.

18. Blair Levin and Larry Downes, "Every Company Needs a Political Strategy Today," *MIT Sloan Management Review*, November 9, 2022, https://sloanreview.mit.edu/article/every-company-needs-a-political-strategy-today/.

19. Donald Sull, Stefano Turconi, and Charles Sull, "When It Comes to Culture, Does Your Company Walk the Talk?" *MIT Sloan Management Review*, July 21, 2020, https://sloanreview.mit.edu/article/when-it-comes-to-culture-does-your-company-walk-the-talk/.

20. Luigi Guiso, Paola Sapienza, and Luigi Zingales, "The Value of Corporate Culture," *Journal of Financial Economics* 117, no. 1 (July 1, 2015): 60–76.

21. Alastair Marsh, "World's Biggest Green Finance Club Condemns 'Political Attacks,'" Bloomberg, May 26, 2023, https://www.bloomberg.com/news/articles/2023-05-26/world-s-biggest-green-finance-club-condemns-political-attacks.

22. The Ethics Centre, "What Is Ethics?" accessed 19 June 2023, https://ethics.org.au/about/what-is-ethics/.

Chapter 1

1. "What It Takes to Be a CEO in the 2020s," *Economist*, February 6, 2020, https://www.economist.com/leaders/2020/02/06/what-it-takes-to-be-a-ceo-in-the-2020s.

2. Chip Cutter and Emily Glazer, "Disney's Clash with Florida Has CEOs on Alert," *Wall Street Journal*, May 1, 2022, https://www.wsj.com/articles/disneys-clash-with-florida-has-ceos-on-alert-11651440367.

3. Samuel J. Brannen, Christian S. Haig, and Katherine Schmidt, "The Age of Mass Protests," Center for Strategic and International Studies, March 2020, https://csis-website-prod.s3.amazonaws.com/s3fs-public/publication/200303_MassProtests_V2.pdf.

4. EncyclopediaBritannica.com, accessed June 7, 2023, https://www.britannica.com/topic/Scylla-and-Charybdis.

5. Robb Mandelbaum, "The Viral List That Turned a Yale Professor into an Enemy of the Russian State," Bloomberg, December 6, 2022, https://www.bloomberg.com/news/articles/2022-12-06/list-of-companies-doing-business-in-russia-made-by-yale-professor; Elisabeth Braw, "Russia's Clueless New Oligarchs," *Foreign Policy* (blog), September 29, 2022, https://foreignpolicy.com/2022/09/29/russias-clueless-new-oligarchs/.

6. Elisabeth Braw, "It's Just Not Easy Saying Goodbye to China and Russia," Politico, March 15, 2023, https://www.politico.eu/article/easy-goodbye-china-russia-west-war-ukraine/.

7. Primrose Riordan, "Political Pressure Weighs on HSBC over Hong Kong Activists," *Financial Times*, January 5, 2021, https://www.ft.com/content/75313efa-e44b-4f73-9cd0-41a045f62749.

8. Chloe Cornish and John Reed, "Myanmar Rights Groups Complain to OECD over Telenor Sale," *Financial Times*, July 27, 2021, https://www.ft.com/content/f7631bfb-25b5-48d8-9c15-39650c6b7f85.

9. Nicole Goodkind, "Forget Disney and Florida, Companies Won't Be Able to Stay Silent on Abortion," CNN, May 4, 2022, https://www.cnn.com/2022/05/04/economy/abortion-roe-wade-companies-disney/index.html.

10. James Mackintosh, "What I Learned about 'Woke Capital' and Milton Friedman at the University of Chicago," *Wall Street Journal*, June 9, 2023, https://www.wsj.com/articles/to-get-politics-out-of-business-get-business-out-of-politics-ce492e1c. This comment was used in a class lecture attended by Mackintosh, confirmed directly with Professor Zingales.

11. "Ten Years after Spain's Indignados Protests," *Economist*, accessed June 5, 2023, https://www.economist.com/europe/2021/05/06/ten-years-after-spains-indignados-protests.

12. Lily Kuo and Quartz, "Why Hong Kong's Protesters Have Their Hands Up," *Atlantic*, September 29, 2014, https://www.theatlantic.com/international/archive/2014/09/why-hong-kongs-protesters-have-their-hands-up/380903/.

13. Melissa Lemieux, "Chilean Government Blames K-Pop for Recent Protests," *Newsweek*, December 24, 2019, https://www.newsweek.com/chilean-government-blames-k-pop-recent-protests-1479151.

14. Esteban Ortiz-Ospina and Max Roser, "Trust," Our World in Data, July 22, 2016, https://ourworldindata.org/trust.

15. Robin Miller, "ESG Performance Tops List of Corporate Affairs Risk Priorities Globally for Organisations," GlobeScan, July 15, 2021, https://globescan.com/2021/07/15/report-oxford-globescan-global-corporate-affairs-survey-2021/.

16. David Gelles, "C.E.O. Activism Has Become the New Normal," *New York Times*, July 25, 2018, https://www.nytimes.com/2018/07/25/business/dealbook/ceo-activism-study.html.

17. "We Are Still In," accessed June 5, 2023, https://www.wearestillin.com/.

18. Jia Wertz, "Taking Risks Can Benefit Your Brand—Nike's Kaepernick Campaign Is a Perfect Example," *Forbes*, September 30, 2018, https://www.forbes.com/sites/jiawertz/2018/09/30/taking-risks-can-benefit-your-brand-nikes-kaepernick-campaign-is-a-perfect-example/; Rachel Sugar, "Chick-fil-A's Controversial Politics Haven't Stopped It from Becoming One of the Biggest Fast-Food Chains in America," Vox, December 20, 2018, https://www.vox.com/the-goods/2018/12/20/18146316/chick-fil-a-growth-controversy.

19. Aaron K. Chatterji and Michael W. Toffel, "The New CEO Activists," *Harvard Business Review*, January 1, 2018, https://hbr.org/2018/01/the-new-ceo-activists.

20. See Sarah Kessler, "A Third of Basecamp's Workers Resign after a Ban on Talking Politics," *New York Times*, April 30, 2021, https://www.nytimes.com/2021/04/30/technology/basecamp-politics-ban-resignations.html; Kim Lyons, "Basecamp Implodes as Employees Flee Company, Including Senior Staff," *Verge*, April 30, 2021, https://www.theverge.com/2021/4/30/22412714/basecamp-employees-memo-policy-hansson-fried-controversy; and Abigail Johnson Hess, "Companies Like Basecamp and Coinbase Have Tried to Ban Political Discussions at Work—Experts Say It's Not That Simple," CNBC, May 5, 2021, https://www.cnbc.com/2021/05/05/banning-political-discussions-at-work-isnt-that-simple-experts-say.html.

21. Robert Eccles and Eli Lehrer, "It's Time to Call a Truce in the Red State/Blue State Culture War," *Harvard Corporate Governance* (blog), May 29, 2023, https://corpgov.law.harvard.edu/2023/05/29/its-time-to-call-a-truce-in-the-red-state-blue-state-esg-culture-war/.

22. Daniel Arkin, "Why Disney Brought Back Bob Iger and Booted His Handpicked Replacement," *NBC News*, November 21, 2022, https://www.nbcnews.com/pop-culture/pop-culture-news/why-disney-replaced-ceo-brought-back-bob-iger-rcna58156.

23. "Home—Center for Political Accountability," accessed June 5, 2023, https://www.politicalaccountability.net/.

24. Amnesty International, "Trafigura: A Toxic Journey," April 11, 2016, https://www.amnesty.org/en/latest/news/2016/04/trafigura-a-toxic-journey/.

25. Robert Booth, "Trafigura: A Few Tweets and Freedom of Speech Is Restored," *Guardian*, October 13, 2009, https://www.theguardian.com/media/2009/oct/13/trafigura-tweets-freedowm-of-speech.

26. This turned out to be too optimistic. An Amnesty International 2016 investigation found that the vast majority of those affected reported ongoing health issues, and the UN estimated that almost a third of victims had received no compensation at all. Amnesty International, "Trafigura"; OHCHR, "Ten Years on, the Survivors of

Toxic Waste Dumping in Côte d'Ivoire Remain in the Dark," press release, August 17, 2016, https://www.ohchr.org/en/press-releases/2016/08/ten-years-survivors-illegal-toxic-waste-dumping-cote-divoire-remain-dark.

27. Daniel Victor and Matt Stevens, "United Airlines Passenger Is Dragged from an Overbooked Flight," *New York Times*, April 10, 2017, https://www.nytimes.com/2017/04/10/business/united-flight-passenger-dragged.html.

28. Michael Etter, Davide Ravasi, and Elanor Colleoni, "Social Media and the Formation of Organizational Reputation," *Academy of Management Review* 44, no. 1 (January 2019): 28–52, https://doi.org/10.5465/amr.2014.0280.

29. Emily Chasan, "New York Pushes JPMorgan, BofA, Visa to Reconsider Gun Sales," Bloomberg, April 4, 2018, https://www.bloomberg.com/news/articles/2018-04-04/new-york-pushes-jpmorgan-bofa-visa-to-reconsider-gun-sale-risk.

30. Amanda Albright and Danielle Moran, "BofA, Citi, JPMorgan See Texas Muni Business Halt after Gun Law," Bloomberg, October 1, 2021, https://www.bloomberg.com/news/articles/2021-10-01/bofa-citi-jpmorgan-see-texas-muni-business-halt-after-gun-law.

31. Alli Joseph, "Running for Their Lives: Native American Relay Tradition Revived to Protest Dakota Access Pipeline," Salon, September 12, 2016, https://www.salon.com/2016/09/12/running-for-their-lives-native-american-relay-tradition-revived-to-protest-dakota-access-pipeline/.

32. Democracy Now, "Standing Rock Special: Unlicensed #DAPL Guards Attacked Water Protectors with Dogs & Pepper Spray," YouTube, November 24, 2016, https://www.youtube.com/watch?v=cxcYNM9o6go.

33. Alleen Brown, "Medics Describe How Police Sprayed Standing Rock Demonstrators with Tear Gas and Water Cannons," Intercept, November 21, 2016, https://theintercept.com/2016/11/21/medics-describe-how-police-sprayed-standing-rock-demonstrators-with-tear-gas-and-water-cannons/.

34. "Investor Statement to Banks Financing the Dakota Access Pipeline," February 16, 2017, https://www.calpers.ca.gov/docs/investor-statement-to-banks-financing-dakota-access-pipeline.pdf.

35. Su T. Fitterman, "The Dakota Access Pipeline (DAPL)—Environmental & Energy Law Program," Harvard Law School, October 25, 2017, https://eelp.law.harvard.edu/2017/10/dakota-access-pipeline/; Carla Fredericks, Mark Meaney, Nick Pelosi, and Kathleen Finn, "Social Cost and Material Loss: The Dakota Access Pipeline" (SSRN scholarly paper, Rochester, NY, November 19, 2018), https://doi.org/10.2139/ssrn.3287216.

36. ING.com, "ING and the Dakota Access Pipeline," May 19, 2017, https://www.ing.com/Sustainability/ING-and-the-Dakota-Access-pipeline-1.htm.

37. Fitterman, "The Dakota Access Pipeline (DAPL)"; Clark Mindock, "Judge Orders Enbridge to Shut Down Portions of Wisconsin Pipeline within Three Years," Reuters, June 20, 2023, https://www.reuters.com/world/us/us-judge-orders-enbridge-shut-down-portions-wisconsin-pipeline-within-3-years-2023-06-17/.

38. Alison Taylor, "Employees Have Given Rise to Something Far More Powerful Than 'CEO Activism,'" Quartz, September 6, 2019, https://qz.com/work/1703005/ceo-activism-has-given-way-to-employee-activism.

39. Nitasha Tiku, "Three Years of Misery Inside Google, the Happiest Company in Tech," *Wired*, August 13, 2019, https://www.wired.com/story/inside-google-three-years-misery-happiest-company-tech/.

40. Casey Newton, "The Secret Lives of Facebook Moderators in America," *Verge*, February 25, 2019, https://www.theverge.com/2019/2/25/18229714/cognizant-facebook-content-moderator-interviews-trauma-working-conditions-arizona.

41. Annie Connell-Bryan, "'We're Just F---ing Illegal': Leaked Documents Show Uber Thwarted Police and Secretly Courted Politicians," Politico, July 10, 2022, https://www.politico.com/news/2022/07/10/uber-investigation-global-expansion-00044914.

42. Mia Sato and Alex Heath, "Hundreds of Employees Say No to Being Part of Elon Musk's 'Extremely Hardcore' Twitter," *Verge*, November 17, 2022, https://www.theverge.com/2022/11/17/23465274/hundreds-of-twitter-employees-resign-from-elon-musk-hardcore-deadline.

43. Irina Ivanova, "Wayfair Employees Walk Out after Company's Sales to Migrant Children Holding Facility," *CBS News*, June 26, 2019, https://www.cbsnews.com/news/wayfair-employees-plan-walkout-after-companys-sales-to-detention-centers/.

44. Sara Fischer and Courtenay Brown, "Employees Revolt over Immigration," Axios, August 16, 2019, https://www.axios.com/2019/08/16/employees-revolt-corporate-ties-trump-immigration; Karen Sloan, "Harvard Law Students Protest Paul Weiss over Exxon Ties," Law.com, January 16, 2020, https://www.law.com/2020/01/16/harvard-law-students-protest-paul-weiss-over-exxon-ties/.

45. Sui-Lee Wee and Raymond Zhong, "China Pressures Business over Hong Kong. Workers Get Caught in the Middle," *New York Times*, August 18, 2019, https://www.nytimes.com/2019/08/18/business/economy/hong-kong-china-business-workers.html.

46. Luz Corona, "Former PR Exec Makes the Earth Her Client as Eco-Activist," *Adweek*, January 11, 2022, https://www.adweek.com/inside-the-brand/former-pr-exec-makes-the-earth-her-client-as-eco-activist/.

47. Madison Marriage, "KPMG's UK Boss Steps Aside as Firm Probes Comments That Offended Staff," *Financial Times*, February 10, 2021, https://www.ft.com/content/3c3c07d1-ffb9-4288-aea4-41acf3f3bbff.

48. Farah Ghouri, "KPMG Encourages Whistleblowing to Avoid Media Leaks after CEO's Exit," CityAM, August 26, 2021, https://www.cityam.com/kpmg-encourages-whistleblowing-to-avoid-media-leaks-after-ceos-exit/.

49. Herbert Smith Freehills, "The New World of Work: 2019 Report Warned of an Unprecedented Rise in Workplace Activism," November 26, 2019, https://www.herbertsmithfreehills.com/latest-thinking/the-new-world-of-work-report-warns-of-an-unprecedented-rise-in-workplace-activism-v2.

50. Allison Schrager, "America's MBAs Are the Latest Skeptics of Capitalism," Bloomberg, June 28, 2022, https://www.bloomberg.com/opinion/articles/2022-06-28/america-s-mbas-are-the-latest-skeptics-of-capitalism.

51. Anya Meyerowitz, "The Real Impact of NDA Abuse: 'I Struggled with Reading My Emails or Answering the Door. Being Silenced Is Choking,'" *Glamour UK*, January 14, 2022, https://www.glamourmagazine.co.uk/article/non-disclosure-agreement-abuse.

52. Michael Barbaro, "The Rise of Workplace Surveillance," *The Daily*, August 24, 2022, https://www.nytimes.com/2022/08/24/podcasts/the-daily/workplace-surveillance-productivity-tracking.html.

53. Deloitte, "A Call for Accountability and Action: The Deloitte Global 2021 Millennial and Gen Z Survey," 2021, https://www.deloitte.com/content/dam/assets-shared/legacy/docs/insights/2022/2021-deloitte-global-millennial-survey-report.pdf.

54. Zapier editorial team, "Misunderstood Generations: What Millennials and Gen Z Actually Think about Work," *Zapier* (blog), January 27, 2020, https://zapier.com/blog/digital-natives-report/.

55. Kim Parker, Nikki Graf, and Ruth Igielnik, "Generation Z Looks a Lot Like Millennials on Key Social and Political Issues," *Pew Research Center's Social & Demographic Trends Project* (blog), January 17, 2019, https://www.pewresearch.org/social-trends/2019/01/17/generation-z-looks-a-lot-like-millennials-on-key-social-and-political-issues/.

56. The Institute of Politics at Harvard University, "Institute of Politics Spring 2018 Youth Poll," accessed June 5, 2023, https://iop.harvard.edu/spring-2018-poll.

57. Jena McGregor, "Employers Are Adding High-Tech Solutions to Solve a Low-Tech Problem: Getting More Sleep," *Washington Post*, March 9, 2020, https://www.washingtonpost.com/business/2020/02/14/sleep-wellness-employer-oura/.

58. Deloitte, "The Deloitte Global 2023 Gen Z and Millennial Survey," accessed June 6, 2023, https://www.deloitte.com/global/en/issues/work/content/genzmillennialsurvey.html.

59. National Institute of Mental Health (NIMH), "Mental Illness," March 2023, https://www.nimh.nih.gov/health/statistics/mental-illness.

60. Rachel Feintzeig, "Stressed Out at the Office? Therapy Can Come to You," *Wall Street Journal*, January 31, 2020, https://www.wsj.com/articles/the-latest-perk-for-stressed-out-office-workers-therapy-comes-to-you-11580486984.

61. Sumreen Ahmad, "Bring Your Whole Self to Work," ATD, June 15, 2018, https://www.td.org/magazines/ctdo-magazine/bring-your-whole-self-to-work.

62. Frank Dobbin and Alexandra Kalev, "Why Diversity Programs Fail," *Harvard Business Review*, July 1, 2016, https://hbr.org/2016/07/why-diversity-programs-fail.

63. Matthew Boyle, "Walmart's Black Senior Managers Don't Recommend Working There," Bloomberg, July 8, 2021, https://www.bloomberg.com/news/articles/2021-07-08/what-s-it-like-to-work-at-walmart-wmt-black-senior-managers-don-t-recommend.

64. Attracta Mooney and Patrick Temple-West, "Investors Increase Pressure on Companies over Racial Issues," *Financial Times*, July 20, 2021, https://www.ft.com/content/d0987e79-624a-4f95-bc0d-89f74efe8380.

65. Rebecca Knight, "Companies Can't Do Layoffs Right Because They're Trying to Act Like 'Cool Parents,'" *Business Insider*, April 13, 2023, https://www.businessinsider.in/careers/news/companies-cant-do-layoffs-right-because-theyre-trying-to-act-like-cool-parents/articleshow/99473821.cms.

Chapter 2

1. Yvon Chouinard, "Yvon Chouinard Donates Patagonia to Fight Climate Crisis," Patagonia, accessed June 6, 2023, https://www.patagonia.com/ownership/.

2. Scott Nover, "Patagonia's $3 Billion Corporate Gift Is Also a Convenient Way to Avoid Taxes," Quartz, September 16, 2022, https://qz.com/patagonia-s-3-billion-corporate-gift-is-also-a-conveni-1849543678; Norman Vanamee, "The World Reacts to Patagonia Founder's Unprecedented Gift," *Town & Country*, September 16, 2022, https://www.townandcountrymag.com/society/money-and-power/a41234265/yvon-chouinard-patagonia-philanthropy-news/.

3. Adam Waytz, Nicholas Epley, and John T. Cacioppo, "Social Cognition Unbound: Insights into Anthropomorphism and Dehumanization," *Current Directions in Psychological Science* 19, no. 1 (February 2010): 58–62, https://doi.org/10.1177/0963721409359302.

4. Leonardo Davoudi, Christopher McKenna, and Rowena Olegario, "The Historical Role of the Corporation in Society," The British Academy, October 31, 2018, https://www.thebritishacademy.ac.uk/publishing/journal-british-academy/6s1/historical-role-of-corporation-in-society/.

5. Corporate governance scholars have argued that the lack of board approval for this statement was a sign that CEOs were not serious. Lucian Bebchuk and Roberto Tallarita, "The Illusory Promise of Stakeholder Governance," *The Harvard Law School Forum on Corporate Governance* (blog), March 2, 2020, https://corpgov.law.harvard.edu/2020/03/02/the-illusory-promise-of-stakeholder-governance/.

6. ProMarket Writers, "eBook: Milton Friedman 50 Years Later, a Reevaluation," *ProMarket* (blog), November 18, 2020, https://www.promarket.org/2020/11/17/ebook-milton-friedman-50-years-later/.

7. Charles J. Fombrun, Naomi A. Gardburg, and Michael L. Barnett, "Opportunity Platforms and Safety Nets: Corporate Citizenship and Reputational Risk," *Business and Society Review* 105, no. 1 (n.d.): 85–106; https://cmapspublic2.ihmc.us/rid=1NBX3QCQT-20Z9NTZ-25ZZ/Fombrun%20et%20al%202002%20on%20reputational%20risk.pdf.

8. Larry Fink, "A Sense of Purpose," *The Harvard Law School Forum on Corporate Governance* (blog), January 17, 2018, https://corpgov.law.harvard.edu/2018/01/17/a-sense-of-purpose/.

9. In truth, the jury is still debating the potential financial rewards of ESG strategies. Countless academic studies on the business case for ESG have been published in the past decade, and there is some evidence that a well-executed strategy can bring

financial success in the long run. But because correlation is not causation, and ESG metrics are so inconsistent and immature, concrete evidence is lacking. With advocates and skeptics free to cherry-pick appealing arguments and statistics—and admissions of uncertainty rare—confusion has multiplied.

10. Michael E. Porter and Mark R. Kramer, "Strategy and Society: The Link between Competitive Advantage and Corporate Social Responsibility," *Harvard Business Review*, December 1, 2006, https://hbr.org/2006/12/strategy-and-society-the-link-between -competitive-advantage-and-corporate-social-responsibility.

11. Kelsey Miller, "The Triple Bottom Line: What It Is & Why It's Important," *Business Insights* (blog), December 8, 2020, https://online.hbs.edu/blog/post/what-is -the-triple-bottom-line.

12. Andrew Crane et al., "Contesting the Value of 'Creating Shared Value,'" *California Management Review* 56, no. 2 (February 2014): 130–153, https://doi.org/10.1525/cmr .2014.56.2.130.

13. Saijel Kishan, Alastair Marsh, and Frances Schwartzkopff Bloomberg, "How Did ESG Funds Wind Up Investing in Putin's Russia?" *Los Angeles Times*, March 7, 2022, https://www.latimes.com/business/story/2022-03-06/esg-funds-ukraine-russia.

14. Mike Pence, "Republicans Can Stop ESG Political Bias," *Wall Street Journal*, May 26, 2022, https://www.wsj.com/articles/only-republicans-can-stop-the-esg -madness-woke-musk-consumer-demand-free-speech-corporate-america-11653574189.

15. James D. Wolfensohn and Andrew Kircher, *Voice for the World's Poor: Selected Speeches and Writings of World Bank President James D. Wolfensohn, 1995–2005* (Washington, DC: World Bank, 2005).

16. For examples, see "FCPA Resource Guide," March 29, 2023, https://www.justice .gov/criminal-fraud/fcpa-resource-guide; "The Bribery Act 2010—Guidance," Ministry of Justice, Gov.UK, March 2011, https://www.justice.gov.uk/downloads/legislation/bribery -act-2010-guidance.pdf.

17. Yousuf Aftab and Jonathan Drimmer, "Expert ESG Attorneys: How Corporate Sustainability Creates Legal Risk—CorpGov," CorpGov, accessed June 6, 2023, https:// corpgov.com/lessons-from-cobalt-in-the-congo-how-corporate-sustainability-creates -legal-risk/.

18. Ideas of impact, based on the UN Guiding Principles on Business and Human Rights, form the basis of emerging EU regulations on ESG, so this is far from a niche perspective.

19. UN Guiding Principles on Business and Human Rights, 2011, https://www.ohchr.org/sites/default/files/documents/publications/guidingprinciples businesshr_en.pdf.

20. Raghuram Rajan, "'50 Years Later, It's Time to Reassess': Raghuram Rajan on Milton Friedman and Maximizing Shareholder Value," *ProMarket* (blog), September 18, 2020, https://www.promarket.org/2020/09/18/50-years-later-its-time-to-reassess -raghuram-rajan-on-milton-friedman-and-maximizing-shareholder-value/.

21. BlackRock, "Larry Fink's Annual 2022 Letter to CEOs," accessed June 6, 2023, https://www.blackrock.com/corporate/investor-relations/larry-fink-ceo-letter.

22. Talia Varley, "Is Your Company Prepared for the Effect of Wildfires?" hbr.org, June 13, 2023, https://hbr.org/2023/06/is-your-company-prepared -for-the-effects-of-wildfires.

23. "Why Disclose as a Company," CDP, accessed June 6, 2023, https://www.cdp .net/en/companies-discloser.

24. Kenneth P. Pucker, "Overselling Sustainability Reporting," *Harvard Business Review*, May 1, 2021, https://hbr.org/2021/05/overselling-sustainability-reporting.

25. Brayden King and Mary-Hunter McDonnell, "Good Firms, Good Targets: The Relationship between Corporate Social Responsibility, Reputation, and Activist Targeting," *SSRN Electronic Journal*, 2012, https://doi.org/10.2139/ssrn.2079227.

26. Investopedia, "Principal-Agent Problem Causes, Solutions, and Examples Explained," February 15, 2023, https://www.investopedia.com/terms/p/principal-agent -problem.asp.

27. Naomi Nix and Elizabeth Dwoskin, "Search Warrants for Abortion Data Leave Tech Companies Few Options," *Washington Post*, August 12, 2022, https://www .washingtonpost.com/technology/2022/08/12/nebraska-abortion-case-facebook/.

28. Steve Hatfield, Jen Fisher, and Paul H. Silverglate, "The C-Suite's Role in Well-Being," *Deloitte Insights*, June 22, 2022, https://www2.deloitte.com/xe/en/insights /topics/leadership/employee-wellness-in-the-corporate-workplace.html.

29. Todd Haugh, "The Criminalization of Compliance," *Notre Dame Law Review* 92, no. 3 (January 1, 2017): 1215, https://scholarship.law.nd.edu/ndlr/vol92/iss3/5.

30. Cass R. Sunstein, "Sludge Audits," *Behavioural Public Policy* 6, no. 4 (October 2022): 654–673, https://doi.org/10.1017/bpp.2019.32.

31. Paul Polman and Adi Ignatius, "Former Unilever CEO Paul Polman Says Aiming for Sustainability Isn't Good Enough—the Goal Is Much Higher," hbr.org, November 19, 2021, https://hbr.org/2021/11/former-unilever-ceo-paul-polman -says-aiming-for-sustainability-isnt-good-enough-the-goal-is-much-higher.

32. Jeff Harrison, review of *On Bullshit*, by Harry G. Frankfurt, *Literature and Theology* 19, no. 4 (November 1, 2005): 412–414, https://doi.org/10.1093/litthe/fri049.

Chapter 3

1. Esme Stallard, "COP27: Activists 'Baffled' That Coca-Cola Will Be Sponsor," *BBC News*, October 5, 2022, https://www.bbc.com/news/science-environment -63096760.

2. "Coca-Cola Reveals How Much Plastic It Uses," *BBC News*, March 14, 2019, https://www.bbc.com/news/newsbeat-47569233.

3. Judith Evans, "Coca-Cola and Rivals Fail to Meet Plastic Pledges," *Financial Times*, September 16, 2020, https://www.ft.com/content/bb189a2a-57ca-44ce-82ab -1d015a20ca1c; Ellen MacArthur Foundation, "The Coca-Cola Company," accessed June 8, 2023, https://ellenmacarthurfoundation.org/the-coca-cola-company; World Wildlife Fund, "The Coca-Cola Company," accessed June 8, 2023, https://www.worldwildlife.org /business/the-coca-cola-company.

4. Stallard, "COP27."

5. Alice Delemare Tangpuori et al., "The Corporate Playbook of False Solutions to the Plastic Crisis," Talking Trash, September 2020, https://talking-trash.com/wp-content /uploads/2021/01/TalkingTrash_FullVersion.pdf.

6. Rachel Wolcott, "'Reputation Launderers,' Disinformation Campaigns Hinder Sanctions and Financial Crime Compliance Efforts," Thomson Reuters Institute, June 9, 2022, https://www.thomsonreuters.com/en-us/posts/news-and-media/reputation-launderers -evade-sanctions/.

7. Andrew C. Wicks, Shawn L. Berman, and Thomas M. Jones, "The Structure of Optimal Trust: Moral and Strategic Implications," *Academy of Management Review* 24, no. 1 (1999): 99–116, https://doi.org/10.2307/259039.

8. Sinziana Dorobantu, Witold J. Henisz, and Lite Nartey, "Not All Sparks Light a Fire: Stakeholder and Shareholder Reactions to Critical Events in Contested Markets," *Administrative Science Quarterly* 62, no. 3 (September 2017): 561–597, https://doi.org /10.1177/0001839216687743.

9. European Commission, "Corporate Sustainability Reporting," accessed August 20, 2023, https://finance.ec.europa.eu/capital-markets-union-and-financial-markets/company -reporting-and-auditing/company-reporting/corporate-sustainability-reporting_en; UN Guiding Principles on Business and Human Rights, 2011, https://shiftproject .org/wp-content/uploads/2020/06/GuidingPrinciplesBusinessHR_EN-7.pdf.

10. R. Edward Freeman, *Strategic Management: A Stakeholder Approach* (Cambridge, UK: Cambridge University Press, 2010), https://doi.org/10.1017/CBO9781139192675.

11. Business Roundtable, "Business Roundtable Redefines the Purpose of a Corporation to Promote 'An Economy That Serves All Americans,'" August 19, 2019, https://www.businessroundtable.org/business-roundtable-redefines-the-purpose-of-a -corporation-to-promote-an-economy-that-serves-all-americans.

12. Judy Samuelson, "Why I Don't Love the Term Stakeholder," Arthur W. Page Society, April 21, 2022, https://page.org/blog/why-i-don-t-love-the-term-stakeholder.

13. Muel Kaptein, "The Limits of the Ethical Responsibilities of Corporations: In Search of Boundary Principles," June 14, 2023, https://www.researchgate.net/publication/364329660_The_Limits_of_the_Ethical_Responsibilities_of_Companies_In_Search_of_Boundary_Principles.

14. Business Roundtable, "Business Roundtable Redefines the Purpose of a Corporation to Promote 'An Economy That Serves All Americans.'"

15. Peter Gassmann and Will Jackson-Moore, "The CEO's ESG Dilemma," *The Harvard Law School Forum on Corporate Governance* (blog), January 23, 2023, https://corpgov.law.harvard.edu/2023/01/23/the-ceos-esg-dilemma/.

16. Investor Alliance for Human Rights, "The Investor Case for Mandatory Human Rights Due Diligence," n.d., https://investorsforhumanrights.org/sites/default/files/attachments/2020-04/The%20Investor%20Case%20for%20mHRDD%20-%20FINAL_0.pdf; OHCHR, "OHCHR Response to Request from BankTrack for Advice Regarding the Application of the UNGPs on Business and Human Rights in the Context of the Banking Sector," June 12, 2017, https://www.ohchr.org/sites/default/files/Documents/Issues/Business/InterpretationGuidingPrinciples.pdf.

17. United Nations, "Free Prior and Informed Consent—an Indigenous Peoples' Right and a Good Practice for Local Communities—FAO," October 14, 2016, https://www.un.org/development/desa/indigenouspeoples/publications/2016/10/free-prior-and-informed-consent-an-indigenous-peoples-right-and-a-good-practice-for-local-communities-fao/.

18. Antofagasta PLC, "Social Management: Our Community Engagement and Social Investment Practices," December 2021, https://www.antofagasta.co.uk/media/4212/reporte_social_eng.pdf.

19. Stavros Gadinis and Amelia Miazad, "A Test of Stakeholder Governance" (SSRN scholarly paper, Rochester, NY, June 15, 2021), https://doi.org/10.2139/ssrn.3869176.

20. Estefania Amer and Jean-Philippe Bonardi, "Firms, Activist Attacks, and the Forward-Looking Management of Reputational Risks," *Strategic Organization* (September 6, 2022), https://doi.org/10.1177/14761270221124941.

21. Sara Enright and Alison Taylor, "The Future of Stakeholder Engagement," BSR, October 2016, https://www.bsr.org/reports/BSR_Future_of_Stakeholder_Engagement_Report.pdf.

22. Dunstan Allison-Hope, "What Does the Global Network Initiative Tell Us about the Value of Multi-Stakeholder Initiatives?" *BSR* (blog), July 9, 2010, https://www.bsr.org/en/blog/what-does-the-global-network-initiative-tell-us-about-the-value-of-multi-st.

23. World Economic Forum, "First Movers Coalition," accessed June 8, 2023, https://www.weforum.org/first-movers-coalition/.

24. Bella Webb, "Puma Opens Up Supply Chain, Sustainability Efforts to Gen Z Scrutiny," Vogue Business, April 6, 2023, https://www.voguebusiness.com/sustainability/puma-opens-up-supply-chain-sustainability-efforts-to-gen-z-scrutiny.

25. Meta, "Product Policy Forum Minutes," November 15, 2018, https://about.fb.com/news/2018/11/content-standards-forum-minutes/.

26. Dunstan Allison-Hope, Lindsey Andersen, and Joanna Lovatt, "A Human Rights-Based Approach to Content Governance," BSR, March 2021, https://www.bsr.org/reports/A_Human_Rights-Based_Approach_to_Content_Governance.pdf.

27. Rio Tinto and Georgetown University conducted a Stakeholder Engagement Academy from 2012 until around 2016; the company's well-documented scandal in Australia arose in 2020. Alison Taylor and Sara Enright, "Is It Time to Overhaul Stakeholder Engagement?" *BSR* (blog), October 4, 2016, https://www.bsr.org/en/blog/is-it-time-to-overhaul-stakeholder-engagement.

28. Elisa Farri, Paolo Cervini, and Gabriele Rosani, "The 8 Responsibilities of Chief Sustainability Officers," hbr.org, March 2, 2023, https://hbr.org/2023/03/the-8-responsibilities-of-chief-sustainability-officers.

29. Daniel Korschun, "Boundary-Spanning Employees and Relationships with External Stakeholders: A Social Identity Approach," *Academy of Management Review* 40, no. 4 (October 2015): 611–629, https://doi.org/10.5465/amr.2012.0398.

30. Employee ownership is one of the most effective and meaningful commitments to stakeholder capitalism you can make, see here for more detail: Hans Taparia, "How to Make Stakeholder Capitalism Work," *Stanford Social Innovation Review*, summer 2021, https://ssir.org/articles/entry/how_to_make_stakeholder_capitalism_work.

31. Dieter Holger, "Vodafone and Nestle Created Panels to Avoid 'Greenwashing' Allegations," *Wall Street Journal*, May 23, 2023, https://www.wsj.com/articles/vodafone-and-nestle-created-panels-to-avoid-greenwashing-allegations-63fff965.

Chapter 4

1. Owen Walker, "The Long and Short of the Quarterly Reports Controversy," *Financial Times*, July 2, 2018, https://www.ft.com/content/e61046bc-7a2e-11e8-8e67-1e1a0846c475.

2. Richa Naidu and Ross Kerber, "Unilever under Pressure to Show Sustainability Focus Is Good for Business," Reuters, February 9, 2022, https://www.reuters.com/business/retail-consumer/unilever-under-pressure-show-sustainability-focus-is-good-business-2022-02-09/.

3. Unilever, "Unilever's Purpose-Led Brands Outperform," June 11, 2019, https://www.unilever.com/news/press-and-media/press-releases/2019/unilevers-purpose-led-brands-outperform/.

4. Judith Evans and Eva Szalay, "Activist Investor Nelson Peltz to Join Board of Unilever," *Financial Times*, May 31, 2022, https://www.ft.com/content/f7e72c63-9531-4d2b-9206-6e723dd1b3f0.

5. Cassie Werber, "Corporate Purpose Took a Step Backward This Week," Quartz, August 24, 2022, https://qz.com/ben-and-jerrys-israel-palestinian-territories-unilever-1849450069.

6. Margaret Sutherlin, "Corporate Giants Promised to Clean Up Their Plastic Mess—They Haven't," Bloomberg, August 19, 2022, https://www.bloomberg.com/news/newsletters/2022-08-19/big-take-toxic-trash-spurs-blame-game-in-west-africa; Joe Brock and John Geddie, "Unilever's Plastic Playbook," Reuters, June 22, 2022, https://www.reuters.com/investigates/special-report/global-plastic-unilever/.

7. Maggie Astor, "A Wealthy 'Anti-Woke' Activist Joins the 2024 Presidential Field," *New York Times*, February 22, 2023, https://www.nytimes.com/2023/02/21/us/politics/vivek-ramaswamy-presidential-candidate-2024.html.

8. Alex Edmans, "How Business Can and Should Solve Social Problems," *Business Fights Poverty* (blog), March 4, 2020, https://businessfightspoverty.org/grow-the-pie-how-great-companies-deliver-both-purpose-and-profit/.

9. Ernst & Young, "Enough: A Review of Corporate Sustainability, in a World Running Out of Time," 2022, https://assets.ey.com/content/dam/ey-sites/ey-com/en_au/pdfs/ey-au-enough-report-june_2022.pdf.

10. CFI Team, "Externality," Corporate Finance Institute, May 30, 2023, https://corporatefinanceinstitute.com/resources/economics/externality/.

11. Alison Taylor, "We Shouldn't Always Need a 'Business Case' to Do the Right Thing," hbr.org, September 19, 2017, https://hbr.org/2017/09/we-shouldnt-always-need-a-business-case-to-do-the-right-thing.

12. V. F. Ridgway, "Dysfunctional Consequences of Performance Measurements," *Administrative Science Quarterly* 1, no. 2 (September 1956): 240, https://doi.org/10.2307/2390989.

13. Alison Taylor, "The Corporate Responsibility Facade Is Finally Starting to Crumble," Quartz, March 4, 2020, https://qz.com/work/1812245/the-corporate-responsibility-facade-is-finally-starting-to-crumble.

14. In 2022, a study by the Governance and Accountability Institute found that 96% of the S&P 500 did. G&A Institute. "2022 Sustainability Reporting in Focus," 2022,

https://www.ga-institute.com/research/ga-research-directory/sustainability-reporting
-trends/2022-sustainability-reporting-in-focus.html.

15. Tensie Whelan, "ESG Reports Aren't a Replacement for Real Sustainability," hbr.org, July 27, 2022, https://hbr.org/2022/07/esg-reports-arent-a
-replacement-for-real-sustainability.

16. Martha Carter, Matt Filosa, and Rhea Brennan, "What's ESG Got to Do with It?" *The Harvard Law School Forum on Corporate Governance* (blog), October 13, 2022, https://corpgov.law.harvard.edu/2022/10/13/whats-esg-got-to-do-with-it/.

17. Michael Moss, "The Extraordinary Science of Addictive Junk Food," *New York Times*, February 20, 2013, https://www.nytimes.com/2013/02/24/magazine/the
-extraordinary-science-of-junk-food.html.

18. Sarah George, "PMI CSO: ESG Reporting Risks Becoming 'Moot' If Corporates Keep Hiding Their 'Elephants in the Room,'" Edie, August 25, 2022, https://www.edie
.net/pmi-cso-esg-reporting-risks-becoming-moot-if-corporates-keep-hiding-their
-elephants-in-the-room/.

19. Martin Neubert and Christer Tryggestad, "Ørsted's Renewable-Energy Transformation," McKinsey, July 10, 2020, https://www.mckinsey.com/capabilities
/sustainability/our-insights/orsteds-renewable-energy-transformation; Georgia Makridou, "Lessons from the World's Most Sustainable Energy Companies," *LSE Business Review* (blog), June 9, 2022, https://blogs.lse.ac.uk/businessreview/2022/06/09/lessons-from
-the-worlds-most-sustainable-energy-companies/.

20. SASB, "SASB," accessed June 9, 2023, https://sasb.org/.

21. Rodney Irwin, "Sustainability and Enterprise Risk Management: The First Step towards Integration," World Business Council for Sustainable Development, January 2017, https://www.wbcsd.org/contentwbc/download/2548/31131/1.

22. Alison Taylor, "How Aligning Sustainability and Risk Can Overcome Organizational Blind Spots," *BSR* (blog), August 19, 2019, https://www.bsr.org/en/blog
/how-aligning-sustainability-and-risk-can-overcome-organizational-blind-spot.

23. Alison Taylor, "Aligning Sustainability and Risk Management," *Risk Management Magazine*, November 1, 2019, http://www.rmmagazine.com/articles
/article/2019/11/01/-Aligning-Sustainability-and-Risk-Management-.

24. Estefania Amer and Jean-Philippe Bonardi, "Firms, Activist Attacks, and the Forward-Looking Management of Reputational Risks," *Strategic Organization* (September 6, 2022), https://doi.org/10.1177/14761270221124941.

25. This is again a story of siloed thinking in many companies.

26. Kim Schumacher, "Environmental, Social, and Governance (ESG) Factors and Green Productivity: The Impacts of Greenwashing and Competence Greenwashing on Sustainable Finance and ESG Investing," *APO* (blog), 2022, https://www.apo-tokyo.org
/publications/environmental-social-and-governance-esg-factors-and-green-productivity
-the-impacts-of-greenwashing-and-competence-greenwashing-on-sustainable-finance
-and-esg-investing/.

27. "Engine No. 1 Announces Support for General Motors Co.'s Transformative Electric Vehicle Plan in Advance of Automaker's," Bloomberg, October 4, 2021, https://
www.bloomberg.com/press-releases/2021-10-04/engine-no-1-announces-support-for
-general-motors-co-s-transformative-electric-vehicle-plan-in-advance-of-automaker-s.

28. Emily Glazer and Theo Francis, "CEO Pay Increasingly Tied to Diversity Goals," *Wall Street Journal*, June 2, 2021, https://www.wsj.com/articles/ceos-pledged-to-increase
-diversity-now-boards-are-holding-them-to-it-11622626380.

29. Susan Berfield, "How McDonald's Made Enemies of Black Franchisees," Bloomberg, December 17, 2021, https://www.bloomberg.com/news/features/2021-12-17
/black-mcdonald-s-franchise-owners-face-off-with-fast-food-restaurant-over-racism.

30. Cisco, "Cisco Social Justice," accessed June 19, 2023, https://www.cisco.com/c
/en/us/about/social-justice.html.

31. Ross Kerber, "Climate Pay Links for CEOs Do Little to Cut Emissions, Study Finds," Reuters, September 29, 2022, https://www.reuters.com/business/sustainable
-business/climate-pay-links-ceos-do-little-cut-emissions-study-finds-2022-09-29/.

32. Douglas MacMillan and Julia Ingram, "Despite Spills and Air Pollution, Fossil Fuel Companies Award CEOs for Environmental Records," *Washington Post*, October 10, 2021, https://www.washingtonpost.com/business/interactive/2021/fossil-fuel-climate-bonus/.

33. Robert Eccles and Alison Taylor, "The Evolving Role of Chief Sustainability Officers," *Harvard Business Review*, July–August 2023, https://hbr.org/2023/07/the-evolving-role-of-chief-sustainability-officers.

Chapter 5

1. Siri Schubert and T. Christian Miller, "At Siemens, Bribery Was Just a Line Item," *New York Times*, December 20, 2008, https://www.nytimes.com/2008/12/21/business/worldbusiness/21siemens.html.

2. "How New Regulations Are a Game-Changer in Just and Sustainable Business," BSR, accessed June 13, 2023, https://www.bsr.org/en/sustainability-insights/insights-plus/how-new-regulations-are-a-game-changer-in-just-and-sustainable-business.

3. "Second Consolidated Amended Class Action Complaint for Violations of the Federal Securities Laws," United States District Court Southern District of Texas Houston Division, March 15, 2017, https://static.blbglaw.com/docs/Cobalt%20%5B200%5D%20031517%20Second%20Am.%20Class%20Action%20Complaint.pdf.

4. Global Witness, "Goldman Sachs Backs Angolan Oil Deal Despite Corruption Risks," May 20, 2010, https:///en/archive/goldman-sachs-backs-angolan-oil-deal-despite-corruption-risks/.

5. Tom Burgis and Cynthia O'Murchu, "Spotlight Falls on Cobalt's Angola Partner," *Financial Times*, April 15, 2012, https://www.ft.com/content/1225e3de-854d-11e1-a394-00144feab49a.

6. Tom Burgis and Cynthia O'Murchu, "Angola Officials Held Hidden Oil Stakes," *Financial Times*, April 15, 2012, https://www.ft.com/content/effd6a98-854c-11e1-a394-00144feab49a.

7. Tom Burgis, "Cobalt Cuts Ties with Two Angola Oil Partners," *Financial Times*, August 28, 2014, https://www.ft.com/content/c6c7028a-2e94-11e4-bffa-00144feabdc0; Tom Burgis, "Cobalt's $1.8bn Angola Buyer Pulls Out," *Financial Times*, August 2, 2016, https://www.ft.com/content/66b512ae-58ce-11e6-9f70-badea1b336d4.

8. Kerry A. Dolan, "How Isabel dos Santos, Once Africa's Richest Woman, Went Broke," *Forbes*, January 22, 2021, https://www.forbes.com/sites/kerryadolan/2021/01/22/the-unmaking-of-a-billionaire-how-africas-richest-woman-went-broke/.

9. Stephen Eisenhammer, "Angola's Ruling MPLA Wins Election with 61 Percent of Vote: Electoral Commission," Reuters, September 6, 2017, https://www.reuters.com/article/us-angola-election-idUSKCN1BH2LR.

10. "Angola Court Orders Seizure of Isabel dos Santos' Assets," December 31, 2019, https://www.bbc.com/news/world-africa-50956370; *BBC News*, "Isabel dos Santos: EuroBic Severs Ties with Angola Billionaire," January 21, 2020, https://www.bbc.com/news/world-africa-51192729.

11. Estelle Maussion, "Angola: Is Lourenço Using His Anti-Corruption Fight to Settle Scores?" The Africa Report.com, May 12, 2021, https://www.theafricareport.com/87503/angola-is-lourenco-using-anti-corruption-fight-to-settle-scores/.

12. Maussion, "Angola."

13. Ben Hallman et al., "Western Advisers Helped an Autocrat's Daughter Amass and Shield a Fortune," International Consortium of Investigative Journalists, January 19, 2020, https://www.icij.org/investigations/luanda-leaks/western-advisers-helped-an-autocrats-daughter-amass-and-shield-a-fortune/.

14. Will Fitzgibbon, "Banking Documents Reveal Consulting Giants' Cash Windfall under Angolan Billionaire Isabel dos Santos," International Consortium of Investigative Journalists, February 15, 2021, https://www.icij.org/investigations/luanda-leaks/banking-documents-reveal-consulting-giants-cash-windfall-under-angolan-billionaire-isabel-dos-santos/.

15. "Corruption: The Unrecognized Threat to International Security," Carnegie Endowment for International Peace, June 2014, https://carnegieendowment.org/files /corruption_and_security.pdf.

16. Samuel P. Huntington, *Political Order in Changing Societies* (New Haven, CT: Yale University Press, 1968).

17. Jane Ellis, *Corruption, Social Sciences and the Law: Exploration across the Disciplines* (Oxfordshire, UK: Routledge, 2020).

18. Ellis, *Corruption*.

19. "Wolfensohn Cancer of Corruption Speech," 1986, https://www.worldbank.org /en/news/video/2022/08/12/wolfensohn-cancer-of-corruption.

20. SEC, "SEC Enforcement Actions: FCPA Cases," May 17, 2023, https://www.sec .gov/enforce/sec-enforcement-actions-fcpa-cases.

21. OECD, "International Co-Operation in Combating Foreign Bribery," n.d., https:// www.oecd.org/corruption/international-co-operation-in-combating-foreign-bribery .htm.

22. Jasper Jolly, "Mining Giant Glencore Flew Cash Bribes to Africa via Private Jet, UK Court Hears," *Guardian*, November 2, 2022, https://www.theguardian.com/business/2022 /nov/02/mining-giant-glencore-flew-cash-bribes-to-africa-via-private-jet-uk-court-hears.

23. "Foreign Corrupt Practices Act: Statistics & Analytics," accessed June 13, 2023, https://fcpa.stanford.edu/statistics-top-ten.html.

24. For examples, see "FCPA Resource Guide," June 9, 2015, https://www.justice .gov/criminal-fraud/fcpa-resource-guide and "The Bribery Act 2010," Ministry of Justice, Gov.UK, 2010, https://www.justice.gov.uk/downloads/legislation/bribery-act -2010-guidance.pdf.

25. "The Anti-Bribery Business," *Economist*, May 9, 2015, https://www.economist .com/business/2015/05/09/the-anti-bribery-business.

26. "Corruption Is Getting Worse in Many Poor Countries," *Economist*, January 25, 2022, https://www.economist.com/graphic-detail/2022/01/25/corruption-is-getting -worse-in-many-poor-countries; Pew Research Center's Global Attitudes Project, "Crime and Corruption Top Problems in Emerging and Developing Countries," November 6, 2014, https://www.pewresearch.org/global/2014/11/06/crime-and-corruption-top -problems-in-emerging-and-developing-countries/; Richard Wike et al., "Many in U.S., Western Europe Say Their Political System Needs Major Reform," *Pew Research Center's Global Attitudes Project* (blog), March 31, 2021, https://www.pewresearch .org/global/2021/03/31/many-in-us-western-europe-say-their-political-system-needs -major-reform/; and Henry Ridgwell, "Global Corruption on the Rise Amid 'Democratic Decline,'" VOA, January 26, 2022, https://www.voanews.com/a/global-corruption-on -the-rise-amid-democratic-decline-/6413643.html.

27. Naomi Larsson, "Anti-Corruption Protests around the World—in Pictures," *Guardian*, March 18, 2016, http://www.theguardian.com/global-development -professionals-network/gallery/2016/mar/18/anti-corruption-protests-around-the-world-in -pictures.

28. Freedom House, "Government Accountability & Transparency," April 20, 2022, https://freedomhouse.org/issues/government-accountability-transparency.

29. Jeffrey Frankel, "The Natural Resource Curse," April 2012, https://www.hks .harvard.edu/centers/cid/publications/faculty-working-papers/natural-resource-curse.

30. Sarah Chayes, *Thieves of State: Why Corruption Threatens Global Security* (New York: Norton, 2015).

31. S. Ramakrishna Velamuri, William S. Harvey, and S. Venkataraman, "Being an Ethical Business in a Corrupt Environment," hbr.org, March 23, 2017, https://hbr .org/2017/03/being-an-ethical-business-in-a-corrupt-environment.

32. Interview conducted on August 5, 2021, when Galvin was in this role.

33. Robert Klitgaard, *Controlling Corruption* (Berkeley: University of California, 1988).

34. MACN, "MACN—Maritime Anti-Corruption Network," June 12, 2023, https://macn.dk/home/.

Chapter 6

1. Daina Lawrence, "Do Human Rights Get Enough Attention from ESG Investors?" *Globe and Mail*, November 15, 2022, https://www.theglobeandmail.com/investing /article-do-human-rights-get-enough-attention-from-esg-investors/.

2. OHCHR, "International Bill of Human Rights," accessed June 14, 2023, https:// www.ohchr.org/en/what-are-human-rights/international-bill-human-rights.

3. International Labour Organization, "Conventions and Recommendations," accessed June 14, 2023, https://www.ilo.org/global/standards/introduction-to -international-labour-standards/conventions-and-recommendations/lang--en/index.htm.

4. Tim Bartley, "Institutional Emergence in an Era of Globalization: The Rise of Transnational Private Regulation of Labor and Environmental Conditions," *American Journal of Sociology* 113, no. 2 (September 2007): 297–351, https://doi.org/10.1086 /518871.

5. Bartley, "Institutional Emergence in an Era of Globalization."

6. David Vogel, *The Market for Virtue: The Potential and Limits of Corporate Social Responsibility*, rev. ed. (Washington, DC: Brookings Institution Press, 2006).

7. Judith Schrempf-Stirling, Harry J. Van Buren, and Florian Wettstein, "Human Rights: A Promising Perspective for Business & Society," *Business & Society* 61, no. 5 (May 2022): 1282–1321, https://doi.org/10.1177/00076503211068425.

8. Shift, "UN Guiding Principles 101," accessed June 14, 2023, https://shiftproject .org/resources/ungps101/.

9. UN Guiding Principles on Business and Human Rights, 2011, https://www.ohchr.org /sites/default/files/documents/publications/guidingprinciplesbusinesshr_en.pdf.

10. Toby Nangle, "A Trillion-Dollar Blind Spot for Asset Managers," *Financial Times*, January 13, 2023, https://www.ft.com/content/92e9ab44-a852-4c96-86e6 -3b10f796e858.

11. OHCHR, "Access to Remedy," accessed June 14, 2023, https://www.ohchr.org /en/special-procedures/wg-business/access-remedy.

12. Janne Mende, "Are Human Rights Western—and Why Does It Matter? A Perspective from International Political Theory," *Journal of International Political Theory* 17, no. 1 (February 2021): 38–57, https://doi.org/10.1177/1755088219832992.

13. IISD, "UNGA Recognizes Human Right to Clean, Healthy, and Sustainable Environment," August 3, 2022, https://sdg.iisd.org:443/news/unga-recognizes-human -right-to-clean-healthy-and-sustainable-environment/.

14. Columbia Center on Sustainable Investment, "Enabling a Just Transition: Protecting Human Rights in Renewable Energy Projects," April 2023, https://ccsi .columbia.edu/sites/default/files/content/docs/publications/final_Renewables AndHumanRights%20(Brief).pdf.

15. Christian Stirling Haig, Katherine Schmidt, and Samuel Brannen, "The Age of Mass Protests: Understanding an Escalating Global Trend," CSIS, March 2, 2020, https://www.csis.org/analysis/age-mass-protests-understanding-escalating-global-trend.

16. Chloé Farand, "Philippines Inquiry Finds Polluters Liable for Rights Violations, Urging Litigation," *Climate Home News*, May 10, 2022, https://www.climatechangenews .com/2022/05/10/philippines-inquiry-finds-polluters-liable-for-rights-violations-urging -litigation/.

17. Kate Selig, "Judge Rules in Favor of Montana Youth in Landmark Climate Decision," *Washington Post*, August 14, 2023, https://www.washingtonpost.com /climate-environment/2023/08/14/youths-win-montana-climate-trial/.

18. Dunstan Allison-Hope et al., "Human Rights Everywhere All at Once," *BSR* (blog), September 8, 2022, https://www.bsr.org/en/blog/human-rights-everywhere-all-at-once.

19. See chapter 10 of "Human Rights Impact Assessment: Meta's Expansion of End-to-End Encryption," BSR, 2022, https://www.bsr.org/reports/bsr-meta-human-rights -impact-assessment-e2ee-report.pdf.

20. See, for example, BSR, "Summary of Vattenfall's Human Rights Assessment by BSR," Vattenfall, 2021, https://group.vattenfall.com/dk/siteassets/danmark/om-os /baeredygtighed/summary_of_human_rights_assessment.pdf.

21. Diageo, "Human Rights," accessed June 14, 2023, https://www.diageo.com/en /esg/doing-business-the-right-way-from-grain-to-glass/human-rights.

22. Dunstan Allison-Hope, Hannah Darnton, and Michaela Lee, "Google's Human Rights by Design," *BSR* (blog), October 30, 2019, https://www.bsr.org/en/blog/google -human-rights-impact-assessment-celebrity-recognition; BSR, "Marlin Mine at Closure: A Review of Goldcorp Commitments to the 2010 Human Rights Assessment," June 2017, https://ilas.sas.ac.uk/sites/default/files/reports/BSR-Report-Marlin-Mine-at -Closure.pdf.

23. Alison Taylor, "FIFA and Bribery in Qatar: It's Time to Approach Corruption and Human Rights Together," *BSR* (blog), June 25, 2015, https://www.bsr.org/en /blog/fifa-and-bribery-in-qatar-its-time-to-approach-corruption-and-human-rights.

24. See, for example, "Human Rights Impact Assessment Guidance and Toolbox," August 25, 2020, https://www.humanrights.dk/tools/human-rights-impact-assessment -guidance-toolbox; and Oxfam Policy & Practice, "Human Rights Impact Assessment Archives," accessed June 14, 2023, https://policy-practice.oxfam.org/keyword/human -rights-impact-assessment/.

25. Jenny Vaughan, "Human Rights Assessments: Identifying Risks, Informing Strategy," BSR, December 9, 2021, https://www.bsr.org/en/reports/human-rights -assessments-identifying-risks-informing-strategy.

26. Stuart Lau, Joshua Posaner, and Hans Von Der Burchard, "What Genocide? Volkswagen's Morally Expensive Bet on China," Politico, June 20, 2023, https://www .politico.eu/article/volkswagen-china-xinjiang-forced-labor-how-to-get-away-with-genocide/.

27. Impact-Weighted Accounts Project, "Mission Statement," Harvard Business School, accessed June 14, 2023, https://www.hbs.edu/impact-weighted-accounts/Pages /default.aspx.

28. Vestas, "Corporate Social Responsibility," n.d., https://www.vestas.com/en /sustainability/corporate-integrity/csr.

29. Vincent Brusse and Kai von Carnap, "Amended Anti-Espionage Law Aims to Curate China's Own Narrative," Mercator Institute for China Studies, May 25, 2023, https://merics .org/en/comment/amended-anti-espionage-law-aims-curate-chinas-own-narrative.

30. US Department of Labor, "Child Labor in the Production of Cocoa," accessed June 14, 2023, http://www.dol.gov/agencies/ilab/our-work/child-forced-labor-trafficking /child-labor-cocoa.

31. Peter Whoriskey and Rachel Siegel, "Cocoa's Child Laborers," *Washington Post*, June 5, 2019, https://www.washingtonpost.com/graphics/2019/business/hershey-nestle -mars-chocolate-child-labor-west-africa/.

32. Etelle Higonnet, Marisa Bellantonio, and Glenn Hurowitz, "Chocolate's Dark Secret: How the Cocoa Industry Destroys National Parks," Mighty Earth, September 12, 2017, https://www.mightyearth.org/wp-content/uploads/2017/09/chocolates_dark _secret_english_web.pdf.

33. BSR, "Stephen Badger, Chairman, Board of Directors, Mars Incorporated | BSR19," YouTube, November 18, 2019, https://www.youtube.com/watch?v=LnIt0RPmL24.

34. Tan Hui Yee, "Effects of Myanmar Coup Especially Devastating for Women: UN Survey," *Straits Times*, March 8, 2022, https://www.straitstimes.com/asia/se-asia /effects-of-myanmar-coup-especially-devastating-for-women-un-survey.

35. Suein Hwang, "4 Experts on How Workplaces Will Respond to the Loss of Roe v. Wade," Charter, June 27, 2022, https://www.charterworks.com/4-experts-on-how -workplaces-will-respond-to-the-loss-of-roe-v-wade/.

Chapter 7

1. Paul Polman, "Ohio Is Close to Abolishing the Death Penalty. Here's Why Businesses Should Help," *Fast Company*, October 10, 2022, https://www.fastcompany.com/90793439 /ohio-is-close-to-abolishing-the-death-penalty-heres-why-businesses-should-help?.

2. Tim Quinson, "Russia's War Casts Huge Shadow Over the Future of ESG," Bloomberg, March 9, 2022, https://www.bloomberg.com/news/newsletters/2022 -03-09/russia-s-war-casts-huge-shadow-over-esg-s-future-green-insight.

3. Megan Cerullo, "Thousands of Salesforce Workers Urge Software Makers to Cut Ties with NRA," *CBS News*, June 1, 2022, https://www.cbsnews.com/news/uvalde -texas-shooting-salesforce-employees-ask-company-to-cut-ties-with-nra/.

4. Salesforce, "Environmental Sustainability at Salesforce," accessed June 15, 2023, https://www.salesforce.com/company/sustainability/; Shervin Khodabandeh and Sam Ransbotham, "Technology as a Force for Good: Salesforce's Paula Goldman," *Me, Myself, and AI*, November 30, 2021, https://sloanreview.mit.edu/audio /technology-as-a-force-for-good-salesforces-paula-goldman/.

5. Twitter, @SquawkStreet, May 25, 2022, https://twitter.com/SquawkStreet/status /1529489704684511240?s=20&t=si35Jr526IuRrbaFHWpLog.

6. Sarah Roach, "Salesforce Will Keep Working with the NRA," Protocol, June 9, 2022, https://www.protocol.com/bulletins/salesforce-nra-policy.

7. Richard Edelman, "The Belief-Driven Employee," Edelman, August 31, 2021, https://www.edelman.com/trust/2021-trust-barometer/belief-driven-employee/new -employee-employer-compact.

8. Edelman, "2022 Edelman Trust Barometer," https://www.edelman.com/sites/g /files/aatuss191/files/2022-01/2022%20Edelman%20Trust%20Barometer_FullReport .pdf.

9. Michael Sheetz, "This Is the Letter Nearly 400 US Executives Signed Asking Trump to Save Immigration Protection," CNBC, September 1, 2017, https://www.cnbc .com/2017/09/01/the-letter-us-executives-signed-asking-trump-to-save-daca.html.

10. Judd Legum, *Popular Information*, Substack, accessed June 15, 2023, https:// popular.info/; InfluenceMap, home page, accessed June 15, 2023, https://influencemap .org/index.html; and Center for Political Accountability, home page, accessed June 15, 2023, https://www.politicalaccountability.net/.

11. Nathan Layne, "Retailer Target Says Transgender People Can Use Bathroom of Their Choice," Reuters, April 19, 2016, https://www.reuters.com/article/us-target-lgbt -idUSKCN0XG2VU; Matthew J. Belvedere, "Target CEO to Critics: What You're Missing about Our Inclusive Bathroom Policy," CNBC, May 11, 2016, https://www.cnbc .com/2016/05/11/target-ceo-to-conservative-critics-on-our-inclusive-bathrom-policy .html.

12. Paul Blumenthal, "Companies Opposed to North Carolina's Anti-LGBT Law Helped Elect Its Supporters," HuffPost, April 27, 2016, https://www.huffpost.com /entry/corporations-lgbt-north-carolina_n_5720f5f4e4b0b49df6a9d76d.

13. Center for Political Accountability, "Conflicted Consequences," July 21, 2020, https://politicalaccountability.net/hifi/files/Conflicted-Consequences.pdf; Center for Political Accountability, "Collision Course: The Risks Companies Face When Their Political Spending and Core Values Conflict and How to Address Them," June 19, 2018, https://politicalaccountability.net/hifi/files/Collision-Course-Report.pdf.

14. Alison Taylor, "The Corporate Responsibility Facade Is Finally Starting to Crumble," Quartz, March 4, 2020, https://qz.com/work/1812245/the-corporate -responsibility-facade-is-finally-starting-to-crumble.

15. Tim Lau, "Citizens United Explained," Brennan Center for Justice, December 12, 2019, https://www.brennancenter.org/our-work/research-reports/citizens-united-explained.

16. Daniel I. Weiner, "Citizens United Five Years Later," Brennan Center for Justice, January 15, 2015, https://www.brennancenter.org/our-work/research-reports/citizens -united-five-years-later.

17. Aswath Damodaran, "Musings on Markets: META Lesson 1: Corporate Governance," *Musings on Markets* (blog), November 4, 2022, https:// aswathdamodaran.blogspot.com/2022/11/meta-lesson-1-corporate-governance.html.

18. LibertyPen, "Milton Friedman—Big Business, Big Government," YouTube, September 14, 2012, https://www.youtube.com/watch?v=R_T0WF-uCWg.

19. Alan S. Blinder, "Financial Entropy and the Optimality of Over-Regulation," paper prepared for the 17th Annual International Banking Conference, November 2014, https://www.hbs.edu/faculty/Shared%20Documents/conferences/2015-crisis-in-theory -of-firm/Blinder_Finance%20and%20Regulation.pdf.

20. Julie Johnsson and Ryan Beene, "Boeing Messages Describe Efforts to Dodge FAA Scrutiny of MAX," *Time*, January 10, 2020, https://time.com/5762666/boeing-max-faa-messages-clowns/.

21. Ian Duncan, Luz Lazo, and Michael Laris, "Before Ohio Derailment, Norfolk Southern Lobbied against Safety Rules," *Washington Post*, February 19, 2023, https://www.washingtonpost.com/transportation/2023/02/18/norfolk-southern-derailment-ohio-train-safety/.

22. This chapter contains further discussion of this study: Michael Hadani and Douglas A. Schuler, "In Search of El Dorado: The Elusive Financial Returns on Corporate Political Investments," *Strategic Management Journal* 34, no. 2 (2013): 165–181, https://www.jstor.org/stable/23362694.

23. John Tozzi, "Americans Are Dying Younger, Saving Corporations Billions," Bloomberg, August 8, 2017, https://www.bloomberg.com/news/articles/2017-08-08/americans-are-dying-younger-saving-corporations-billions.

24. Andrew Howard, "SustainEx: Examining the Social Value of Corporate Activities," Schroders, April 2019, https://prod.schroders.com/en/sysglobalassets/digital/insights/2019/pdfs/sustainability/sustainex/sustainex-short.pdf.

25. Justin H. Vassallo, "When It Becomes Too Hot to Work," *Noema*, November 17, 2022, https://www.noemamag.com/how-to-protect-the-economy-when-it-becomes-too-hot-to-work.

26. "The Brazilian Amazon Has Been a Net Carbon Emitter Since 2016," *Economist*, May 21, 2022, https://www.economist.com/interactive/graphic-detail/2022/05/21/the-brazilian-amazon-has-been-a-net-carbon-emitter-since-2016.

27. Frederick Alexander, "From Meta to Twitter, What Everyone Gets Wrong about ESG—and Why It Matters," *Institutional Investor*, August 24, 2022, https://www.institutionalinvestor.com/article/b1zh8gsv8hssjh/From-Meta-to-Twitter-What-Everyone-Gets-Wrong-About-ESG-And-Why-It-Matters.

28. Robert G. Eccles, and Svetlana Klimenko, "The Investor Revolution," *Harvard Business Review*, May 1, 2019, https://hbr.org/2019/05/the-investor-revolution.

29. David Zuluaga Martinez, Madeleine Michael, and Martin Reeves, "Breaking the Vicious Cycle of Corporate Entanglement," BCG Henderson Institute, January 3, 2023, https://www.bcghendersoninstitute.com/breaking-the-vicious-cycle-of-corporate-entanglement/.

30. Luigi Zingales and Bethany McLean, "The Political Polarization of Corporate America," *Capitalisn't*, December 16, 2021, https://www.capitalisnt.com/episodes/the-political-polarization-of-corporate-america.

31. Jennifer Tonti, "Survey: Here's What Americans Expect from Corporate America in the Wake of the Capitol Riot," JUST Capital, January 15, 2021, https://justcapital.com/news/survey-heres-what-americans-expect-from-corporate-america-in-the-wake-of-the-capitol-riot/.

32. John Dunbar and Aaron Kessler, "Several Big Trade Associations Still Backing Election Objectors," Bloomberg Law, February 10, 2021, https://news.bloomberglaw.com/banking-law/several-big-trade-associations-still-backing-election-objectors.

33. Lawrence Norden and Daniel I. Weiner, "Corporations and Fixing Campaign Finance," Brennan Center for Justice, January 21, 2021, https://www.brennancenter.org/our-work/analysis-opinion/corporations-and-fixing-campaign-finance.

34. OECD, "Lobbying in the 21st Century: Transparency, Integrity and Access," May 20, 2021, https://www.oecd.org/corruption/ethics/lobbying-21-century.htm.

35. Erb Institute at the University of Michigan, "The Erb Principles for Corporate Political Responsibility," 2022, https://erb.umich.edu/wp-content/uploads/2023/03/Erb-Principles-for-CPR_v1_0.pdf; Bruce Freed, Karl Sandstrom, and William Laufer, "The CPA-Wharton Zicklin Model Code of Conduct," *The Harvard Law School Forum on Corporate Governance* (blog), November 28, 2020, https://corpgov.law.harvard.edu/2020/11/28/the-cpa-wharton-zicklin-model-code-of-conduct/.

36. Leo E. Strine, Jr., "Good Corporate Citizenship We Can All Get Behind?: Toward a Principled, Non-Ideological Approach to Making Money the Right Way"

(SSRN scholarly paper, Rochester, NY, December 7, 2022), https://papers.ssrn.com/abstract=4296287.

37. Richard Levick, "The Handmaid's Tale," *The Shadow* (blog), May 19, 2022, https://medium.com/the-shadow/the-handmaids-tale-5bcf008ed2e0.

38. Ford Motor Company, "Integrated Sustainability and Financial Report 2021," 2021, https://media.ford.com/content/dam/fordmedia/North%20America/US/2021/03/31/Ford-Integrated-Report-2021.pdf; First Energy Corp., "Corporate Political Activity Policy," accessed June 16, 2023, https://firstenergycorp.com/investor/corporate_governance/responsibility/corporate_political_activity_policy.html.

39. Jaclyn Diaz, "An Energy Company behind a Major Bribery Scandal in Ohio Will Pay a $230 Million Fine," NPR, July 23, 2021, https://www.npr.org/2021/07/23/1019567905/an-energy-company-behind-a-major-bribery-scandal-in-ohio-will-pay-a-230-million-.

40. Edison International, "Edison International Political Contribution Policy," April 12, 2021, https://www.edison.com/content/dam/eix/documents/investors/corporate-governance/eix-political-contribution-policy.pdf.

41. Voters choose among available candidates, though their views are unlikely to align fully.

42. Erb Institute, "The Erb Principles for Corporate Responsibility."

43. Peter Vanham, "The Promise and Peril of Microsoft's ESG Policy Plays," Yahoo Finance, May 11, 2023, https://finance.yahoo.com/news/promise-peril-microsoft-esg-policy-152305832.html.

44. Peter Eavis, "Microsoft's Pursuit of Climate Goals Runs into Headwinds," *New York Times*, March 10, 2022, https://www.nytimes.com/2022/03/10/business/microsoft-climate-carbon-emissions.html.

45. Bill Weihl, "Why Microsoft Is a Company to Watch on Climate Policy," GreenBiz, October 18, 2022, https://www.greenbiz.com/article/why-microsoft-company-watch-climate-policy.

46. US SIF Foundation, "2022 Report on US Sustainable Investing Trends," December 2022, https://www.ussif.org/Files/Trends/2022/Trends%202022%20Executive%20Summary.pdf.

47. Brendan Fischer, "ALEC Is Not Where Visa Wants to Be," PR Watch, December 4, 2013, https://www.prwatch.org/news/2013/12/12332/alec-not-where-visa-wants-be.

48. Josh Dickey, "Netflix Investor Demands More Transparency for Streaming Giant's Political Lobbying," Yahoo, May 19, 2022, https://www.yahoo.com/entertainment/netflix-investor-demands-more-transparency-134001081.html.

49. Steven Mufson, "BP Is Pulling Out of Three Trade Groups over Climate Policies," *Washington Post*, February 26, 2020, https://www.washingtonpost.com/climate-environment/2020/02/25/bp-pull-out-trade-groups-over-climate-policies/.

50. Hadani and Schuler, "In Search of El Dorado."

51. Andrew Ross Sorkin, "'An Epiphany Moment' for Corporate Political Donors May Have Arrived," *New York Times*, July 20, 2021, https://www.nytimes.com/2021/01/12/business/dealbook/political-donations-ibm.html.

52. Jesse Eisinger, Jeff Ernsthausen, and Paul Kiel, "The Secret IRS Files: Trove of Never-Before-Seen Records Reveal How the Wealthiest Avoid Income Tax," ProPublica, June 8, 2021, https://www.propublica.org/article/the-secret-irs-files-trove-of-never-before-seen-records-reveal-how-the-wealthiest-avoid-income-tax.

53. World Economic Forum, "The Role and Responsibilities of Gatekeepers in the Fight against Illicit Financial Flows: A Unifying Framework," June 2021, https://www3.weforum.org/docs/WEF_Gatekeepers_A_Unifying_Framework_2021.pdf.

54. "The Rise and Fall of Londongrad," *Economist*, March 5, 2022, https://www.economist.com/Britain/2022/03/05/the-rise-and-fall-of-londongrad.

55. Robert Barrington, "A Profession Close to 'Moral Bankruptcy,'" *Law Society Gazette*, March 11, 2022, https://www.lawgazette.co.uk/practice-points/a-profession-close-to-moral-bankruptcy/5111900.article.

56. Muel Kaptein, "The Limits of the Ethical Responsibilities of Companies: In Search of Boundary Principles," working paper, June 2023, https://www.researchgate.net /publication/364329660_The_Limits_of_the_Ethical_Responsibilities_of_Companies _In_Search_of_Boundary_Principles.

57. Oxfam, "Dollars and Sense," April 12, 2018, https://www.oxfamamerica.org /explore/research-publications/dollars-and-sense/.

58. Michael R. Bloomberg, "On Climate Change, Republicans Need a Crash Course in Capitalism," Bloomberg, September 6, 2022, https://www.bloomberg.com/opinion /articles/2022-09-06/on-climate-change-republicans-need-a-crash-course-in-capitalism; Mike Pence, "Republicans Can Stop ESG Political Bias," *Wall Street Journal*, May 26, 2022, https://www.wsj.com/articles/only-republicans-can-stop-the-esg-madness-woke -musk-consumer-demand-free-speech-corporate-america-11653574189.

59. Liam Denning, "The Tricky Politics of Anti-ESG Investing," Bloomberg, May 19, 2022, https://www.bloomberg.com/opinion/articles/2022-05-19/the-tricky-politics-of-a -new-asset-firm-backed-by-peter-thiel.

60. Vivia Chen, "Big Law's 'Wokeness' Is Driving Conservatives Batty," Bloomberg Law, November 18, 2022, https://news.bloomberglaw.com/business-and-practice/big -laws-wokeness-is-driving-conservatives-batty.

Chapter 8

1. Jennifer Rubin, "Feel Free to Spill the Beans, Ex-Employees. Your Former Boss Can't Stop You," *Washington Post*, April 2, 2023, https://www.washingtonpost.com /opinions/2023/04/02/nlrb-ruling-nondisparagement-agreements/.

2. Paige Smith, "Wall Street's Silencing of Sexual Harassment Curbed by US 'Speak Out Act,'" Bloomberg, November 16, 2022, https://www.bloomberg.com/news /articles/2022-11-16/wall-street-s-silencing-of-sexual-harassment-cut-back-by-new-law.

3. Kim Elsesser, "Congress Passes Law Restoring Victims' Voices, Banning NDAs in Sexual Harassment Cases," *Forbes*, November 16, 2022, https://www.forbes.com/sites /kimelsesser/2022/11/16/congress-passes-law-restoring-victims-voices-banning-ndas-in -sexual-harassment-cases/.

4. Cristina Rouvalis, "NYC Employers Adapting to Pay Transparency Law," SHRM, November 15, 2022, https://www.shrm.org/resourcesandtools/hr-topics/talent-acquisition /pages/nyc-employers-adapting-to-pay-transparency-law.aspx.

5. European Commission, "Just and Sustainable Economy: Commission Lays Down Rules for Companies to Respect Human Rights and Environment in Global Value Chains," February 23, 2022, https://ec.europa.eu/commission/presscorner/home/en.

6. Bloomberg Law, "Proposed SEC Climate Disclosure Rule," August 15, 2022, https://pro.bloomberglaw.com/brief/proposed-sec-climate-disclosure-rule/.

7. Hunton Andrews Kurth LLP, "Treasury Issues Final Rule on Beneficial Ownership Reporting Requirements under the Corporate Transparency Act," November 1, 2022, https://www.huntonak.com/en/insights/treasury-issues-final-rule-on-beneficial -ownership-reporting-requirements-under-the-corporate-transparency-act.html.

8. Rana Foroohar, "Corporations Can No Longer Remain Black Boxes," *Financial Times*, November 6, 2022, https://www.ft.com/content/3ab3ec60-dcba-4fd7-846f -0acbe36ffa65.

9. Amitai Etzioni, "Is Transparency the Best Disinfectant?," *Journal of Political Philosophy* 18, no. 4 (December 2010): 389–404, https://doi.org/10.1111/j.1467 -9760.2010.00366.x.

10. Christopher Hood, *Transparency: The Key to Better Governance?* (London: British Academy, 2006).

11. Don Tapscott and David Ticoll, *The Naked Corporation: How the Age of Transparency Will Revolutionize Business* (New York: Free Press, 2003).

12. Hood, *Transparency*.

13. Marilyn Strathern, "The Tyranny of Transparency," *British Educational Research Journal* 26, no. 3 (2000): 309–321, https://www.jstor.org/stable/1501878.

14. Lars Thøger Christensen and Joep Cornelissen, "Organizational Transparency as Myth and Metaphor," *European Journal of Social Theory* 18, no. 2 (May 2015): 132–149, https://doi.org/10.1177/1368431014555256.

15. Paul Dickinson, "Celebrating CDP at 20: A Q&A with Co-Founder Paul Dickinson," CDP, September 25, 2020, https://www.cdp.net/en/articles/climate/cdpat20-a-qa-with-paul-dickinson.

16. Pablo Berrutti, "It's Time to Talk about Net Zero Bullsh*t," Climate and Capital Media, July 28, 2022, https://www.climateandcapitalmedia.com/its-time-to-talk-about-net-zero-bullshit/.

17. CDP, "Disclosing as a Company," accessed June 19, 2023, https://www.cdp.net/en/companies-discloser.

18. Nadia Ameli, Sumit Kothari, and Michael Grubb, "Misplaced Expectations from Climate Disclosure Initiatives," *Nature Climate Change* 11, no. 11 (November 2021): 917–924, https://doi.org/10.1038/s41558-021-01174-8.

19. Daniel Roth, "Road Map for Financial Recovery: Radical Transparency Now!," *Wired*, February 23, 2009, https://www.wired.com/2009/02/wp-reboot/.

20. Daylian M. Cain, George Loewenstein, and Don A. Moore, "The Dirt on Coming Clean: Perverse Effects of Disclosing Conflicts of Interest," *Journal of Legal Studies* 34, no. 1 (2005): 1–25, https://doi.org/10.1086/426699.

21. Louis Gore-Langton, "Alliance to End Plastic Waste Defends Failures after Achieving 0.2% of Its Targets," *Packaging Insights*, February 10, 2023, https://pi.cnsmedia.com/a/bU6hqEi8VpA=.

22. Charles J. Fombrun, Naomi A. Gardberg, and Michael L. Barnett, "Opportunity Platforms and Safety Nets: Corporate Citizenship and Reputational Risk," *Business and Society Review* 105, no. 1 (January 2000): 85–106, https://doi.org/10.1111/0045-3609.00066.

23. Ross Brennan, "The End of Corporate Social Responsibility: Crisis & Critique, by Peter Fleming and Marc T. Jones," *Journal of Business-to-Business Marketing* 21, no. 2 (April 3, 2014): 141–143, https://doi.org/10.1080/1051712X.2014.874262.

24. Benjamin Hart, "A Crisis-PR Veteran on Sam Bankman-Fried's Odd Media Strategy," Intelligencer, *New York Magazine*, December 9, 2022, https://nymag.com/intelligencer/2022/12/a-crisis-pr-expert-on-sam-bankman-frieds-odd-media-strategy.html.

25. Apple App Store, "Exxchange," n.d., https://apps.apple.com/us/app/exxchange/id1438743004.

26. Hiroko Tabuchi, "How One Firm Drove Influence Campaigns Nationwide for Big Oil," *New York Times*, November 11, 2020, https://www.nytimes.com/2020/11/11/climate/fti-consulting.html.

27. Yousuf Aftab and Jonathan Drimmer, "Expert ESG Attorneys: How Corporate Sustainability Creates Legal Risk," Corp Gov, 2020, https://corpgov.com/lessons-from-cobalt-in-the-congo-how-corporate-sustainability-creates-legal-risk/.

28. SEC, "Activision Blizzard to Pay $35 Million for Failing to Maintain Disclosure Controls Related to Complaints of Workplace Misconduct and Violating Whistleblower Protection Rule," February 3, 2023, https://www.sec.gov/news/press-release/2023-22.

29. This review paper states, for example: "Reputation involves both beliefs and judgments held by people in the general public or special niche groups outside the organization." Alan Clardy, "Organizational Reputation: Issues in Conceptualization and Measurement," *Corporate Reputation Review* 15, no. 4 (November 2012): 285–303, https://doi.org/10.1057/crr.2012.17.

30. Jeffrey K. Liker, *The Toyota Way: 14 Management Principles from the World's Greatest Manufacturer* (New York: McGraw-Hill, 2004).

31. Ethan Bernstein, "The Transparency Trap," *Harvard Business Review*, October 2014, https://hbr.org/2014/10/the-transparency-trap.

32. James D'Angelo and Brent Ranalli, "The Dark Side of Sunlight," *Foreign Affairs*, April 16, 2019, https://www.foreignaffairs.com/united-states/dark-side-sunlight.

33. Forrest Briscoe and Abhinav Gupta, "Business Disruption from the Inside Out," *Stanford Social Innovation Review* 19 (2020): 4854, https://doi.org/10.48558/4EHP -4D02.

34. Byung-Chul Han, *The Transparency Society* (Stanford, CA: Stanford Briefs, 2015), 48.

35. Margie Mason et al., "Global Supermarkets Selling Shrimp Peeled by Slaves," Associated Press, December 14, 2015, http://www.ap.org/explore/seafood-from-slaves /global-supermarkets-selling-shrimp-peeled-by-slaves.html.

36. Associated Press, "Nestlé Admits to Forced Labour in Its Seafood Supply Chain in Thailand," *Guardian*, November 24, 2015, https://www.theguardian.com/global -development/2015/nov/24/nestle-admits-forced-labour-in-seafood-supply-chain.

37. Cecilia Jamasmie, "Rio Tinto Sorry for Blasting 46,000-Year-Old Aboriginal Site," Mining.com, June 1, 2020, https://www.mining.com/rio-tinto-sorry-for-blasting -of-46000-year-old-aboriginal-site/.

38. "Rio Tinto and the Problem of Toxic Culture," *Economist*, February 12, 2022, https://www.economist.com/business/rio-tinto-and-the-problem-of-toxic-culture/21807599.

39. Dunstan Allison-Hope and Aditi Mohapatra, "Five Insights on the Future of Reporting from Uber's Safety Report," *BSR* (blog), January 21, 2020, https://www.bsr .org/en/blog/five-insights-on-the-future-of-reporting-from-ubers-safety-report.

40. "Uber Fined $59 Million, May Pay Just $150,000 over Sexual Assault Data— CBS San Francisco," *CBS News*, July 16, 2021, https://www.cbsnews.com/sanfrancisco /news/uber-fined-59-million-may-pay-just-150000-sexual-assault-data/.

41. Kari Paul, "Lyft Admits It Recorded 4,000 Sexual Assault Claims in Long-Awaited Report," *Guardian*, October 22, 2021, https://www.theguardian.com /technology/2021/oct/22/lyft-sexual-assault-reports-uber-ridesharing; Jeff Green, "Microsoft's Unprecedented New Report Puts Pressure on Companies to Release More Harassment Data," Bloomberg, November 17, 2022, https://www.bloomberg.com /news/newsletters/2022-11-17/microsoft-s-unprecedented-new-report-puts-pressure-on -companies-to-release-more-harassment-data.

42. Google, "Google Transparency Report," accessed June 19, 2023, https:// transparencyreport.google.com/.

43. Dunstan Allison-Hope, "A New Transparency Challenge for Business and Human Rights," *BSR* (blog), February 25, 2019, https://www.bsr.org/en/blog /transparency-business-and-human-rights-government-law-enforcement.

44. Access Now, "Transparency Reporting Index," accessed June 19, 2023, https:// www.accessnow.org/campaign/transparency-reporting-index/.

45. David Wallace-Wells, "What's Worse: Climate Denial or Climate Hypocrisy?" *New York Times*, June 22, 2022, https://www-nytimes-com.cdn.ampproject.org/c/s /www.nytimes.com/2022/06/22/opinion/environment/climate-hypocrisy-larry-fink.amp .html.

46. Irina Anghel and Akshat Rathi, "Net-Zero Plans of the Biggest Global Companies Do Not Add Up to Net Zero," Bloomberg, February 8, 2022, https://www.bloomberg .com/news/articles/2022-02-08/net-zero-plans-of-the-biggest-global-companies-do-not -add-up-to-net-zero.

47. Peter Gassmann and Will Jackson-Moore, "The CEO's ESG Dilemma," *The Harvard Law School Forum on Corporate Governance* (blog), January 23, 2023, https://corpgov.law.harvard.edu/2023/01/23/the-ceos-esg-dilemma/.

48. Graham Readfearn and Australian Associated Press, "'Don't F&*! The Planet': Atlassian Issues Net Zero Guide for Companies Cutting Climate Impact," *Guardian*, May 24, 2023, https://www.theguardian.com/environment/2023/may/24/dont-f-the -planet-atlassian-issues-net-zero-guide-for-companies-cutting-climate-impact.

49. Atlassian, "Atlassian Sustainability Report Fiscal Year 2022," 2022, https://s28 .q4cdn.com/541786762/files/doc_downloads/sustainability/2022/12/FY22-Atlassian -Sustainability-Report.pdf.

50. Athalie Williams, "The Road to Gender Balance," BHP, February 8, 2022, https://www.bhp.com/news/articles/2022/02/the-road-to-gender-balance.

51. Sarah Krouse, "The New Ways Your Boss Is Spying on You," *Wall Street Journal*, July 19, 2019, https://www.wsj.com/articles/the-new-ways-your-boss-is-spying-on-you-11563528604.

52. Danielle Abril and Drew Harwell, "Keystroke Tracking, Screenshots, and Facial Recognition: The Boss May Be Watching Long after the Pandemic Ends," *Washington Post*, September 24, 2021, https://www.washingtonpost.com/technology/2021/09/24/remote-work-from-home-surveillance/.

53. J. S. Nelson, "Management Culture and Surveillance" (SSRN scholarly paper, Rochester, NY, December 16, 2019), https://papers.ssrn.com/abstract=3504408.

54. David Heald, *Transparency: The Key to Better Governance?* (London: British Academy, 2006).

Chapter 9

1. BrewDog UK, "The World F*Cup," accessed June 19, 2023, https://www.brewdog.com/uk/anti-sponsor-qatar.

2. Gregor Young, "BrewDog Protests against Qatar World Cup with New Scheme," *National*, November 7, 2022, https://www.thenational.scot/news/23106561.brewdog-protests-qatar-world-cup-new-scheme/.

3. Jack Mendel, "BrewDog Signed Beer Distribution Deal in Qatar Despite 'Anti-Sponsorship' Campaign," CityAM, November 8, 2022, https://www.cityam.com/brewdog-signed-beer-distribution-deal-in-qatar-despite-anti-sponsorship-campaign/; Mark Daly, "The Truth about BrewDog," BBC, January 21, 2022, https://www.bbc.co.uk/programmes/m0013yfj; and g50p, "BBC Disclosure—The Truth about BrewDog," YouTube, March 28, 2022, https://www.youtube.com/watch?v=XamxzvGm8YQ.

4. Mark Sweney and Rob Davies, "BrewDog Loses Its Ethical B Corp Certificate," *Guardian*, December 1, 2022, https://www.theguardian.com/business/2022/dec/01/brewdog-loses-its-ethical-b-corp-certificate.

5. Gallup, "Indicator: ESG," Gallup.com, accessed June 19, 2023, https://www.gallup.com/395216/indicator-esg.aspx.

6. Edgar H. Schein, *Organizational Culture and Leadership*, 3rd ed. (San Francisco: Jossey-Bass, 2004).

7. Jo Constantz, "'I Got This Wrong': CEO Apologies Abound amid Mass Layoffs and Losses," Bloomberg, November 11, 2022, https://www.bloomberg.com/news/articles/2022-11-11/apologies-from-tech-ceos-abound-amid-mass-layoffs-and-losses.

8. "What It Takes to Be a CEO in the 2020s," *Economist*, February 6, 2020, https://www.economist.com/leaders/2020/02/06/what-it-takes-to-be-a-ceo-in-the-2020s.

9. "Testimony of John Stumpf," Washington, DC, September 20, 2016, https://www.banking.senate.gov/imo/media/doc/092016_Stumpf%20Testimony.pdf.

10. Pradnya Joshi and Danny Hakim, "VW's Public Relations Responses and Flubs," *New York Times*, February 26, 2016, https://www.nytimes.com/interactive/2016/02/26/business/volkswagen-public-relations-flubs.html.

11. Lynn S. Paine, "Managing for Organizational Integrity," *Harvard Business Review*, March 1, 1994, https://hbr.org/1994/03/managing-for-organizational-integrity.

12. Ralph Hertwig and Christoph Engel, eds., *Deliberate Ignorance: Choosing Not to Know* (Cambridge, MA: MIT Press, 2020).

13. Alison Taylor, "5 Signs Your Organization Might Be Headed for an Ethics Scandal," hbr.org, December 18, 2017, https://hbr.org/2017/12/5-signs-your-organization-might-be-headed-for-an-ethics-scandal.

14. Taylor, "5 Signs Your Organization Might Be Headed for an Ethics Scandal."

15. Andres Schipani and Neil Hume, "Vale under Scrutiny after Second Mine Disaster in Brazil," *Financial Times*, January 28, 2019, https://www.ft.com/content/3f82b07c-2263-11e9-8ce6-5db4543da632.

16. Vikas Anand et al., "Business as Usual: The Acceptance and Perpetuation of Corruption in Organizations [and Executive Commentary]," *Academy of Management Executive (1993–2005)* 18, no. 2 (2004): 39–55, https://www.jstor.org/stable/4166061.

17. Don A. Moore et al., "Conflicts of Interest and the Case of Auditor Independence: Moral Seduction and Strategic Issue Cycling," *Academy of Management Review* 31, no. 1 (January 2006): 10–29, https://doi.org/10.5465/amr.2006.19379621.

18. Mark Seal, "The Madoff Chronicles, Part I: Inside the Ponzi Schemer's Life and Financial Façade," *Vanity Fair*, March 4, 2009, https://www.vanityfair.com/news/2009/04/bernard-madoff-friends-family-profile.

19. Jerry Useem, "How Corporations Become Evil," *Atlantic*, December 22, 2015, https://www.theatlantic.com/magazine/archive/2016/01/what-was-volkswagen-thinking/419127/.

20. Siri Schubert and T. Christian Miller, "At Siemens, Bribery Was Just a Line Item," *New York Times*, December 20, 2008, https://www.nytimes.com/2008/12/21/business/worldbusiness/21siemens.html.

21. Rani Molla, "How Remote Work Is Quietly Remaking Our Lives," Vox, October 9, 2019, https://www.vox.com/recode/2019/10/9/20885699/remote-work-from-anywhere-change-coworking-office-real-estate.

22. Matthew Boyle, "Microsoft's CEO Warns of the Impact of All Those Late-Night Emails," Bloomberg, April 7, 2022, https://www.bloomberg.com/news/articles/2022-04-07/microsoft-ceo-warns-of-the-impact-of-all-those-late-night-emails.

23. Matt Robinson and Benjamin Bain, "Whistle-Blowing Soars to Record with Americans Working from Home," Bloomberg, January 12, 2021, https://www.bloomberg.com/news/articles/2021-01-12/whistle-blowing-soars-to-record-with-americans-working-from-home.

24. Henry Kronk, "Retaliation against Whistleblowers Is on the Rise: ECI's Patricia Harned in Conversation," *Corporate Compliance Insights* (blog), March 16, 2021, https://www.corporatecomplianceinsights.com/rising-retaliation-whistleblowers/.

25. Douglas J. Cumming et al., "Work-from-Home and the Risk of Securities Misconduct" (SSRN scholarly paper, Rochester, NY, April 5, 2023), https://papers.ssrn.com/abstract=4428145.

26. Thegoodcult, "#thegoodcult on TikTok," TikTok, accessed November 22, 2022, https://www.tiktok.com/@.thegoodcult/video/7163318873326931246?.

27. Adam Bryant, "Is It Time to Retire the Title of Manager?" *strategy+business* (blog), January 30, 2020, https://www.strategy-business.com/blog/Is-it-time-to-retire-the-title-of-manager.

28. Alexia Fernández Campbell, "Google Will Extend Some Benefits to Contract Workers after Internal Protest," Vox, April 4, 2019, https://www.vox.com/2019/4/4/18293900/google-contractors-benefits-policy.

29. Sarah Murray, "So You Think You Know Your Supply Chain?" *Financial Times*, March 24, 2023, https://www.ft.com/content/687c2a10-403b-4a93-85c0-3ede41af5d09.

30. US EPA, "Scope 3 Inventory Guidance," February 14, 2023, https://www.epa.gov/climateleadership/scope-3-inventory-guidance.

31. Morwenna Coniam, "Unilever CEO Has 'No Idea' How It Will Meet Full Net-Zero Target," Bloomberg, June 21, 2022, https://www.bloomberg.com/news/articles/2022-06-21/jope-has-no-idea-how-unilever-will-meet-full-net-zero-target.

32. Kristi Hedges, "How to Tell If a Prospective Employer Shares Your Values," hbr.org, October 12, 2020, https://hbr.org/2020/10/how-to-tell-if-a-prospective-employer-shares-your-values.

33. Joan Michelson, "Align Your Corporate Giving with Employee Values to Help Retain Talent," *Forbes*, November 23, 2022, https://www.forbes.com/sites/joanmichelson2/2022/11/23/align-your-corporate-giving-with-employee-values/.

34. Jeff Green, "CEOs Who Are All Talk and No Action on Inclusion Still Benefit," Bloomberg, January 19, 2023, https://www.bloomberg.com/news/articles/2023-01-19/diversity-washing-funds-can-aid-companies-even-if-they-don-t-improve-hiring.

35. Ethical Systems, "Ethical Culture Survey," 2021, https://www.ethicalsystems.org/wp-content/uploads/2021/07/Ethical-Culture-Survey.pdf.

36. Henry Engler, "Novartis Applies Behavioral Science to Code of Ethics, Unearthing Biases and Compliance Gaps," Reuters, November 10, 2020, https://www.reuters.com/article/bc-finreg-novartis-behavioral-science-in-idUSKBN27Q2MD.

Chapter 10

1. "Live Updates: Zelenskyy Declines US Offer to Evacuate Kyiv," Associated Press, February 25, 2022, https://apnews.com/article/russia-ukraine-business-europe-united-nations-kyiv-6ccba0905f1871992b93712d3585f548.

2. Howard Gardner and Emma Laskin, *Leading Minds: An Anatomy of Leadership* (New York: Basic Books, 2011).

3. Enxhi Myslymi, "Covid-19 Impact Reveals Global Leadership Crisis, According to New Global Survey," Milken Institute, October 11, 2020, https://milkeninstitute.org/article/covid-19-impact-reveals-global-leadership-crisis-according-new-global-survey.

4. Aaron K. Chatterji and Michael W. Toffel, "The New CEO Activists," *Harvard Business Review*, January 2018, https://hbr.org/2018/01/the-new-ceo-activists.

5. World Economic Forum, "Implementing Stakeholder Capitalism Part 2, Davos Agenda 2021," YouTube, January 26, 2021, https://www.youtube.com/watch?v=pniLJIpkEU0.

6. David Gelles, "Marc Benioff's $25 Million Blitz to Buy Protective Gear from China," *New York Times*, April 28, 2020, https://www.nytimes.com/2020/04/28/business/coronavirus-marc-benioff-salesforce.html.

7. Patricia Cohen, "No Federal Taxes for Dozens of Big, Profitable Companies," *New York Times*, April 2, 2021, https://www.nytimes.com/2021/04/02/business/economy/zero-corporate-tax.html.

8. Sarah Murray, "How to Pay Executives in the Age of Stakeholder Capitalism," *Financial Times*, December 14, 2022, https://www.ft.com/content/d4aedc19-93c4-4fee-ae51-acac48ed13b7.

9. Kif Leswing, "Here's How Much Money Apple CEO Tim Cook Made in 2021," CNBC, January 6, 2022, https://www.cnbc.com/2022/01/06/apple-ceo-tim-cook-compensation-fy-2021.html.

10. David F. Larcker et al., "Are Narcissistic CEOs All That Bad?," Stanford Closer Look Series, Corporate Governance Research Initiative, Stanford Graduate School of Business, October 7, 2021, https://www.gsb.stanford.edu/faculty-research/publications/are-narcissistic-ceos-all-bad#:~:text=The%20role%20that%20a%20CEO's,is%20associated%20with%20worse%20outcomes. Overall, this suggests that our notions of ESG still focus on grandiose, self-serving PR rather than strategic questions of integrity.

11. Heidrick & Struggles, "Route to the Top 2021," accessed June 20, 2023, https://www.heidrick.com/en/insights/chief-executive-officer/route-to-the-top-2021.

12. Stephen Hansen et al., "The Demand for Executive Skills" (NBER working paper, Cambridge, MA: National Bureau of Economic Research, June 2021), https://doi.org/10.3386/w28959.

13. David Enrich and Rachel Abrams, "McDonald's Sues Former C.E.O., Accusing Him of Lying and Fraud," *New York Times*, August 10, 2020, https://www.nytimes.com/2020/08/10/business/mcdonalds-ceo-steve-easterbrook.html. Legal jeopardy came later, when he was found to have lied: SEC, "SEC Charges McDonald's Former CEO for Misrepresentations about His Termination," January 9, 2023, https://www.sec.gov/news/press-release/2023-4; "Juukan Gorge: Rio Tinto Investors in Pay Revolt over Sacred Cave Blast," *BBC News*, May 7, 2021, https://www.bbc.com/news/business-57018473.

14. Aimee Picchi, "Estée Lauder Fires Senior Executive for Offensive Instagram Post," *CBS News*, March 1, 2022, https://www.cbsnews.com/news/john-demsey-estee-lauder-fired-instagram-post/.

15. Rebecca Henderson, *Reimagining Capitalism in a World on Fire* (New York: PublicAffairs, 2020), 45.

16. Michael Blanding, "The Hard Truth about Being a CEO," Harvard Business School, May 12, 2021, http://hbswk.hbs.edu/item/the-hard-truth-about-being-a-ceo.

17. Linda Klebe Treviño, Laura Pincus Hartman, and Michael Brown, "Moral Person and Moral Manager: How Executives Develop a Reputation for Ethical Leadership," *California Management Review* 42, no. 4 (July 2000): 128–142, https://doi.org/10.2307/41166057.

18. David Mayer, "Why Leading by Example Isn't Always Enough," *Fast Company*, January 20, 2016, https://www.fastcompany.com/3055598/why-leading-by-example-isnt-always-enough.

19. Robert G. Eccles and Alison Taylor, "The Evolving Role of Chief Sustainability Officers," *Harvard Business Review*, July 2023, https://hbr.org/2023/07/the-evolving-role-of-chief-sustainability-officers.

20. This framing is common. See, for example: Alex Woolgar, "ESG: The Journey to beyond Compliance," Passle, September 29, 2022, https://legalbriefs.deloitte.com//post/102hxwe/esg-the-journey-to-beyond-compliance; Glenn Steinberg, "How a Comprehensively Sustainable Approach Reaches beyond Compliance," EY.com, May 27, 2022, https://www.ey.com/en_gl/consulting/how-a-comprehensively-sustainable-approach-reaches-beyond-compliance; and Thomson Reuters Institute, "Corporate ESG Commitments Are Moving beyond Compliance Requirements to Values-Based Commitments," March 18, 2022, https://www.thomsonreuters.com/en-us/posts/investigation-fraud-and-risk/corporate-esg-commitments/.

21. World Economic Forum, "The Rise and Role of the Chief Integrity Officer: Leadership Imperatives in an ESG-Driven World," December 2021, https://www3.weforum.org/docs/WEF_The_Rise_and_Role_of_the_Chief_Integrity_Officer_2021.pdf.

22. Eccles and Taylor, "The Evolving Role of Chief Sustainability Officers."

23. Brian Harward, "Why You Should Spotlight Exemplary Ethical Behavior at Work," *Ethical Systems* (blog), July 6, 2021, https://www.ethicalsystems.org/how-spotlighting-exemplary-workplace-behavior-can-strengthen-ethical-culture/.

24. I interviewed Galvin on August 5, 2021, while he was still at AB InBev.

25. J. Robert Brown Jr., "The Demythification of the Board of Directors," *American Business Law Journal* 52, no. 1 (March 2015): 131–200, https://doi.org/10.1111/ablj.12043.

26. Brown Jr., "The Demythification of the Board of Directors."

27. See Z. Jill Barclift, "Corporate Governance and CEO Dominance," *Washburn Law Journal* 50 (2011, 2010): 611, https://heinonline.org/HOL/Page?handle=hein.journals/wasbur50&id=665&div=&collection=; Bryan Ford, "In Whose Interest: An Examination of the Duties of Directors and Officers in Control Contests," *Arizona State Law Journal* 26, no. 1 (Spring 1994): 91–162; and Marleen O'Connor, "The Enron Board: The Perils of Groupthink," *University of Cincinnati Law Review* 71 (2003), https://papers.ssrn.com/abstract=1791848.

28. PwC and The Conference Board, "Board Effectiveness: A Survey of the C-Suite," November 2021, https://www.pwc.com/us/en/services/governance-insights-center/pwc-board-effectiveness-a-survey-of-the-c-suite-final.pdf.

29. Jamie Smith, "How Committees Are Evolving to Meet Changing Oversight Needs," EY.com, October 17, 2022, https://www.ey.com/en_us/board-matters/how-committees-are-evolving-to-meet-changing-oversight-needs.

30. Tensie Whelan, "U.S. Corporate Boards Suffer from Inadequate Expertise in Financially Material ESG Matters," NYU Stern Center for Sustainable Business, January 2021, https://www.stern.nyu.edu/sites/default/files/assets/documents/U.S.%20Corporate%20Boards%20Suffer%20From%20Inadequate%20Expertise%20in%20Financially%20Material%20ESG%20Matters.docx%20%282.13.21%29.pdf.

31. Theo Francis and Emily Glazer, "Newest Class of Corporate Directors Is the Most Diverse Yet, but Gains Are Uneven," *Wall Street Journal*, October 19, 2021, https://www.wsj.com/articles/newest-class-of-corporate-directors-is-the-most-diverse-yet-but-gains-are-uneven-11634644801.

32. Francis and Glazer, "Newest Class of Corporate Directors Is Most Diverse."

33. Vyacheslav Fos, Elisabeth Kempf, and Margarita Tsoutsoura, "The Political Polarization of Corporate America" (SSRN scholarly paper, Rochester, NY, May 22, 2023), https://doi.org/10.2139/ssrn.3784969.

34. Robin J. Ely and David A. Thomas, "Getting Serious about Diversity: Enough Already with the Business Case," *Harvard Business Review*, November 2020, https://hbr.org/2020/11/getting-serious-about-diversity-enough-already-with-the-business-case.

35. Jennifer Miller, "Why Some Companies Are Saying 'Diversity and Belonging' Instead of 'Diversity and Inclusion,'" *New York Times*, May 13, 2023, https://www.nytimes.com/2023/05/13/business/diversity-equity-inclusion-belonging.html.

36. PwC's 2022 annual corporate directors survey, "Charting the Course through a Changing Governance Landscape," 2022, https://www.pwc.com/us/en/services/governance-insights-center/assets/pwc-2022-annual-corporate-directors-survey.pdf.

37. Maja Pawinska Sims, "Rio Tinto Corporate Affairs Head Steps Down after Aboriginal Cave Blast," ProvokeMedia.com, September 11, 2020, https://www.provokemedia.com/latest/article/rio-tinto-corporate-relations-head-steps-down-after-aboriginal-cave-blast.

38. Brian Gallagher, "Why Promotion Is a Moral Hazard," *Ethical Systems* (blog), March 25, 2021, https://www.ethicalsystems.org/why-even-promotion-is-a-moral-hazard/.

39. Jessica A. Kennedy, "Does Getting Promoted Alter Your Moral Compass?," hbr.org, February 9, 2021, https://hbr.org/2021/02/does-getting-promoted-alter-your-moral-compass.

Chapter 11

1. Oliver Bevan et al., "Benchmarking the Compliance Function," McKinsey, January 7, 2019, https://www.mckinsey.com/capabilities/risk-and-resilience/our-insights/the-compliance-function-at-an-inflection-point.

2. Uri Berliner, "Wells Fargo Admits to Nearly Twice as Many Possible Fake Accounts—3.5 Million," NPR, August 31, 2017, https://www.npr.org/sections/thetwo-way/2017/08/31/547550804/wells-fargo-admits-to-nearly-twice-as-many-possible-fake-accounts-3-5-million.

3. Bethany McLean, "How Wells Fargo's Cutthroat Corporate Culture Allegedly Drove Bankers to Fraud," *Vanity Fair*, May 31, 2017, https://www.vanityfair.com/news/2017/05/wells-fargo-corporate-culture-fraud.

4. J. S. Nelson, "The Dark Side of Compliance" (SSRN scholarly paper, Rochester, NY, September 10, 2019), https://doi.org/10.2139/ssrn.3451586.

5. James Fanelli, "At Trial, Lawyers Present Clashing Portraits of Goldman Sachs Banker," *Wall Street Journal*, February 14, 2022, https://www.wsj.com/articles/trial-for-former-goldman-sachs-banker-set-to-begin-11644840001.

6. Indeed, a survey of 3,000 executives in 2016 found that 42 percent believed they could justify unethical behavior to meet financial targets. (The proportion was higher among younger executives.) EY, Global Fraud Survey, "Corporate Misconduct—Individual Consequences," 2016, https://www.comunicarseweb.com/sites/default/files/ey-corporate-misconduct-individual-consequences.pdf.

7. Markus Jüttner, "Corporate Compliance and Business Ethics between Claim and Reality—Why Academic-Bureaucratic Compliance Programs Fail," 2021, https://doi.org/10.11588/HEIBOOKS.592.C11625.

8. Ann E. Tenbrunsel, Kristin Smith-Crowe, and Elizabeth E. Umphress, "Building Houses on Rocks: The Role of the Ethical Infrastructure in Organizations," *Social Justice Research* 16, no. 3 (2003): 285–307, https://doi.org/10.1023/A:1025992813613.

9. Todd Haugh, "The Criminalization of Compliance," *Notre Dame Law Review* 92, no. 3 (January 1, 2017): 1215, https://scholarship.law.nd.edu/ndlr/vol92/iss3/5.

10. Richard Bistrong, "Will Incentive Time Bombs Blow Up Your Company?" *The FCPA Blog* (blog), June 15, 2016, https://fcpablog.com/2016/06/15/richard-bistrong-will-incentive-time-bombs-blow-up-your-comp/.

11. Cass R. Sunstein, "Sludge Audits," *Behavioural Public Policy* 6, no. 4 (October 2022): 654–673, https://doi.org/10.1017/bpp.2019.32.

12. James Hutton, "Animals Feel What's Right and Wrong, Too," *Nautilus*, April 13, 2022, https://nautil.us/animals-feel-whats-right-and-wrong-too -238458/.

13. Government Finance Officers Association, "What's Fair?," accessed June 21, 2023, https://www.gfoa.org/fairness.

14. Leaving this question unresolved seems to place many ethics and compliance officers under unacceptable levels of stress.

15. Hui Chen and Eugene Soltes, "Why Compliance Programs Fail—and How to Fix Them," *Harvard Business Review*, March 2018, https://hbr.org/2018/03/why-compliance -programs-fail.

16. Emanuel Moss, "Too Big a Word," *Data & Society*, April 29, 2020, https:// points.datasociety.net/too-big-a-word-13e66e62a5bf.

17. Emanuel Moss and Jacob Metcalf, "Ethics Owners," *Data & Society*, September 23, 2020, https://datasociety.net/library/ethics-owners/.

18. Brian Harward, "Why You Should Spotlight Exemplary Ethical Behavior at Work," *Ethical Systems* (blog), July 6, 2021, https://www.ethicalsystems.org/how -spotlighting-exemplary-workplace-behavior-can-strengthen-ethical-culture/.

Chapter 12

1. Jessica DiNapoli and Richa Naidu, "Oreo-Maker, Nestle, Pepsi Face Pressure from European Employees over Russia," Reuters, April 14, 2022, https://www.reuters .com/business/oreo-maker-nestle-pepsi-face-pressure-european-employees-over-russia -2022-04-14/.

2. Jennifer Sey, "Yesterday I Was Levi's Brand President. I Quit So I Could Be Free," The Free Press, February 14, 2022, https://www.thefp.com/p/yesterday-i-was-levis-brand -president.

3. Jeff Horwitz, "The Facebook Whistleblower, Frances Haugen, Says She Wants to Fix the Company, Not Harm It," *Wall Street Journal*, October 3, 2021, https://www .wsj.com/articles/facebook-whistleblower-frances-haugen-says-she-wants-to-fix-the -company-not-harm-it-11633304122.

4. Chris Hamby et al., "McKinsey Opened a Door in Its Firewall between Pharma Clients and Regulators," *New York Times*, April 13, 2022, https://www.nytimes.com /2022/04/13/business/mckinsey-purdue-fda-records.html.

5. Vittoria Elliott, "Ex-Twitter Employees Plan to 'Bombard' Company with Legal Claims," *Wired*, December 6, 2022, https://www.wired.com/story/twitter-employee -arbitration/.

6. Casey Newton, "Breaking Camp," *Verge*, April 28, 2021, https://www.theverge .com/2021/4/27/22406673/basecamp-political-speech-policy-controversy.

7. Casey Newton, "Inside the All-Hands Meeting That Led to a Third of Basecamp Employees Quitting," *Verge*, May 3, 2021, https://www.theverge.com/2021/5/3 /22418208/basecamp-all-hands-meeting-employee-resignations-buyouts-implosion.

8. Zoe Schiffer, "Apple Just Banned a Pay Equity Slack Channel but Lets Fun Dogs Channel Lie," *Verge*, August 30, 2021, https://www.theverge.com/2021/8/31/22650751 /apple-bans-pay-equity-slack-channel.

9. Carl Karlsson and Alison Taylor, "The Pitfalls of 'Cool Parent' Leadership," Welcome to the Jungle, January 3, 2023, https://www.welcometothejungle.com/en/articles /empathetic-leadership.

10. Javier E. David, "The Financial Toll of Right-Wing Backlash: At Least $28B in Market Value," Axios, June 16, 2023, https://www.axios.com/2023/06/16/corporate -america-pride-backlash-stocks.

11. Brown University, "U.S. Is Polarizing Faster Than Other Democracies, Study Finds," January 21, 2020, https://www.brown.edu/news/2020-01-21 /polarization.

12. Vyacheslav Fos, Elisabeth Kempf, and Margarita Tsoutsoura, "The Political Polarization of Corporate America" (SSRN scholarly paper, Rochester, NY, May 22, 2023), https://doi.org/10.2139/ssrn.3784969.

13. Saijel Kishan, "Executives Find They're Ill-Equipped to Stem Worker Polarization," Bloomberg, November 2, 2022, https://www.bloomberg.com/news/articles/2022-11-02/gen-zs-bringing-politics-to-work-managers-don-t-know-how-to-handle-it.

14. Adam Bonica, "Mapping the Ideological Marketplace," *American Journal of Political Science* 58, no. 2 (April 2014): 367–386, https://doi.org/10.1111/ajps.12062.

15. Ryan Grim, "Elephant in the Zoom: Meltdowns Have Brought Progressive Advocacy Groups to a Standstill at a Critical Moment in World History," The Intercept, June 13, 2022, https://theintercept.com/2022/06/13/progressive-organizing-infighting-callout-culture/.

16. Jaclyn Peiser and Jacob Bogage, "Emboldened Shoppers Threaten Target Workers over Pride Month Items," *Washington Post*, June 5, 2023, https://www.washingtonpost.com/business/2023/06/04/target-lgbtq-culture-wars/.

17. Julie Creswell, Kevin Draper, and Rachel Abrams, "At Nike, Revolt Led by Women Leads to Exodus of Male Executives," *New York Times*, April 28, 2018, https://www.nytimes.com/2018/04/28/business/nike-women.html.

18. Vault, "Workplace Misconduct and Speak Up Solution," accessed June 22, 2023, https://vaultplatform.com/.

19. Ellen Cushing, "Slackers of the World, Unite!," *Atlantic*, October 12, 2021, https://www.theatlantic.com/magazine/archive/2021/11/slack-office-trouble/620173/.

20. James R. Detert and Amy C. Edmondson, "Implicit Voice Theories: Taken-for-Granted Rules of Self-Censorship at Work," *Academy of Management Journal* 54, no. 3 (June 2011): 461–488, https://doi.org/10.5465/amj.2011.61967925.

21. Barry Ritholtz, "Transcript: Robert Cialdini," *The Big Picture* (blog), November 4, 2018, https://ritholtz.com/2018/11/transcript-robert-cialdini/.

22. Zoe Schiffer, "LinkedIn Employees Use Forum about Diversity to Defend Racism," *Verge*, June 5, 2020, https://www.theverge.com/2020/6/4/21279739/linkedin-employees-racist-comments-george-floyd-protest.

23. Nico Grant and Ian King, "Cisco Fires Workers for Racial Comments during Diversity Forum," Bloomberg, July 17, 2020, https://www.bloomberg.com/news/articles/2020-07-17/cisco-fires-workers-for-racial-comments-during-diversity-forum.

24. Katherine Bindley, "A Tech Company Tried to Limit What Employees Talk about at Work. It Didn't Go Well," *Wall Street Journal*, May 2, 2021, https://www.wsj.com/articles/a-tech-company-tried-to-limit-what-employees-talk-about-at-work-it-didnt-go-well-11619967600.

25. "To Save America, Argue Better," *Atlantic*, accessed June 22, 2023, https://www.theatlantic.com/sponsored/allstate-2020/save-america-argue-better/3337/.

26. Megan Reitz and John Higgins, "Leading in an Age of Employee Activism," *MIT Sloan Management Review* 63, no. 3 (January 19, 2022), https://sloanreview.mit.edu/article/leading-in-an-age-of-employee-activism/.

27. Re_Generation, "Company Transition Toolkit," accessed June 22, 2023, https://www.re-generation.ca/company-transition-toolkit/.

28. Jesus Jiménez, "Why Chick-fil-A Is Drawing Fire over a 'Culture of Belonging,'" *New York Times*, May 31, 2023, https://www.nytimes.com/2023/05/31/business/chick-fil-a-woke-dei.html.

29. Becky Sullivan, "Hertz Will Pay $168 Million to Customers It Falsely Accused of Stealing Its Cars," NPR, December 6, 2022, https://www.npr.org/2022/12/06/1140998674/hertz-false-accusation-stealing-cars-settlement.

30. Ariel Zilber, "Amazon Employees Rage over Being Forced to Work after Colleague Died from Heart Attack," *New York Post*, January 10, 2023, https://nypost.com/2023/01/10/amazon-employees-rage-over-treatment-of-coworker-who-died-in-warehouse/.

Conclusion

1. In 2021, the Conference Board reported that 223 companies in the S&P Global 1200 index produced purpose statements, up from just 80 five years earlier. The number of companies that "identify as purpose-driven" had increased more than tenfold: Paul Washington and Thomas Singer, "Putting Purpose into Practice: How Companies Can Deliver," *Management and Business Review* 1, no. 2 (Spring 2021): 16–19, https://mbrjournal.com/wp-content/uploads/2021/10/016_MBR-Paper-9-Washington-Singer.pdf.

2. Lynn A. Stout, "The Problem of Corporate Purpose," Issues in Governance Studies, Brookings, June 2012, https://www.brookings.edu/wp-content/uploads/2016/06/Stout_Corporate-Issues.pdf.

3. William Ocasio, Matthew Kraatz, and David Chandler, "Making Sense of Corporate Purpose," *Strategy Science*, June 13, 2023, https://doi.org/10.1287/stsc.2023.0054. See here: Victoria Hurth, Charles Ebert, and Jaideep Prabhu, "Organisational Purpose: The Construct and Its Antecedents and Consequences" (working paper, Cambridge Judge Business School, 2018), https://ideas.repec.org//p/jbs/wpaper/201802.html; The British Academy, "Principles for Purposeful Business," November 2019, https://www.thebritishacademy.ac.uk/documents/224/future-of-the-corporation-principles-purposeful-business.pdf; and Arne Gast et al., "Corporate Purpose: Shifting from Why to How," McKinsey, April 22, 2020, https://www.mckinsey.com/capabilities/people-and-organizational-performance/our-insights/purpose-shifting-from-why-to-how.

4. Hurth, Ebert, and Prabhu, "Organisational Purpose."

5. *Harvard Business Review* and EY, "The Business Case for Purpose," 2015, https://assets.ey.com/content/dam/ey-sites/ey-com/en_gl/topics/digital/ey-the-business-case-for-purpose.pdf.

6. Kwasi Mitchell, "The Power of the Purpose-Driven C-Suite," Deloitte, accessed June 23, 2023, https://www2.deloitte.com/us/en/pages/about-deloitte/articles/the-power-of-the-purpose-driven-c-suite.html.

7. The British Academy, "Future of the Corporation," accessed June 23, 2023, https://www.thebritishacademy.ac.uk/programmes/future-of-the-corporation/.

8. Alex Edmans, *Grow the Pie: How Great Companies Deliver Both Purpose and Profit* (Cambridge, UK, and New York: Cambridge University Press, 2020).

9. Coca-Cola Company, "Our Purpose," accessed June 23, 2023, https://investors.coca-colacompany.com/about/our-purpose.

10. Meta, "Meta—Resources," accessed June 23, 2023, https://investor.fb.com/resources/default.aspx.

11. Quartz, "Jeff Bezos's Legacy," accessed June 23, 2023, https://qz.com/guide/bezos/.

12. Atlassian, "Who We Are," accessed June 14, 2023, https://www.atlassian.com/company.

13. Emily Ketchen, "How to Make Your Next Purpose-Driven Campaign Resonate with Gen Z," *Forbes*, January 26, 2023, https://www.forbes.com/sites/forbescommunicationscouncil/2023/01/26/how-to-make-your-next-purpose-driven-campaign-resonate-with-gen-z/.

14. Mark A. O'Brien, "A Principle Isn't a Principle Until It Costs You Something," *Huffington Post*, October 4, 2011, https://www.huffpost.com/entry/advertising-agencies-intellectual-property_b_994091.

15. Brian Gallagher, "Rachel Ruttan on Business' Role in Eroding Sacred Values," accessed June 23, 2023, https://www.ethicalsystems.org/rachel-ruttan-on-business-role-in-eroding-sacred-values/.

16. Hubert Joly, "Creating a Meaningful Corporate Purpose," hbr.org, October 28, 2021, https://hbr.org/2021/10/creating-a-meaningful-corporate-purpose.

17. Donald Sull, Charles Sull, and Ben Zweig, "Toxic Culture Is Driving the Great Resignation," *MIT Sloan Management Review*, January 11, 2022, https://sloanreview.mit.edu/article/toxic-culture-is-driving-the-great-resignation/.

18. Gallup, "State of the Global Workplace: 2023 Report," 2023, https://www.gallup.com/workplace/349484/state-of-the-global-workplace.aspx.

19. Shawn Achor et al., "9 Out of 10 People Are Willing to Earn Less Money to Do More-Meaningful Work," hbr.org, November 6, 2018, https://hbr.org /2018/11/9-out-of-10-people-are-willing-to-earn-less-money-to-do-more-meaningful -work.

20. Shannon G. Taylor and Lauren R. Locklear, "A Little Rudeness Goes a Long Way," *MIT Sloan Management Review*, January 24, 2022, https://sloanreview.mit.edu /article/a-little-rudeness-goes-a-long-way/.

21. Marjolein Lips-Wiersma and Lani Morris, "Discriminating between 'Meaningful Work' and the 'Management of Meaning,'" *Journal of Business Ethics* 88, no. 3 (September 2009): 491–511, https://doi.org/10.1007/s10551-009-0118-9.

22. Rani Molla, "How a Bunch of Starbucks Baristas Built a Labor Movement," Vox, April 8, 2022, https://www.vox.com/recode/22993509/starbucks-successful -union-drive.

23. Te-Ping Chen, "What CEOs Are Getting Wrong about the Future of Work—and How to Make It Right," *Wall Street Journal*, February 17, 2023, https://www.wsj.com /articles/what-ceos-are-getting-wrong-about-the-future-of-workand-how-to-make-it -right-8a84e279.

24. Starbucks, "Our Mission," accessed June 23, 2023, https://stories.starbucks .com/mission/.

25. Steven Greenhouse, "'Old-School Union Busting': How US Corporations Are Quashing the New Wave of Organizing," *Guardian*, February 26, 2023, https://www .theguardian.com/us-news/2023/feb/26/amazon-trader-joes-starbucks-anti-union-measures.

26. Remy Tumin and Amanda Holpuch, "Starbucks Is under Scrutiny over Removal of Pride Decorations," *New York Times*, June 15, 2023, https://www.nytimes.com /2023/06/15/business/starbucks-pride-decorations.html; Jaclyn Peiser, "Starbucks Accuses Union of a 'Smear Campaign' over Pride Decorations," *Washington Post*, June 27, 2023, https://www.washingtonpost.com/business/2023/06/27/starbucks-union -charges-pride/; Danielle Wiener-Bronner, "Starbucks Promises 'Clearer' Guidelines after Pride Month Décor Clash with Union," CNN.com, June 27, 2023, https://www .cnn.com/2023/06/27/business/starbucks-pride-decorations-clarity/index.html.

27. Hilary Russ, "Starbucks Shareholders Seek Input on Labor Rights Review," Reuters, June 8, 2023, https://www.reuters.com/sustainability/sustainable-finance -reporting/starbucks-shareholders-seek-input-labor-rights-review-letter-2023-06-08/.

28. Trillium Asset Management, "The Investor Case for Supporting Worker Organizing Rights," July 2022, https://www.trilliuminvest.com/whitepapers/the-investor -case-for-supporting-worker-organizing-rights.

29. Starbucks Investor Relations, "Investor Relations Home," accessed June 1, 2023, https://investor.starbucks.com/corporate-governance/board-of-directors/default.aspx.

30. Roy E. Bahat, Thomas A. Kochan, and Liba Wenig Rubenstein, "The Labor-Savvy Leader," *Harvard Business Review*, July–August 2023, https://hbr.org/2023/07 /the-labor-savvy-leader.

31. Chobani, "The Chobani Way," accessed June 27, 2023, http://prod.chobani.sdny .in/impact/the-chobani-way/.

32. Stephanie Strom, "At Chobani, Now It's Not Just the Yoghurt That's Rich," *New York Times*, April 26, 2016, https://www.nytimes.com/2016/04/27/business/a -windfall-for-chobani-employees-stakes-in-the-company.html.

33. Nicole Goodkind, "Chobani CEO Says He Won't Be Captive to Profit Demands," CNN, May 1, 2023, https://www.cnn.com/2023/05/01/investing/premarket-stocks -trading/index.html.

34. Foodingredientsfirst.com, "Fair Trade USA and Chobani Partner on First-of-Its-Kind Certification Program for US Dairy," May 7, 2021, https://www.foodingredientsfirst .com/news/fair-trade-usa-and-chobani-partner-on-first-of-its-kind-certification-program -for-us-dairy.html.

35. Jeanne Sahadi and Matt Egan, "Ahead of World Refugee Day, Dozens of Big Companies Pledge to Hire and Train over 250,000 Refugees in Europe," CNN, June 19, 2023, https://edition.cnn.com/2023/06/19/success/refugees-europe-jobs-training/index .html.

ACKNOWLEDGMENTS

I would never have written this book without the support and encouragement of Jonathan Haidt, whom I have been lucky enough to work with since 2019 and whose brilliance and integrity is a constant inspiration. It was Jonathan who introduced me to Jeff Kehoe, and Jeff who spotted an article I wrote for the *Wall Street Journal*, commissioned by Larry Rout, and who approached me with the idea to write a book on business ethics for the twenty-first century. Jeff's patience and the clarity of his advice are unparalleled, and I am deeply grateful to him for his impeccable judgment and for all his help in shaping this book. I'm also grateful to Stephani Finks for a perfect, distinctive cover on the first shot, to Cheyenne Paterson for her help through the process, and to the production and publicity teams, including Jennifer Waring, Sally Ashworth, Felicia Sinusas, and Julie Devoll. Finally, massive thanks to Heather Landy and Sarah Green Carmichael for publishing my early articles and building my confidence.

I'm deeply grateful for the support of my small but mighty team at Ethical Systems, whose friendship, good humor, and brilliance helped maintain my sanity through the pandemic. I am so grateful to Noel Boyland, Brian Harward, Brian Gallagher, and most of all Mitchell Simoes, who supported me with research for this book with professionalism and judgment far beyond what I could ever hope for from an intern. I'm also grateful to my colleagues in the Business and Society Program at Stern, including Batia Wiesenfeld, Michael Posner, Tensie Whelan, Rachel Kowal, Matthew Statler, Dorothée Baumann-Pauly, and Maria Paterson, for welcoming and encouraging me.

I owe more love and thanks than I can express to my parents, Maggie and Steve Morgan, my brother and sister-in-law, Henry and Helen Morgan, and their gorgeous children, Robyn and Ted. Thank you for believing in me and for letting me hole up to write for months at a time in London. My beloved stepmother, Nancy, and my Aunty Gill are no longer with us, but I'm so grateful to them for helping to shape my childhood and for making me who I am. Thanks to my beloved, terrible kitties, Munkus and Squidley, for their cuddles, purrs, yowling during Zoom interviews, and bringing tributes to my desk. Munkus, I love you so much and will miss you forever.

I've had a weird and wonderful career and worked with many talented people in deeply stressful situations. All of these experiences shaped my perspective and formed the foundations of this book. I owe particular thanks to Dunstan Allison-Hope, Ouida Chichester, Beth Richmond, Alex Maddy, Charles Hecker, Geert Aalbers, Jonathan Morris, Daniel Rudder, Christine Sowder, Charlotte Bancilhon, Roger McElrath, Ralph Stobwasser, Tara Norton, John Hodges, David Korngold, Aron Cramer, Lisa Osofsky, and Laura Gitman. So many more people have inspired me with their efforts to make business better and drive transformational change.

Thank you to the wonderful people who agreed to read and critique early drafts of this book. Anna Romberg, Forrest Deegan, Morgan Hamel, Siobhan Cleary, Bob Eccles, Bettina Palazzo, Susan Ray, Vladimir Borodin, Cristina Tebar Less, Sam Wilkin, and Megan Reitz, you all helped so much. I'm especially grateful to Bob Eccles for his friendship and collaboration, and for introductions to so many brilliant women, especially Clara Miller, Allison Binns, and Jenny Motles.

I owe huge thanks to everyone I interviewed, both on and off the record, and to everyone I quoted in this book. Thanks also to Robert Mascola, Guido Palazzo, Ellen Hunt, Katharina Weghmann, Ron Carucci, Toni Dechario, Praveen Gupta, Lyel Resner, Johannes Lenhard, and Jim Massey for your friendship and insight. Thank you to my dear friends Richard Bistrong and Tom Hardin for teaching me about self-awareness and redemption. And thank you to my collaborators at BCG BrightHouse, qb. consulting, the FT Moral Money team, and the World Economic Forum, especially Andrew Edgecliffe-Johnson, Emilie Prattico, Anna Tunkel, Jane Nelson, Klaus Moosmayer, Gonzalo Guzman, Nicola Bonucci, Nicole Bigby, Daniel Malan, Birgit Kurtz, and Jon Drimmer.

Writing a book is hard—and isolating at the best of times—and I happened to write this book during a period of great personal pain and turmoil. I am so thankful for my dear, dear friends for keeping me going and cheering me up. Clare Gustavsson, I have no idea what I'd have done without our Riverside Park raccoon visits, your baking, singing, love, and friendship. Jonas Gustavsson, thank you for the pictures! Misha Lepetic, thank you for helping me see the future in a new way. Ashley Kelloff, Michael Wiener, and Elizabeth Hodur, thank you for making me love New York. Heidi Sjursen and Jeffrey Abell, thank you for being the best neighbors ever. Simone Ross, thanks for the Il Posto evenings. Justin Frishberg, Ellie Naughten, Patty Goodwin, Jerome Tagger, and Ben Wootliff, Talya Boston, Rebecca Page, Kym Canter, Janet Stilson, Louise Troman, I love you all and am so grateful for your support.

Last but not least, thank you to the leaders trying to reach higher ground and to my past, current, and future students. I learn so much from you every day, and you make me believe in a better future for business. Thank you.

ABOUT THE AUTHOR

ALISON TAYLOR is a clinical associate professor at NYU Stern School of Business, where she teaches sustainability and business ethics classes to undergraduate, MBA, and executive MBA students. Taylor is also executive director at Ethical Systems, a research collaboration based at NYU Stern and focused on harnessing research from leaders in academia in order to transform the ethical practice of business in the corporate world. Previously, she was a managing director at the nonprofit sustainable business network and consultancy BSR and a senior managing director at Control Risks. Taylor holds advisory roles on impact and sustainability issues at VentureESG, BSR, Pictet Group, KKR, BCG BrightHouse, and Zai Lab. She is a 2023–24 member of the World Economic Forum Global Future Council on the Future of Good Governance.

Taylor has over two decades of experience advising corporations on strategy, sustainability, political and social risk, organizational culture and behavior, human rights, ethics and compliance, stakeholder engagement, anti-corruption, and professional responsibility. She received her BA in modern history from Balliol College, Oxford University, her MA in international relations from the University of Chicago, and her MA in organizational psychology from Columbia University. She grew up in London but now divides her time between New York City and Woodstock, NY.